MODERN USMC AIR POWER

Aircraft and Units of the Flying 'Leathernecks'

Joe Copalman

HARPIA PUBLISHING

Meynertgasse 8/8, 1090 Wien, Austria
enquiries@harpia-publishing.com

Consulting and inspiration by Kerstin Berger

Front cover artwork by Ugo Crisponi, Aviation Graphic shows an AV-8B Harrier II Plus from Marine Attack Squadron 214 'Blacksheep'.
Rear cover artworks by Ugo Crisponi, Aviation Graphic show (from top to bottom): AH-1Z Viper from Marine Light Attack Helicopter Squadron 267 'Stingers', KC-130J Super Hercules from Marine Aerial Refueler Transport Squadron 234 'Ranger', and MV-22B Osprey from Marine Medium Tiltrotor Squadron 261 'Raging Bulls'.

Editorial by Thomas Newdick

Layout by Norbert Novak

Maps by James Lawrence

Printed at finidr, Czech Republic

ISBN 978-1-950394-02-9

Harpia Publishing is a member of

MODERN USMC AIR POWER, Aircraft and Units of the Flying 'Leathernecks'

Joe Copalman

Contents

Introduction: a force in transition

US Marine Corps aviation has been undergoing three concurrent transitions since the turn of the 21st Century, with a service-wide focus on enhancing lethality, survivability, range, lift, connectivity, and versatility. Given the US Department of Defence's recent strategic shift from combatting global insurgencies to organizing, equipping, and orienting its forces for the kind of peer-state competition that characterized the Cold War, these upgrades have taken on even greater importance.

Foremost among these transitions is that from older legacy aircraft to newer, more capable types. Every community within Marine Corps aviation – from fighter attack to heavy lift helicopter, to unmanned aerial vehicles – is either in the midst of an upgrade from a legacy platform to a new one, or has already completed such a transition. Even the Beech C-12s flown by Marine base flights are being replaced by more modern variants that can carry more passengers over longer distances

The second major transition in Marine Corps aviation has been the various upgrades implemented to keep legacy aircraft as viable as possible through their programmed 'sunset' dates. Delays in development or testing of newer types like the Lockheed F-35 Lightning II or Sikorsky CH-53K King Stallion have only heightened the need for such upgrades. The result of these upgrades is that most Marine aircraft are retired from service at the top of the type's game, demonstrably more capable than when the aircraft were introduced into service

The third transition is the introduction of networked digital communications under the umbrella of digital interoperability, aimed at enhancing the situational awareness of Marines in the air and on the ground, shortening so-called 'kill chains' and enabling Marine aircraft to get kinetic effects onto targets sooner than previously possible.

These transitions have occurred against the backdrop of – and in some cases were driven by – the operational demands of the wars in Iraq, Afghanistan, and Syria, allowing new aircraft, systems, and capabilities to be evaluated in combat. The chapters that follow give a community-by-community insight into how each of these transitions has shaped the ability of USMC aviation to meet the needs of the Marine Corps and the nation in an increasingly unstable world. In each chapter, I have tried to incorporate brief combat histories of each community's legacy types and the newer aircraft replacing them, augmented by personal accounts from pilots and aircrew who flew them and by forward air controllers who relied on air support from the ground.

One of the challenges of writing about the Marine Corps is the integrated nature of how the service operates. It is difficult, for instance, to write about Harriers or 'Hueys' in combat without also writing about what the ground combat element was doing at the time. While I have tried to avoid redundancy, I have written about specific events in multiple chapters to highlight the complementary capabilities different aircraft bring to the mission and how those capabilities were employed in real-world operations. Another challenge is that for many recent operations and capabilities, significant amounts of information remain classified, and for good reason. Though I deliberately refrain from speculating on unpublished capabilities in almost every chapter, the few instances in which I do are entirely my speculation and not from any of the Marines I have interviewed over the years.

My goal is to present an authoritative historical, technological, organisational, and personal overview of USMC aviation in the first two decades of the 21st century without being exhaustive.

Joe Copalman, September 2020

Acknowledgements

Much of the content in this book comes from interviews with active-duty, reserve, and retired Marine aviators and aircrew between 2013 and 2020. The author extends his gratitude to the following personnel for taking the time to answer questions about their platforms, their units and their combat experience:

Gen Harry Blot (Ret), MGen Joe Anderson (Ret), MGen Andrew O'Donnell (Ret), Col James Adams, Col Matt Amidon, Col Allen Broughton (Ret), Col John Kelliher, Col Christopher O'Balle, Col Jim Wellons, Lt Col Tom Carter (Ret), Lt Col Chad Fitzgerald, Lt Col Eric Geyer, Lt Col Shawn Hermley (Ret), Lt Col Chris Holloway, Lt Col Brian Littleton, Lt Col Jason Lower, Lt Col Paul Marko, Lt Col Brett McGregor, Lt Col Steve Mount (Ret), Lt Col Greg Sand, Lt Col Bill Sheridan, Lt Col Andrew Turner, Lt Col Jayson Tiger, Lt Col Chad Vaughn, Maj Ben Apple, Maj Akil Bacchus, Maj Andrew Baxter, Maj Art Bruggeman, Maj Tyler Burnam, Maj Eileen Donovan, Maj Rob Dugan, Maj Garrett Ebey, Maj Trevor Felter, Maj Michael French, Maj Brian Friestman (Ret), Maj Douglas Glover (Ret), Maj Seth Goldstein (Ret), Maj Eric Grunke, Maj Brian Hansell, Maj Tommy Keech, Maj Lynn Larson, Maj Andrew Myers, Maj Christopher Neal, Maj Miguel Pena, Maj Alex Ramthun, Maj Eric Rodriguez, Capt Jack Cronan, Capt Jeffrey Dean, Capt Thomas Frey, Capt Rob Guyette, Capt Mike Harper, Capt James O'Hara, Capt K.C. O'Malley, Capt Sean Rafferty, Capt Syed Rashid, Capt Steve Rogers, MGySgt Mathew Whitacre (Ret), MSgt Brian Norman, MSgt Felix Rosa, GySgt Bill Franceschini, GySgt Mwenya Mundende, GySgt Salisibarra, SSgt Christopher Herr, SSgt Thomas Lara, Sgt Stephen Pullins, Sgt Jonathan Ruiz and Cpl Matt Jordan.

These interviews (and photos) would not have been possible without the assistance of Public Affairs and Communications Strategy (CommStrat) Marines, including Maj Staci Reidinger, Capt Christopher Harrison, Capt Gabriel Adibe, Capt Sarah Burns, Capt Melanie Salinas, 1Lt Frederick Walker, 2nd Lt Greg Cronan, 2nd Lt Casey Littesy, Sgt Bill Waterstreet and Cpl Zach Scanlon, with special thanks to Capt Adara Story at MAWTS-1 Commstrat and Capt Stephanie Leguizamon at Marine Forces Reserve CommStrat and to Mr Kris Haugh at NAF El Centro.

Special thanks to Kevin Whitehead, Scott Youmans, Marcus Jellyman, Taj Backus, Jerry Gunner and Jamie Hunter for the additional images, to Doug Glover for providing clarification on complex issues when needed, and to Simon Jakubowski of The Aviation Enthusiast Book Club for building an outstanding online community.

Lastly, boundless love to my phenomenal wife Jonna and our awesome kids Nora and James for their patience, support and incomparable humour.

Abbreviations

ACE	Aviation Combat Element
ADGR	air-delivered ground refuelling
AirO	Regimental Air Officer
ARG	Amphibious Ready Group
ATARS	Advanced Tactical Aerial Reconnaissance System
C3	command, ontrol and communications
CAS	close air support
CASEVAC	casualty evacuation
CE	Command Element
CLB	Combat Logistics Battalion
CLR	Combat Logistics Regiment
COCO	contractor owned, contractor operated
CONUS	Continental United States
ECMO	Electronic Countermeasures Officer
FAC	forward air controller
FAC(A)	forward air controller (airborne)
FARP	forward arming and refuelling pointt
FRS	Fleet Replacement Squadron
GBU	Guided Bomb Unit
GCE	Ground Combat Element
GPS	Global Positioning System
H&HS	Headquarters and Headquarters Squadron
H&MS	Headquarters and Maintenance Squadron
HMH	Marine Heavy Helicopter Squadron
HMHT	Marine Heavy Helicopter Training Squadron
HMLA	Marine Light Attack Helicopter Squadron
HMLAT	Marine Light Attack Helicopter Training Squadron
HMM	Marine Medium Helicopter Squadron
HMR	Marine Helicopter Transport Squadron
HMX	Marine Helicopter Squadron
IED	improvised explosive device
ISAF	International Stabilisation and Assistance Force
JHMCS	Joint Helmet Mounted Cueing System
JPADS	Joint Precision Air Delivery System
JTAC	Joint Terminal Attack Controller
LAAD	Low Altitude Air Defense
LCE	Logistics Combat Element
MACG	Marine Air Control Group
MACS	Marine Air Control Squadron
MAG	Marine Aircraft Group
MAGTAB	Marine Air-Ground TABlet
MAGTF	Marine Air-Ground Task Force
MALS	Marine Aviation Logistics Squadron
MARDIV	Marine Division
MARFORRES	Marine Forces Reserve

MASS Marine Air Support Squadron
MAW Marine Air Wing
MAWTS Marine Aviation Weapons and Tactics Squadron
MCAS Marine Corps Air Station
MEB Marine Expeditionary Brigade
MEF Marine Expeditionary Force
MEU Marine Expeditionary Unit
MRF Marine Rotational Force
MTACS Marine Tactical Air Command Squadron
MWCS Marine Wing Communications Squadron
MWHS Marine Wing Headquarters Squadron
MWSD Marine Wing Support Detachment
MWSS Marine Wing Support Squadron
NAG Northern Arabian Gulf
NAS Naval Air Station
OT&E Operational Test and Evaluation
RSTA reconnaissance, surveillance and target acquisition
RCT Regimental Combat Team
REIN Reinforced
ROTC Reserve Officer Training Corps
SEAD suppression of enemy air defences
SPMAGTF Special Purpose Marine Air-Ground Task Force
TECOM Training and Education Command
TTPs tactics, techniques and procedures
UAS unmanned aerial system
UAV unmanned aerial vehicle
USD US Dollar
USMC United States Marine Corps
VMA Marine Attack Squadron
VMAT Marine Attack Training Squadron
VMAQ Marine Electronic Warfare Squadron
VMCJ Marine Composite Reconnaissance Squadron
VMF Marine Fighter Squadron
VMFA Marine Fighter Attack Squadron
VMFA(AW) Marine Fighter Attack Squadron(All Weather)
VMFAT Marine Fighter Attack Training Squadron
VMGR Marine Aerial Refueler Transport Squadron
VMM Marine Medium Tiltrotor Squadron
VMMT Marine Medium Tiltrotor Training Squadron
VMR Marine Transport Squadron
VMU Marine Unmanned Aerial Vehicle Squadron
VMX Marine Operational Test and Evaluation Squadron
WSO Weapons Systems Officer
WTI Weapons and Tactics Instructor

HISTORY OF MARINE CORPS AVIATION

Marine Corps aviation traces its origins to 22 May 1912, when the first Marine aviator, First Lieutenant Alfred Cunningham reported for training at the Naval Aviation Camp in Annapolis, Maryland. At the time, the Navy possessed a total of four hydroplanes – two Wright and two Curtiss – none of which were airworthy when Cunningham arrived. Not content to wait for them to be repaired, Cunningham sought out flight training on his own through the Burgess Company, which manufactured Wright hydroplanes, soloing on 20 August 1912 after only two and a half hours of instruction. In January 1913, the Navy demonstrated the airplane's capabilities during fleet exercises off the Cuban coast, with Cunningham and his Navy brethren performing surface reconnaissance, tracking submerged submarines and conducting rudimentary bombing. Another exercise in Puerto Rico in January 1914 saw the first use of aircraft flown by Marine aviators in support of Marines on the ground. By August of that year, the Marine aviators began flying landplanes.

Lt Alfred Cunningham, the first Marine Corps aviator (and the fifth naval aviator) at the controls of a Curtiss hydroplane in 1914. (USMC)

World War I and the 1920s

The Marines went to war in Europe flying the de Havilland DH-4 and DH-9A bombers, though not in support of Marines. Simply getting the aircraft to Europe proved problematic and Cunningham's Marines began flying with the British Royal Air Force (which also flew DH-9As) to gain combat experience alongside seasoned veterans. Cunningham's Marines ended the war with four confirmed kills, eight 'probables', and having conducted aerial resupply and interdiction, attacking targets like German-held railyards.

After the war, Marine aviation struggled in the face of reduced budgets and hostility from senior officers still upset that Cunningham and his pilots did not directly support their Marines fighting in France. In the face of this, Cunningham issued an assurance that to this day remains the core, foundational principle of Marine Corps aviation: '*The only excuse for aviation in any service is its usefulness in assisting the troops on the ground to successfully carry out their operations.*'

The next decade gave Marine aviators ample opportunity to make good on this, with Marines deploying to protect American commercial interests in China, the Dominican Republic, Haiti and Honduras. During this period, Marine aviators flew reconnaissance, medical evacuation, resupply and early close air support missions, as well as pioneering dive-bomb tactics against ground targets.

The crew of a DeHavilland DH-4 of the First Marine Aviation Force in France during World War I.
(USMC)

Major Russ Rowell, led VO-1M in combat operations against guerrillas in Nicaragua in the late 1920s and helped develop early air-ground coordination tactics.
(USMC)

In 1927, Marine aircraft deployed to Nicaragua to help Marine and government forces fight Sandinista guerrillas threatening US agricultural and Nicaraguan government interests throughout the country. This conflict saw the development of early air-ground coordination efforts. At the time, Marine Corps aircraft still lacked proper radios, and those that were available to ground forces were cumbersome and impractical. Instead, the Marines worked out a series of ground panel arrangements and wing-wag manoeuvres to communicate between the air and the ground. For more direct coordination, ground troops could clear 750-foot-long (229m) runways for aircraft to land and allow pilots to communicate face-to-face with the Marines they were supporting.

On 16 July 1927, Major Ross Rowell of Marine Observation Squadron One (VO-1M) 'Ace of Spades' led five World War I-era DH-4s in an attack on Sandinista forces engaged in a battle with Marine and Nicaraguan forces near Otócal. The gun and bomb attacks devastated the Sandinistas. The Nicaraguan campaign also yielded the first Medal of Honor for a Marine aviator, awarded to Lieutenant Christian F. Schilt for making repeated landings under heavy fire to evacuate wounded troops from Quilali between 6 and 8 January 1928.

The 1930s saw considerable organisational momentum that would serve the USMC well in the coming war against Japan. In 1935, the service published its *Tentative Landing Operations Manual*, which codified the role of Marine aviation during amphibious landings. Further clarification came in 1939, when the General Board of the US Navy specified that the mission of Marine aviation was to support the Marines during amphibious operations and continue supporting Marine ground forces as they advanced inland from the beach, with a secondary mission of supporting naval aviation aboard the Navy's growing fleet of aircraft carriers. The 1930s also brought the first monoplane into USMC service, with the Brewster F3A Buffalo entering the inventory in 1939, followed by the vastly superior Grumman F4F Wildcat in 1941.

World War II – fighters reign supreme

World War II proved to be a trial by fire for Marine aviation. Concurrent with the attack on Pearl Harbor, the Imperial Japanese Navy attacked US forces at Wake Island, a small atoll in the central Pacific. Wake Island was defended by a dozen F4Fs from Marine Fighter Squadron 211 (VMF-211). In the initial attack, Japanese bombers destroyed eight of the squadron's Wildcats on the ground, leaving only four to defend against the coming onslaught. Pulling double-duty as fighters and bombers, VMF-211 shot down two bombers the following day, and began bombing Japanese ships on 11 December, sinking the destroyer *Kisaragi*. Captain Henry T. Elrod – killed at Wake on 23 January 1941 organising VMF-211's surviving Marines for beach defence after all the squadron's aircraft were destroyed – was posthumously awarded the Medal of Honor for his actions, which included downing two Japanese aircraft and striking the fatal blow on the *Kisaragi*.

Marine aviators began getting their footing against the Japanese in summer 1942 over Guadalcanal in the Solomon Islands. Operating from Henderson Field, Wildcat and SBD Dauntless aircraft bombed and strafed Japanese troops, bases and shipping, downing dozens of Japanese aircraft as well. Early combat over the Solomons pro-

A pair of Vought F4U-1A Corsairs from VMF-113 'Whistling Devils' over the Pacific near Eniwetok in July 1944. The Corsair was Marine air's workhorse in the Pacific, keeping Japanese fighters at bay and attacking ground targets during the 'island hopping' campaign. (US Navy)

duced the first two Marine aces – Captain Marion Carl and Major John Smith, both of VMF-224 'Fighting Wildcats'. Over the course of numerous naval battles and attacks by Japanese troops on Guadalcanal, Marine aviators helped to successfully thwart all enemy attempts to retake the island and its strategically critical airfield. The Japanese eventually withdrew from the area in February 1943.

That same month, the Vought F4U-1 Corsair entered the Solomons campaign. With its distinctive bent wing, the Corsair held speed and firepower advantages over the nimbler but far less robust Japanese Zero. By September 1943, all VMF squadrons in the Pacific had transitioned from the Wildcat to the Corsair. Hard-won combat experience and a target-rich environment created opportunities for Marine aviators to become aces, some many times over. By late 1943, Captain Joe Foss of VMF-121 had amassed 26 kills, more than any other pilot would accrue in USMC service. Major Gregory 'Pappy' Boyington, legendary commander of the misfit VMF-214 'Black Sheep', who had entered the war with six kills from his time in China with the American Volunteer Group, accrued 20 more kills in December 1943 alone, matching Foss for career shootdowns. On 3 January 1944, Boyington became the top Marine ace of the war, downing two Zeros over Rabaul before bailing out of his stricken Corsair and being taken prisoner for the rest of the war.

The Solomons campaign also saw the introduction of dedicated night fighters into Marine aviation, tasked with defending Guadalcanal against Japanese bombers harassing the Americans at night, depriving them of much-needed rest. Employing radar-equipped Lockheed PV-1 Venturas and Vought F4U-2 Corsairs, VMF(N)-531 'Grey Ghosts' and VMF(N)-532 'Night Fighters' had little to show in terms of kills but succeeded in reducing the effectiveness of Japanese night raids. North American PBJ bombers also fought at night, utilising radar equipment to attack Japanese ships at anchor under cover of darkness.

Marine aviation's success operating from land bases in the Solomons led to its absence in several key amphibious operations on islands too distant to reach from their land bases. The solution to this was placing Marine fighter and torpedo squadrons

A Marine Douglas SBD Dauntless en route to a bombing mission over Rabaul during the New Guinea campaign. (USMC)

aboard Navy escort carriers, enabling Marine aviators to support their infantry brethren on the ground. The arrangement bore its first fruit on 12 January 1945, when Marine Corsairs from USS *Essex* (CV 9) shot down several Japanese aircraft near Okinawa.

In February 1945, Marine pilots finally had a chance to prove the service's close air support (CAS) capabilities during the Army-led campaign to force the Japanese from the Philippines. Radiomen in USMC jeeps integrated with Army mechanised units, enabling pilots to stay connected with the troops they supported. This link to the infantry worked both ways – Marine SBD crews could perform visual reconnaissance and inform ground forces of threats ahead, and the troops could direct pilots onto Japanese positions using bombs, machine guns and napalm cannisters. The Corsairs, capable of carrying bombs and rockets, joined the SBDs in providing CAS when attention shifted from the northern Philippines to the south.

After the Philippines, American attention turned towards Iwo Jima. Though arguably the most well-known battle in USMC history, Marine aviation played a relatively minor role, with eight Corsair squadrons contributing to a much larger Army/Navy ground support effort. During the battle, the Marines launched and recovered Stinson OY-1 spotter planes from modified landing craft to provide aerial spotting for naval gunfire and shore-based artillery.

During the battle of Okinawa – seen as the final domino that needed to fall before US forces could invade the Japanese home islands – Marine aviators provided some CAS for Marines on the ground but were primarily tasked with defending the US fleet from suicide attacks by kamikaze pilots. Okinawa proved to be the Marines' final battle of World War II, with the Japanese surrendering on 2 September 1945.

Post-war developments – into the jet (and rotor) age

Though early jets and helicopters both saw service in World War II, the Marines only began operating their own jets and rotorcraft after the war. Between the end of World War II and the beginning of the Korean conflict, three jet fighters entered Marine Corps service – the McDonnell FH-1 Phantom, Grumman F9F-2 Panther and McDonnell F2H Banshee, with the service's first jet night fighter, the Douglas F3D Skyknight, entering service after the war began.

Having witnessed an atomic bomb test in the south Pacific, Lieutenant General Roy Geiger – himself an early Marine Corps aviator – realised that amphibious landings could be stopped with just one of the new weapons. Fearing this would invalidate the entire concept of amphibious operations, Geiger convinced then-Commandant General Alexander Vandegrift to approve development of a helicopter capability to transport Marines and supplies from ships to distributed landing zones beyond the beach to mitigate the risks of atomic attack. This resulted in the establishment of Marine Helicopter Squadron One (HMX-1) 'The Nighthawks' in December 1947 with the mission of developing USMC helicopter doctrine. The first two aircraft flown by HMX-1 were Piasecki's tandem-rotor HRP and Sikorsky's H03S. The squadron used these aircraft to develop tactics, techniques and procedures for helicopter employment and to demonstrate the capabilities of both aircraft to the Marine Corps. Putting together a 'wish list' of capabilities, the Marines sought a two-aircraft solution to its problem – a medium-lift helicopter to transport troops from ship to shore, and a heavy-lift helicopter to transport light vehicles, supplies and even artillery pieces ashore.

War in Korea

When North Korea invaded its southern neighbour on 25 June 1950, the USMC lacked any significant presence in the region. Marine aviation assets arrived in Korea in early August, with Corsairs from VMF-214 'Blacksheep' and VMF-323 'Death Rattlers' operating aboard carriers providing CAS with rockets and napalm for beleaguered ground forces around Pusan. Marine HO3S-1 helicopters saw action almost immediately upon arrival, rescuing several downed pilots. With the Pusan perimeter secured, Marine aviation shifted to supporting the amphibious assault on Inchon near Seoul. In support of the landings, Marine Corsairs used rockets, bombs and napalm to neutralise North Korean defensive positions near friendly ground troops.

Marine aviation also began aerial resupply of fielded forces using airdropped loads from Fairchild R4Q-1 cargo aircraft, which were vital to the success of the Chosin Breakout in December 1950. That same month, VMF-311 'Tomcats' began flying the F9F-2 Panther in combat, the first Marine jet to see action in Korea, flying CAS and armed reconnaissance missions in coordination with forward air controllers (FACs) – aviators on ground tours coordinating airstrikes for the infantry. Radar-equipped F4Us and F7F Tigercats found utility as night interdiction and CAS platforms, though two Tigercat pilots also scored night kills against North Korean PO-2 harassment bombers.

The Sikorsky HRS-1 medium-lift helicopter entered the war in September 1951 with Marine Helicopter Transport Squadron 161 (HMR-161), enabling the validation of the Corps' vertical envelopment concept in combat, providing troop transport and resupply of fielded forces. Though limited in number, the Douglas AD Skyraider proved to be a CAS and interdiction powerhouse, capable of hauling two and a half tons of ordnance to distant targets with plenty of loiter time. The photoreconnaissance-tasked F2H-2P Banshee entered the conflict in March 1952, locating enemy ground targets and conducting post-strike battle damage assessment.

Entering combat in November 1952, the Douglas F3D-2 Skyknight served as the Corps' first jet night fighter with the 'Flying Nightmares' of VMF(N)-513. Tasked primarily with escorting Air Force B-29s on night bombing raids over North Korea, the big Skyknights claimed six kills before the end of the war. While not as impressive a number as the hundreds of enemy aircraft downed by Air Force F-86 Sabres (some flown by Marine exchange pilots), F3Ds helped dramatically reduce B-29 losses for the remainder of the war.

The Marine Corps developed and refined helicopter tactics during the Korean Conflict. Here Marine infantrymen disembark from a Sikorsky HRS-1 operated by HMR-161 on a beach near Inchon, South Korea in early 1953. (USMC)

After Korea

Though facing post-war reductions in manpower and aircraft, the Marine Corps continued to develop its vertical envelopment doctrine. The Corps took delivery of its first heavy-lift helicopter, the Sikorsky HR2S-1, in July 1956. That same year, the Marines accepted the service's first air-to-air missile platform, the North American FJ-3M Fury, capable of downing other aircraft with the AIM-9 Sidewinder air-to-air missile. With every service trying to get a piece of the nuclear pie at the time, the Marines gained an atomic attack capability in 1957 with another Fury variant, the FJ-4B.

Also introduced in 1957, the Douglas A4D Skyhawk brought a credible jet attack capability that would make it the Corps' CAS workhorse throughout the Vietnam War. Another stalwart Vietnam-era aircraft entered service in the late 1950s – the Chance-Vought F8U Crusader. Marine Crusaders saw action during the Cuban Missile Crisis in October 1962 when RF-8As (the naval designation system aligned with the Air Force's in 1962) of VMCJ-2 'Playboys' augmented Navy RF-8s conducting photoreconnaissance missions over Cuba. Three other Vietnam staples – the McDonnell Douglas F-4 Phantom II, Lockheed KC-130 Hercules and Sikorsky UH-34 Seahorse – entered service in the early 1960s.

Vietnam

The first Marine aircraft in Vietnam – 24 UH-34Ds and three O-1 Bird Dogs of HMM-362 'Archie's Angels' – arrived in 1962 under Operation Shufly. Tasked with supporting the Army of the Republic of Vietnam (ARVN) against Viet Cong guerrillas, HMM-362 transported troops and supplies to landing zones throughout South Vietnam. Shufly rotations continued until the arrival of the 9th Marine Expeditionary Brigade at Danang in March 1965, signalling the end of the advisory mission and the beginning of overt US combat operations in Vietnam.

The build-up of 1st Marine Air Wing (MAW) assets at Danang began shortly thereafter, with VMFA-531 bringing its F-4Bs and VMCJ-1 'Golden Hawks' bringing EF-10B Skyknight electronic warfare aircraft. By the end of 1965, 1st MAW had F-4s, F-8s, EF-10s and RF-8s flying from Danang, A-4s flying from Chu Lai, and UH-1s, UH-34s and CH-37s operating out of Marble Mountain and Ky Ha. The US Military Assistance Command for Vietnam (USMACV) divided South Vietnam into six areas of responsibility, with the Marines being responsible for I Corps, the northern most zone in South Vietnam. While 1st MAW commanding officer, Brigadier General Keith B McCutcheon advocated for complete control of Marine aviation in-theatre, the Marines lost some degree of control to 7th Air Force in Saigon. As such, Marine F-4s and EF-10s often flew in support of Air Force strikes over North Vietnam. Marine air eventually fell under 7th Air Force as the single manager in 1968, though with flexibility for the Marines to meet their air support needs before yielding sorties to the Air Force.

As the war progressed, the Marines continued introducing new aviation capabilities. With Vietnam's often challenging weather, and the ground forces' continued need for air support regardless of the weather, the Marines needed a means of accurately combing through cloud cover. The solution, introduced in 1965, was a radar-controlled bombing system called TPQ-10, a development of radar bombing systems used in the Korean War, which used known grid coordinates and radar triangulation to command pilots to drop unguided bombs with relative precision.

Though the Marines had successfully conducted forward air control – airborne, or FAC(A) missions using O-1 Bird Dogs and UH-1Es, the service sought a faster, more survivable FAC(A) platform for missions near the demilitarised zone separating North and South Vietnam, and in the A Shau Valley, where North Vietnamese anti-aircraft guns made life particularly troublesome for slow-flying FACs. Known as 'Fast-FAC', this mission was initially fulfilled by Grumman TF-9J Cougars flying with H&MS-11 at Danang and H&MS-13 at Chu Lai in mid-1966. The Marines replaced the Cougars with TA-4F Skyhawks in 1967 to perform the same mission. The all-weather Grumman A-6A Intruder also entered service in 1966, bringing a heavy bombload, ample loiter time and advanced targeting systems to the fight with VMA(AW)-242 'Bats' at Danang. Another variant of the Intruder, the EA-6A Electric Intruder, joined VMCJ-1 in 1966 as the eventual replacement for the EF-10Bs. VMCJ-1 also began replacing its RF-8A Crusaders with the RF-4B Phantom II that same year.

Concurrent with the Tet Offensive in January 1968, the North Vietnamese Army (NVA) laid siege to a remote Marine outpost at Khe Sanh. Cut off from ground support, the defenders at Khe Sanh relied on airpower, with the Air Force and Navy joining USMC aviation units in attacking NVA positions throughout the area. Aerial resupply factored prominently into the defence of Khe Sanh, with KC-130F Hercules employing Low Altitude Parachute Extraction System deliveries to avoid exposure to ground fire and CH-46s and CH-53s escorted by A-4s delivering underslung loads of food, water and ammunition. The TPQ-10 radar bombing system paid dividends as well, helping keep the pressure on the NVA even in marginal weather.

The North American OV-10 Bronco joined VMO-2 at Danang in July 1968, followed by the AH-1G Cobra – on loan from the US Army – the following year. By 1969, most of the older types the Marines started the war with – the H-34, H-37, F-8 and RF-8 and EF-10 – had been fully phased out and replaced by newer types. The twin-engine AH-1J SeaCobra entered service in 1971, escorting helicopters carrying ARVN troops into Laos during Operation Lam Son 719 in March just prior to most USMC units leaving Vietnam in April. The NVA's Easter Offensive in late March 1972 brought Marine air back to Vietnam, with A-4s, A-6s and F-4s flying from Bien Hoa, Danang and Nam Phong in Thailand, and EA-6As supporting strikes from Cubi Point in the Philippines. The only air-to-air kill by a Marine crew flying a Marine aircraft happened on 11 September 1972, when Major Lee Lasseter and Captain John Cummings of VMFA-333 'Fighting Shamrocks' downed a MiG-21 over North Vietnam. The Linebacker II raids, mass USAF B-52 bombing raids aimed at forcing the North Vietnamese government to negotiate an end to the war, saw extensive EW support from Marine EA-6As, with the raids ultimately bearing the desired fruit. The last Marine aircraft to drop bombs in Southeast Asia were A-4E Skyhawks from VMA-311 'Tomcats' on 28 January 1973. The

An A-4E Skyhawk from VMA-121 'Green Knights' taxis out for a ground attack mission at Chu Lai airfield in South Vietnam. The A-4 was the Marine Corps' ground attack mainstay in Vietnam and into the 1980s when it was replaced by the AV-8B Harrier II. (USMC)

Marines returned to Vietnam in April 1975 for Operation Frequent Wind, the evacuation of American diplomatic personnel from the US Embassy in Saigon, with CH-46Es and CH-53Ds escorted by AH-1Js being used to transport them to ships in the South China Sea.

Post-Vietnam – new aircraft, new adversaries

As with every previous war, the Marine Corps faced a drawdown following Vietnam, but also introduced new aircraft into its air wings. The most consequential of these was the British Aerospace (BAE) Harrier, a British-built short take-off and vertical landing (STOVL) attack jet capable of flexible, forward basing and operating from short-decked amphibious assault carriers. Acquisition remained limited, with only VMA-231 'Ace of Spades', VMA-513 'Flying Nightmares' and VMA-542 'Tigers' transitioning as operational squadrons flying the AV-8A, and one training squadron, VMAT-203 'Hawks', flying a mix of AV-8As and two-seat TAV-8A trainers, which only began arriving in 1975. The Marines also took delivery of the ultimate single-seat A-4 variant, the A-4M Skyhawk II, in 1971. The AH-1T Improved SeaCobra, introduced in 1976, brought a precision weapons capability with the BGM-71 Tube-launched Optically tracked Wire-guided missile, or TOW. The Vietnam-era fast-FAC TA-4Fs received an upgrade to OA-4M standard in 1979, equipped with most of the A-4M's mission systems, though without an engine upgrade to accommodate the added weight.

Many of the legacy platforms still serving today entered service in the early 1980s, including the CH-53E Super Stallion, F/A-18 Hornet and the AV-8B Harrier II. After ten years of relative peace, Marine aircraft engaged in combat operations in Grenada during Operation Urgent Fury in 1983, after a power struggle between rival factions within Grenada's communist government put hundreds of American medical students on the island in danger. Though the operation was successful, the Marines lost two AH-1Ts (with three of the four pilots killed in action) and one CH-46E during combat. In 1986, tensions with Libyan dictator Muammar Gaddafi, a state sponsor of terrorism, reached a crescendo with Operation Diablo Canyon, in which Marine EA-6Bs and F/A-18s operating from Navy carriers in the Gulf of Sidra supported Air Force raids against Gaddafi's regime – the first combat operation for both types in USMC service. Also in 1986, the Marines established the service's first and only adversary squadron,

CH-46F BuNo 157711 from HMM-261 'Raging Bulls' on the beach at Grand Anse in Grenada after being downed by anti-aircraft fire. The Grenada invasion, dubbed Operation Urgent Fury, was the Marine Corps' first conflict after Vietnam. (US Army)

An F/A-18D from VMFA(AW)-121 'Green Knights' over Kuwait following Operation Desert Storm in 1991. The two-seat Hornet has been a multi-role workhorse for the Marine Corps for nearly 30 years and is currently being replaced by the F-35. (USMC)

VMFT-401 'Snipers', at MCAS Yuma. Utilising F-21 Kfirs leased from Israel, the 'Snipers' provided dissimilar air combat training for all Marine aviation and air defence units, employing known Soviet fighter tactics to simulate the most likely air threats they would face. The 'Snipers' transitioned to the F-5E Tiger II in 1989 and continue to fly the F-5N in the adversary role at Yuma to this day. The Marine Corps took its first step towards what would prove to be a long and sometimes painful introduction of the revolutionary V-22 Osprey tiltrotor with the type's first flight on 19 March 1989.

Desert Storm and the Balkans in the 1990s

Marine air played a major role in the ejection of Iraqi forces from Kuwait during Operation Desert Storm in January and February 1991. Newer variants of legacy types like the AH-1W SuperCobra, AV-8B Harrier II and F/A-18D Hornet made their combat debuts during Desert Storm. The F/A-18D – a two-seat variant with a missioned rear cockpit intended to replace the A-6E Intruder – flew fast-FAC missions in Kuwait and southern Iraq, directing airstrikes onto Iraqi armour, artillery and infantry ahead of the ground invasion. The A-6E made crucial contributions to the air war in the Gulf in what proved to be its final combat deployment in USMC service – a distinction the Intruder shared with the AH-1J SeaCobra and OV-10 Bronco. The Harriers operated from amphibious assault ships in the Persian Gulf and from austere airfields in northern Saudi Arabia, while Marine helicopters provided reconnaissance, light attack, troop transport, heavy lift and casualty evacuation for the First Marine Expeditionary Force (I MEF) once the ground war started on 24 February. Even unmanned aircraft had a role to play, with Marine RQ-2 Pioneer UAVs used for reconnaissance and adjustment of artillery and naval gunfire.

Throughout the early 1990s, Marine aviation supported peacekeeping and humanitarian operations throughout the world, flying relief missions for Kurdish refugees following Desert Storm, supporting Operation Restore Hope in Somalia, and participating in NATO strikes against Serb forces in Bosnia and Croatia as part of Operations Deny Flight and Deliberate Force.

While assigned to Marine Tactical Electronic Warfare Squadrons (VMAQs), the Corps' Grumman EA-6B Prowlers primarily saw use supporting joint force and coalition air operations over Iraq, the Balkans, Afghanistan, and towards the end of the type's service life, Syria. (Joe Copalman)

The 24th MEU executed a successful TRAP mission (Tactical Recovery of Aircraft and Personnel) on 8 June 1995, using CH-53Es escorted by AH-1Ws to rescue Air Force F-16 pilot Captain Scott O'Grady, who had been shot down over Bosnia six days earlier. An organisational change within the Marine electronic warfare community saw the Corps' sole EA-6B Prowler squadron, VMAQ-2 'Playboys', divided into four squadrons. In addition to supporting rotational deployments in support of Operations Northern Watch and Southern Watch enforcing Iraq's no-fly zones established after Desert Storm, Marine F/A-18s participated in Operation Desert Fox, a series of punitive strikes against Iraqi military and command targets in the face of Saddam Hussein's non-compliance with UN weapons inspectors tasked with verifying that Iraq no longer had weapons of mass destruction or the ability to manufacture them. The final combat missions of the 20th Century for Marine Corps aviation came in May 1999 with Operation Allied Force, another NATO effort aimed at stopping Serb ethno-nationalist violence in the Balkans, this time against ethnic Albanians in Serbia's southern province of Kosovo. Two F/A-18D squadrons and two EA-6B Prowler squadrons contributed to Allied Force, with VMFA(AW)-332 'Moonlighters' executing the first operational employment of the F/A-18D's Advanced Tactical Aerial Reconnaissance System (ATARS) for tactical reconnaissance, a system the Marines would use extensively over Iraq in the coming years.

On the eve of the 21st century, Marine Corps aviation was already in the process of beginning two major transitions – the introduction of the MV-22B Osprey tiltrotor to replace the CH-46E and CH-53D, and the replacement of the service's KC-130F/R/T Hercules refueler/transports – some of which had been in service since the early 1960s – with the KC-130J. The H-1 Upgrade Program that would introduce vastly more capable Huey and Cobra variants from 2008 onward had been initiated with a 1996 contract. The Joint Strike Fighter competition, intended to produce a stealthy, multi-role, STOVL-capable replacement for the Marine Corps' AV-8B Harrier and F/A-18 Hornet (as well as the Navy's F/A-18s and the Air Force's F-16s) had been narrowed down to two competitors – Boeing's X-32 and Lockheed's X-35 – both poised to begin flight testing in 2000.

Additionally, so many of the capability enhancements that made Marine 'legacy' aircraft so effective in combat over Iraq and Afghanistan, particularly in terms of precision ordnance employment, were already operational or in developmental test. Other transitions, such as that from the CH-53E to the CH-53K or the RQ-2 Pioneer to RQ-7B Shadow (and eventually the RQ-21 Blackjack) would not be initiated for several more years.

ORGANISATION AND STRUCTURE OF MARINE AVIATION

First to fight

The United States Marine Corps traces its roots to the establishment of the Continental Marines on 10 November 1775. During the Revolutionary War, the Marines provided the Continental Navy with a maritime infantry force tasked with defending ships from being boarding, conducting boarding operations against Royal Navy vessels and amphibious operations against British coastal installations, and protecting the officers aboard Navy ships from mutiny. With the Continental Marines disbanded in 1783, the newly established United States of America went 15 years without a naval infantry force until the US Congress established the United States Marine Corps on 11 July 1798. Congress formalised the Marine Corps' relationship with the US Navy in 1834 by placing it under the Department of the Navy, a relationship that continues to this day.

Having engaged in numerous maritime and amphibious campaigns during the war against the Barbary Pirates in the early 1800s and the War of 1812, the Marine Corps began participating in expeditionary land warfare in the mid-1800s during the Mexican-American War. In addition to fighting in every major American war since then, the Marine Corps participated in dozens of lower-intensity conflicts throughout the world, primarily protecting US commercial interests abroad. Years of jungle fighting throughout the 1920s and a renewed focus on amphibious operations in the 1930s served the Marines well throughout World War II, where they led the charge against Japanese forces in the Pacific, capturing island after island during a westward campaign that brought them to Japan's doorstep in Okinawa.

The Marine Air-Ground Task Force

Following a strong showing during the Korean War, the Marine Corps effectively became America's amphibious crisis-response force, tasked with being the 'first to fight' in conflict zones around the world and establishing a foothold for follow-on forces. As retired General Harry Blot once told the author, '*The Marine Corps is tasked with being the first to fight. With the Marine Corps, you get there right away and give the powerhouse, the Army and the Air Force, thirty days to get ready.*' To do this, the Marines have relied on their close relationship with the US Navy, utilising specialised shallow-draft amphibious assault ships for transporting battalion-sized elements of Marines to any littoral hot-spot in the world, complete with landing craft to move tanks and artillery ashore and aircraft to provide aerial firepower.

The core concept at the heart of the Marine Corps' post-Korean War organisational model is the Marine Air-Ground Task Force, or MAGTF. The MAGTF is a scalable model of task organisation that is comprised of four elements no matter the size – a command element (CE), a Ground Combat Element (GCE), an Aviation Combat Element (ACE) and a Logistics Combat Element (LCE).

The largest conventional MAGTF is a Marine Expeditionary Force (MEF), comprised of a Marine Division (MARDIV), a Marine Air Wing (MAW) and a Marine Logistics Group (MLG), with the CE being run by a lieutenant general (three-star) and his staff. The second largest form a MAGTF takes is the Marine Expeditionary Brigade (MEB), with the GCE being a Marine infantry regiment, the ACE being a Marine Aircraft Group (MAG) and the LCE being a Combat Logistics Regiment (CLR), all commanded by a brigadier or major general (one-star or two star).

The most common MAGTF is the Marine Expeditionary Unit, or MEU. An MEU consists of a reinforced infantry battalion, a reinforced Marine Medium Tiltrotor Squadron (VMM) and a Combat Logistics Battalion (CLB), all under the command of a colonel. (See page 27 for an example of the MEU/ACE).

In addition to MEFs, MEBs and MEUs, the Marine Corps fields Special Purpose MAGTFs, typically assigned to regional commands for a limited set of missions, vice the MEU's 'any mission anywhere' orientation. Known as SPMAGTFs, these task forces tend to be smaller than MEUs, with less robust tables of organisation. For example, SPMAGTF – Southern Command in Honduras relies on a small detachment of CH-53Es as its ACE, while SPMAGTF – Crisis Response – AFRICOM's ACE consists of a squadron of MV-22s with a two-ship KC-130 detachment.

Marine Air-Ground Task Force (MAGTF)

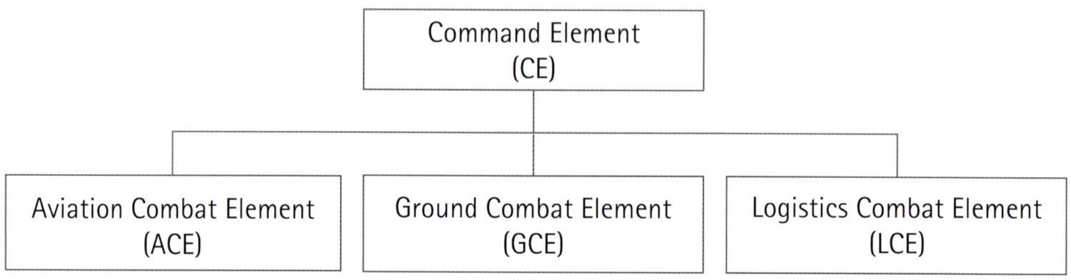

Aviation organisation

Marine Corps aviation is organised into four similar, but not identical Marine Air Wings (MAWs), with multiple Marine Aircraft Groups (MAGs) underneath them, and several squadrons reporting to each MAG. In the three active-component MAWs (1st, 2nd and 3rd MAW), the MAGs are comprised of either fixed-wing or rotor-wing/tiltrotor squadrons. For example, under 3rd MAW at Marine Corps Air Station (MCAS) Miramar, MAG-11 oversees F/A-18, F-35 and KC-130 squadrons, while MAG-16 consists of CH-53E and MV-22 squadrons. The 4th MAW is the aviation element of Marine Forces Reserve, and is structured differently, with two MAGs organised not by aircraft type, but geographically, with MAG-49 responsible for reserve squadrons on the east coast, and MAG-41 responsible for the west coast reserve squadrons. Each of the four MAWs possess a mix of squadron types, each capable of performing one or more of the six functions of Marine Corps aviation. These six functions are assault support, anti-air warfare, offensive air support, electronic warfare, control of aircraft and missiles, and aerial reconnaissance.

Squadrons routinely detach aircraft and personnel to the ACEs for MEUs, SPMAGTFs and other deployments that do not demand the presence of a full squadron. The size of these detachments differs in each aviation community and depends on what capabilities the unit being supported needs. In cases where a detachment separates from a squadron, the larger element is known as a squadron minus, and may be deployed as well, independent of the detachment.

Squadron designations in Marine Corps aviation follow the same naming convention as US naval aviation units, with 'V' designating fixed-wing units and 'H' designating rotor-wing units, with multiple sub-designations indicating a squadron's purpose, be it attack, fighter, transport, etc. The constant in all USMC aviation squadron designations is the letter 'M' for 'Marine'. Below is a list of all deployable, operational squadron types in Marine Corps aviation, most of which can be found under each of the four MAWs:

HMH | Marine Heavy Helicopter (CH-53E, CH-53K): support the MAGTF commander by providing assault support transport of heavy equipment, combat troops and supplies, day or night, under all weather conditions during expeditionary, joint, or combined operations.

HMLA | Marine Light Attack Helicopter (AH-1W, AH-1Z, UH-1Y): support the MAGTF commander by providing offensive air support, utility support, armed escort and airborne supporting arms coordination, day or night under all weather conditions during expeditionary, joint or combined operations.

VMA | Marine Attack (AV-8B): support the MAGTF commander by destroying surface targets and escorting friendly aircraft, day or night, under all weather conditions, during expeditionary, joint, or combined operations. (Only 2nd and 3rd MAW).

VMFA | Marine Fighter/Attack (F/A-18A to D, F-35B/C): **F/A-18** – support the MAGTF commander by providing supporting arms coordination, conducting multi-sensor imagery reconnaissance and destroying surface targets and enemy aircraft, day or night, under all weather conditions, during expeditionary, joint, or combined operations. **F-35** – to attack and destroy surface targets, intercept and destroy enemy aircraft, provide electronic warfare support and network enabled reconnaissance support across the full spectrum of combat operations.

VMGR | Marine Aerial Refueler Transport (KC-130J/T): support the MAGTF commander by providing air-to-air refuelling, assault support, CAS and MIR, day or night under all weather conditions during expeditionary, joint, or combined operations.

VMM | Marine Medium Tiltrotor (MV-22B): support the MAGTF commander by providing day/night all weather assault support by transporting combat troops and equipment during expeditionary, joint, or combined operations.

VMU | Marine Unmanned Aerial Vehicle (MQ-9, RQ-21): support the MAGTF commander by conducting multi-sensor reconnaissance and surveillance, and facilitating the destruction of targets, from unmanned aerial platforms, during expeditionary, joint and combined operations.

Non-Flying MAW Units

In addition to flying squadrons, each MAW oversees numerous non-flying squadrons tasked with various aspects of expeditionary and at-sea aviation operations. Every MAG oversees two of these squadrons – one Marine Aviation Logistics Squadron (MALS) and one Marine Wing Support Squadron (MWSS). The MALS handles intermediate maintenance, which falls between that which can be completed on the flight line or in the hangar by the squadrons, and full teardown maintenance done at the depot level. Intermediate, or 'I-Level' maintenance typically includes repairs that require components to be removed from the aircraft – engine repairs, avionics repairs, etc. Additionally, a MALS will distribute ordnance among the squadrons within a MAG per their training or combat requirements. Tasked with establishing, maintaining and running expeditionary airfields, the MWSS units employ the broadest range of military occupational specialties of any type of squadron within Marine aviation. MWSS Marines are responsible for everything from assessing potential sites for expeditionary airfields and forward arming and refuelling points (FARPs) and setting them up to providing security for them to providing clean drinking water and food for the Marines running and flying from the airfield to crash rescue, salvage and recovery operations.

While the MALS and MWSS squadrons fall under the MAGs, most aviation support squadrons fall under Marine Air Control Groups (MACGs), with each MAW having one MACG. The Marine Tactical Air Command Squadrons (MTACS) operate Tactical Air Control Centres (TACC) from which the MAW command staff manage tactical air operations. From the TACC, the MAW commander manages the actions of the Marine Air Support Squadron (MASS) and Marine Air Control Squadron (MACS). The MASS runs the Direct Air Support Centre (DASC), which coordinates air support for ground units, including deconfliction with supporting arms, while MACS units provide basic air traffic control as well as management of anti-air warfare through the Tactical Air Operations Centre (TAOC), which includes airborne early warning and ground controlled intercept (GCI). Marine Wing Communications Squadrons (MWCS) provide and maintain the communications infrastructure needed to conduct aerial operations.

Flying units outside the MAW

The Marine Corps also operates a few flying squadrons outside of the MAWs. The most common of these units are the Headquarters and Headquarters Squadrons (H&HS) at each Marine Corps Air Station (MCAS) that operate commercial-derivative aircraft like Beech UC-12 Huron and/or Cessna UC-35 Citation in the Operational Support Airlift (OSA) role, primarily used for transporting high-ranking officers. Until recently, some H&HS squadrons also operated small helicopter detachments assigned the search and rescue (SAR) mission, with the last of these – H&HS MCAS Yuma – retiring its HH-1N Twin Hueys and ending its SAR obligation on 15 March 2020.

The highest-profile aviation unit not assigned to a MAW is Marine Helicopter Squadron One (HMX-1), which is assigned directly to Headquarters Marine Corps (HQMC) and tasked with short-haul movement of the President of the United States and other VIPs. Marine Operational Test and Evaluation Squadron One (VMX-1) is also assigned directly to HQMC and performs operational test and evaluation (OT&E) for most aircraft types in USMC service. While not permanently assigned any aircraft, Marine Aviation Weapons and Tactics Squadron One (MAWTS-1) falls under HQMC as well, though as a subordinate unit of the Marine Corps' Training and Education Command (TECOM) rather than directly reporting to Headquarters. As the Corps' aviation centre of excellence, MAWTS-1 creates and revises all training and readiness manuals for USMC aviation units, administers all advanced qualifications for aircrew and aviation support Marines and runs the twice-annual Weapons and Tactics Instructor (WTI) course at MCAS Yuma.

Aviation and the MEU

The MEU has long been the centrepiece of Marine expeditionary operations, sized to fit aboard a three-ship US Navy formation known as an Amphibious Ready Group (ARG). The flagship of each ARG is a flat-topped amphibious assault ship, with two ship classes currently filling this role – the LHA (Landing Helicopter Assault) and the LHD (Landing Helicopter Dock). The largest ship in the ARG, the LHA/LHD carries the MEU's command element, most of the ACE, and a good portion of the GCE. The second-largest ship class in an ARG is the Landing Platform Dock (LPD). In addition to a cavernous well deck to launch amphibious assault vehicles (AAVs, seaworthy armoured personnel carriers) and hovercrafts known as LCACs (Landing Craft, Air Cushion) to transport tanks, trucks and other non-amphibious vehicles ashore, LPDs have a modest flight deck at the rear of the ship to accommodate aviation assets. The smallest ship within an ARG is the Landing Ship Dock, which again, has a well deck capable of launching amphibious vehicles and LCACs and flight deck at the rear of the ship.

The Navy and Marine Corps have two ARG/MEU teams deployed at any given time, with three west coast MEUs (the 11th, 13th and 15th) and three east coast MEUs (22nd, 24th and 26th) each deploying on a regular, rotating cycle, with each deployment typically lasting six months. Additionally, the 31st MEU is permanently forward-deployed in Japan and serves as America's crisis response force in the Indo-Pacific region. Like the CONUS-based MEUs, the 31st will occasionally go out to sea on regional patrols as part of an ARG. The primary mission of MEUs is to provide a mobile, responsive force to conduct amphibious and expeditionary warfare and to secure the ports and airfields needed for the introduction of follow-on forces should the need arise, making the MEU the practical embodiment of the Marine Corps motto, 'First to Fight.' In addition to combat operations, MEUs train for several other missions, including tactical recovery of aircraft and personnel (TRAP), humanitarian assistance/disaster relief (HA/DR), non-combatant evacuation operations (NEO), maritime interdiction operations (MIO) to include counter-piracy, stability operations and theatre security cooperation. As a self-contained force, each MEU is capable of all of the above, with the flexibility to addresses challenges beyond those doctrinally defined. Additionally, MEUs participate in multiple theatre cooperation engagements with allied armed forces around the world. The relationships built through these engagements – some of which are regularly scheduled multinational exercises – have two functions. The first is to establish, reinforce, or refine interoperability procedures with regional allies should an operational need for such cooperation arise. The second is to enhance the training of partner nations to bolster their own self-defence capabilities.

The ACE for each MEU has been standardised for several decades. Having previously centred around a complete Marine Medium Helicopter Squadron (HMM) flying 12 Boeing-Vertol CH-46E Sea Knights, the modern ACE is built around a ten-aircraft Bell-Boeing MV-22B Osprey detachment from a Marine Medium Tiltrotor Squadron

The USS *America* (LHA 6) is the first of a new class of amphibious assault ships and was built without a floodable well deck, as aviation is becoming the Corps' primary ship-to-shore connector. (USN/MCA Theodore C. Lee)

(VMM). Known as a reinforced VMM, or VMM(REIN), the modern ACE is comprised of the following:

- 10 × MV-22B Osprey
- 6 × AV-8B Harrier or F-35B Lightning II
- 5 × RQ-21A Blackjack
- 4 × CH-53E Super Stallion (soon to be CH-53K King Stallion)
- 4 × AH-1Z Viper
- 3 or 4 × UH-1Y Venom
- 2 × MH-60S Knighthawk
  (US Navy assets, provide search and rescue and additional utility capability)

The composition of the 26th MEU's ACE during its 2019 cruise:
10 × MV-22B from VMM-365
6 × AV-8B from VMA-542
5 × RQ-21 from VMU-2
4 × CH-53E from HMH-461
4 × AH-1W from HMLA-167
4 × UH-1Y from HMLA-167
2 × MH-60s from HSC-26 and HSC-28, respectively

Additionally, MEUs often rely on two-ship detachments of Lockheed KC-130J Hercules for transport and aerial refuelling. Incapable of operating from amphibious shipping, KC-130s supporting MEUs typically do so on a 'tether', flying from land bases in the region where a MEU is operating and prioritising MEU support over other tasks. Occasionally, a MEU will augment its ACE with extra fixed-wing aircraft for specific operations. The 'Harrier carrier' concept dates back to the 1970s, when the Marines evaluated full-squadron shipboard operations aboard amphibious assault ships with the early AV-8As and has evolved to the 'Lightning carrier' concept currently being evaluated with the F-35B Lightning II.

A MEU's ACE is commanded by the VMM(REIN) squadron commander. Underneath the ACE CO, each detachment is led by a detachment officer-in-charge (OIC), who is typically a senior major from the contributing squadron. While a squadron has aircraft, pilots and maintainers assigned to a MEU det, the rest of the squadron – known as a 'squadron minus', – can still deploy. Often, this takes the form of a Unit Deployment Program (UDP) deployment to Japan, or a 'dirt det' in support of a SPMAGTF, a Marine Rotational Force, or a contingency operation like Operation Inherent Resolve. Sometimes a squadron minus will remain at home and engage in unit-level training while the 'det' is at sea with the MEU, building up newer pilots and adding instructor qualifications for more experienced ones.

A flexible force for the 21st century

Regardless of the size or composition of a MAGTF, the integrated Marine air-ground team gives geographic combatant commanders flexibility to tackle almost any challenge that may present itself, from low-threat humanitarian operations to full-scale combined arms warfare against peer competitor states. Advances in aviation technology give Marine air more range, better sensors, smarter weapons and the ability to share critical information to enhance situational awareness, both with other aircraft and with ground forces, making the Marine Corps of the 21st century even more capable of meeting and defeating most of the threats it will face.

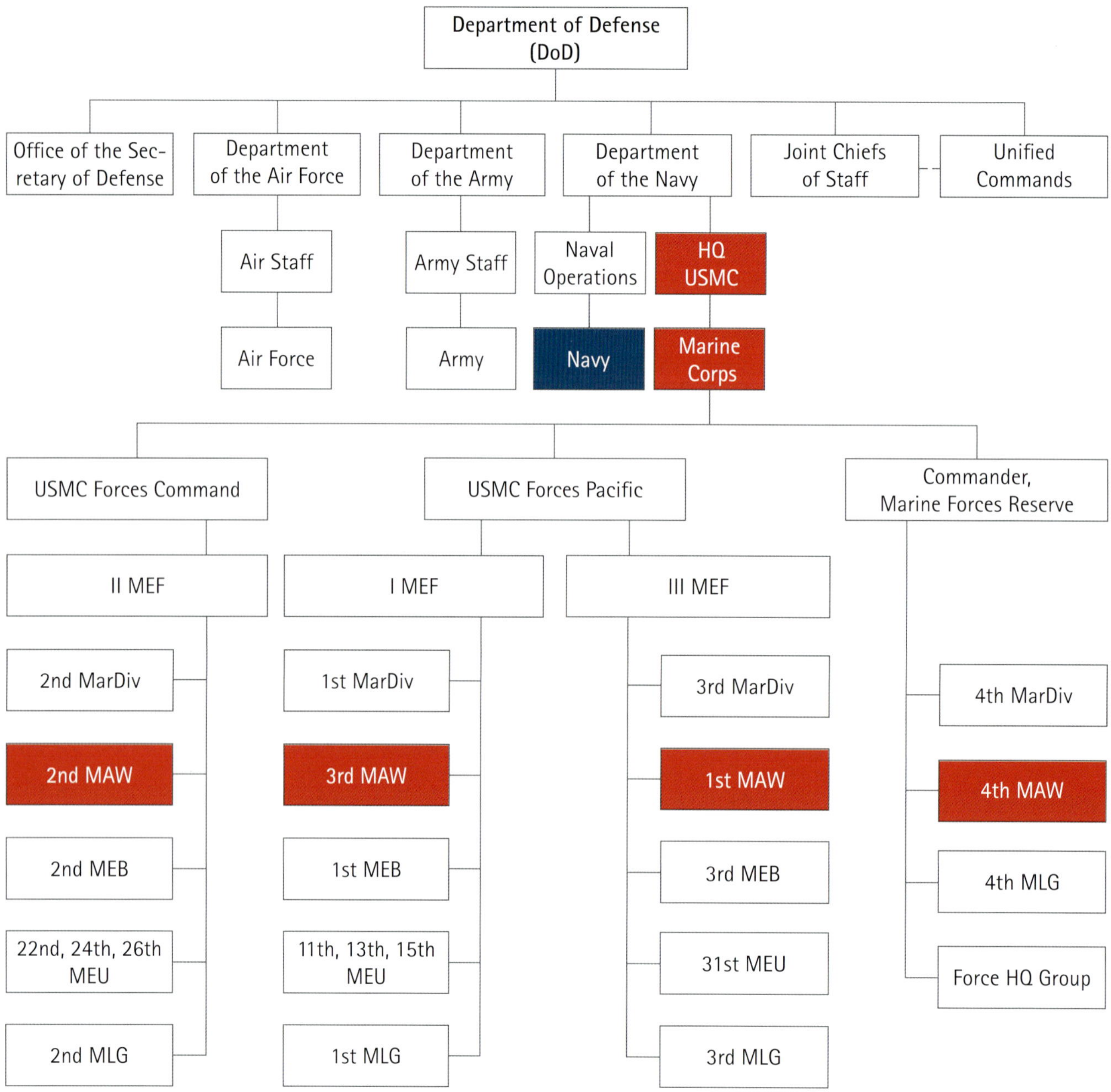

A simplified graph of the USMC's administrative structure.
(Drawing by Dr. Heinz Berger)

USMC ORBAT

Headquarters USMC (HQ USMC, The Pentagon, Arlington, Virginia)

Unit (Wing/Squadron)	Location (MCAS)	Aircraft type	Remarks
HMX-1 'The Nighthawks'	MCAF Quantico, Virginia	VH-3D, VH-60N, VH-92, MV-22B	VH-92 deliveries begin in 2021
MAWTS-1 'none'	MCAS Yuma, Arizona		Reports directly to Training and Education Command under HQ USMC
VMX-1 'Argonauts'	MCAS Yuma, Arizona	F-35B, AH-1Z, UH-1Y, CH-53E, CH-53K, RQ-21A, CQ-24A, MV-22B	

1st Marine Air Wing (1st MAW, Camp Foster, Okinawa, Japan)

Unit (Wing/Squadron)	Location (MCAS)	Aircraft type	Remarks
MWHS-1 'America's Finest'	Camp Foster		
Marine Aircraft Group 12 (MAG-12)			HQ MCAS Iwakuni, Japan
MALS-12 'Marauders'	Iwakuni		
MWSS-171 'The Sentinels'	Iwakuni		
VMFA-121 'Green Knights'	Iwakuni	F-35B	
VMFA-242 'Bats'	Iwakuni	F-35B	Began F/A-18D to F-35B transition in Oct 2020
VMGR-152 'Sumos'	Iwakuni	KC-130J	
Marine Aircraft Group 24 (MAG-24)			HQ Kaneohe Bay, Hawaii
HMH-463 'Pegasus'	Kaneohe Bay	CH-53E	
HMLA-367 'Scarface'	Kaneohe Bay	AH-1Z UH-1Y	
MALS-24 'Warriors'	Kaneohe Bay		
MWSD-24 'Gryphons'	Kaneohe Bay		
VMM-268 'Red Dragons'	Kaneohe Bay	MV-22B	
VMM-363 'Lucky Red Lions'	Kaneohe Bay	MV-22B	
VMU-3 'Phantoms'	Kaneohe Bay	RQ-21A	
Marine Aircraft Group 36 (MAG-36)			HQ MCAS Futenma, Japan
MALS-36 'Bladerunner'	Futenma		
MWSS-172 'Firebirds'	Futenma		
VMM-262 'Flying Tigers'	Futenma	MV-22B	
VMM-265 'Dragons'	Futenma	MV-22B	

Marine Air Control Group 18 (MACG-18)			HQ MCAS Futenma, Japan
MACS-4 'Vice Squad'	Futenma		
MASS-2 'Pacific Vagabonds'	Futenma		
MTACS-18 'Keep Charging'	Futenma		
MWCS-18 'Warriors From The Ground Up'	Futenma		

2nd Marine Air Wing (2nd MAW, MCAS Cherry Point, North Carolina, USA)

Unit (Wing/Squadron)	Location (MCAS)	Aircraft type	Remarks
MWHS-2 'Snake Eyes'			HQ MCAS Cherry Point, Havelock, North Carolina
Marine Aircraft Group 14 (MAG-14)			HQ MCAS Cherry Point, Havelock, North Carolina
MALS-14 'Dragons'	Cherry Point		
MWSS-271 'Workhorse'	Cherry Point		
VMA-223 'Bulldogs'	Cherry Point	AV-8B	
VMA-231 'Ace of Spades'	Cherry Point	AV-8B	
VMA-542 'Tigers'	Cherry Point	AV-8B	
VMAT-203 'Hawks'	Cherry Point	AV-8B, TAV-8B	AV-8B FRS
VMGR-252 'Otis'	Cherry Point	KC-130J	
VMU-2 'Night Owls'	Cherry Point	RQ-21A	
Marine Aircraft Group 26 (MAG-26)			HQ MCAS New River, Jacksonville, North Carolina
MALS-26 'Patriots'	New River		
MWSS-272 'Untouchables'	New River		
VMM-162 'Golden Eagles'	New River	MV-22B	
VMM-261 'Raging Bulls'	New River	MV-22B	
VMM-263 'Thunder Chickens'	New River	MV-22B	
VMM-264 'Black Nights'	New River	MV-22B	Designated for deactivation under Commandant Berger's March 2020 Force Structure Initiative
VMM-266 'Fighting Griffins'	New River	MV-22B	
VMM-365 'Blue Knights'	New River	MV-22B	
VMMT-204 'Raptors'	New River	MV-22B	MV-22 FRS
Marine Aircraft Group 29 (MAG-29)			HQ MCAS New River, Jacksonville, North Carolina
HMH-366 'Hammerheads'	New River	CH-53E	Scheduled to be the first operational squadron to receive the CH-53K King Stallion
HMH-461 'Ironhorse'	New River	CH-53E	
HMH-464 'Condors'	New River	CH-53E	
HMHT-302 'Phoenix'	New River	CH-53E	CH-53E FRS
HMLA-167 'Warriors'	New River	AH-1Z, UH-1Y	

HMLA-269 'The Gunrunners'	New River	AH-1Z, UH-1Y	
MALS-29 'Wolverines'	New River		
MWSS-274 'Ironmen'	New River		
Marine Aircraft Group 31 (MAG-31)			**HQ MCAS Beaufort, South Carolina**
MALS-31 'Stingers'	Beaufort		
MWSS-273 'Sweat Hogs'	Beaufort		
VMFA-115 'Silver Eagles'	Beaufort	F/A-18C	
VMFA-251 'Thunderbolts'	Beaufort	F/A-18C (F-35C)	Deactivated 23 April 2020 in preparation for F-35C transition
VMFA-312 'Checkerboards'	Beaufort	F/A-18C	
VMFA(AW)-224 'Bengals'	Beaufort	F/A-18D	
VMFA(AW)-533 'Hawks'	Beaufort	F/A-18D	
VMFAT-501 'Warlords'	Beaufort	F-35B	
VMFAT-502 'Nightmares'	Beaufort	F-35B	
Marine Air Control Group 28 (MACG-28)			**HQ MCAS Cherry Point, Havelock, North Carolina**
MACS-2 'Eyes of the MAGTF'	Cherry Point		
MASS-1 'Chieftain'	Cherry Point		
MTACS-28 'Olympians'	Cherry Point		
MWCS-28 'Spartans'	Cherry Point		
2nd LAAD Bn 'Death From Below'	Cherry Point		Low-level air defence unit

3rd Marine Air Wing (3rd MAW, MCAS Miramar, California, USA)

Unit (Wing/Squadron)	Location (MCAS)	Aircraft type	Remarks
MWHS-3 'Eagles'			HQ MCAS Miramar, San Diego, California
Marine Aircraft Group 11 (MAG-11)			**HQ MCAS Miramar, San Diego, California**
MALS-11 'Devilfish'	Miramar		
MWSS-373 'Ace Support'	Miramar		
VMFA-225 'Vikings'	Miramar	F-35B	Final F/A-18D flight on 23 January 2020, still awaiting arrival of F-35B
VMFA-232 'Red Devils'	Miramar	F/A-18C	
VMFA-314 'Black Knights'	Miramar	F-35C	First operational USMC F-35C squadron
VMFA-323 'Death Rattlers'	Miramar	F/A-18C	Final F/A-18C squadron to deploy aboard an aircraft carrier, embarking on the USS *Nimitz* (CVN 68) as part of Carrier Air Wing 11 in June 2020
VMFAT-101 'Sharpshooters'	Miramar	F/A-18C, F/A-18D	F/A-18 FRS
VMGR-352 'Raiders'	Miramar	KC-130J	

Marine Aircraft Group 13 (MAG-13)			HQ MCAS Yuma, Arizona
MALS-13 'Black Widows'	Yuma		
MWSS-371 'Sand Sharks'	Yuma		
VMA-214 'Black Sheep'	Yuma	AV-8B	
VMA-311 'Tomcats'	Yuma	AV-8B	
VMFA-122 'Flying Leathernecks'	Yuma	F-35B	
VMFA-211 'Wake Island Avengers'	Yuma	F-35B	
VMU-1 'Watchdogs'	Yuma	MQ-9A, RQ-21A	

Marine Aircraft Group 16 (MAG-16)			HQ MCAS Miramar, San Diego, California
HMH-361 'Flying Tigers'	Miramar	CH-53E	
HMH-462 'Heavy Haulers'	Miramar	CH-53E	designated for deactivation under Commandant Berger's March 2020 Force Structure Initiative
HMH-465 'Warhorse'	Miramar	CH-53E	
HMH-466 'Wolfpack'	Miramar	CH-53E	
MALS-16 'Forerunners'	Miramar		
MWSS-374 'Rhinos'	Miramar		
VMM-161 'Greyhawks'	Miramar	MV-22B	
VMM-163 'Ridge Runners'	Miramar	MV-22B	
VMM-165 'White Knights'	Miramar	MV-22B	
VMM-166 'Sea Elk'	Miramar	MV-22B	
VMM-362 'Ugly Angels'	Miramar	MV-22B	

Marine Aircraft Group 39 (MAG-39)			HQ MCAS Camp Pendleton, Oceanside, California
HMLA-169 'Vipers'	Camp Pendleton	AH-1Z, UH-1Y	
HMLA-267 'Stingers'	Camp Pendleton	AH-1Z, UH-1Y	
HMLA-369 'Gunfighters'	Camp Pendleton	AH-1Z, UH-1Y	
HMLA-469 'Vengeance'	Camp Pendleton	AH-1Z, UH-1Y	
HMLAT-303 'Atlas'	Camp Pendleton	AH-1Z, UH-1Y	AH-1 and UH-1 FRS
MALS-39 'Hellhounds'	Camp Pendleton		
MWSS-372 'Diamondbacks'	Camp Pendleton		
VMM-164 'Knightriders'	Camp Pendleton	MV-22B	
VMM-364 'Purple Foxes'	Camp Pendleton	MV-22B	

Marine Air Control Group 38 (MACG-38)			HQ MCAS Miramar, San Diego, California
MACS-1 'Falconers'	Miramar		
MASS-3 'Blacklist'	Miramar		
MTACS-38 'Phoenix'	Miramar		
MWCS-38 'Red Lightning'	Miramar		
3rd LAAD Bn 'Feel The Sting'	Miramar		Low-level air defence unit

4th Marine Air Wing (4th MAW, New Orleans, Louisiana, USA)

Unit (Wing/Squadron)	Location (MCAS)	Aircraft type	Remarks
VMR Belle Chasse 'Easy'	NAS New Orleans, Louisiana	UC-12W, UC-35C	
Marine Aircraft Group 41 (MAG-41)			**HQ NAS Fort Worth, Texas**
HMLA-775 'Coyotes'	Camp Pendleton, California	AH-1Z, UH-1Y	
MALS-41 'Desperados'	Fort Worth, Texas		
MWSS-471 'Red Wolf'	Minneapolis, Minnesota		
MWSS-473 'The Gargoyles'	Miramar, California		
VMFA-112 'Cowboys'	Fort Worth, Texas	F/A-18A++, F/A-18/C+	Transitioning
VMFT-401 'Snipers'	Yuma, Arizona	F-5F, F-5N	
VMGR-234 'Rangers'	Fort Worth, Texas	KC-130J	
VMM-764 'Moonlight'	Miramar, California	MV-22B	
VMR-1 'Roadrunners'	Fort Worth, Texas	C-40A	Transitioning to C-40
VMU-4 'Evil Eyes'	Camp Pendleton, California	RQ-21A	
Marine Aircraft Group 49 (MAG-49)			**HQ JB McGuire–Dix–Lakehurst, New Jersey**
HMH-772 (-) 'The Hustlers'	McGuire–Dix–Lakehurst	CH-53E	
HMLA-773 'Red Dogs'	McGuire–Dix–Lakehurst New Orleans, Louisiana (Det A)	AH-1W, AH-1Z, UH-1Y	HMLA-773 Det A in New Orleans is the final operator of AH-1W, beginning transition in late 2020
MALS-49 'Magicians'	Stewart ANG, New York		
MWSS-472 'Dragons'	McGuire–Dix–Lakehurst		
VMGR-452 'Yankees'	Stewart ANG, New York	KC-130T, KC-130J	Transitioning
VMM-774 'Wild Goose'	NAS Norfolk, Virginia	MV-22B	

Marine Air Control Group 48 (MACG-48)	HQ NAS Great Lakes, Illinois
MACS-24 'Earthquake'	Virginia Beach, Virginia
MASS-6 'Lighthouse'	Westover ARB, Massachusetts
MTACS-48 'none'	Great Lakes, Illinois
MWCS-48 'Roar of the Corps'	Great Lakes, Illinois

Marine Corps Installations Command

Unit (Wing/Squadron)	Location (MCAS)	Aircraft type	Remarks
Marine Corps Installations – East (MCIEAST)			
H&HS Beaufort 'Swamp Foxes'	Beaufort, South Carolina	UC-12M	
H&HS Cherry Point 'Rams'	Cherry Point, North Carolina	UC-35D	
H&HS New River 'Ka-Bar'	New River, North Carolina	UC-12F, UC-12W	
Marine Corps Installations – West (MCIWEST)			
H&HS Miramar 'Grizzlies'	Miramar, California	UC-12W, UC-35D	
H&HS Camp Pendleton 'Stampede'	Camp Pendleton, California	UC-12W	Commenced UC-12 operations on 4 August 2020
H&HS Yuma 'Guardians'	Yuma, Arizona	UC-12F	
Marine Corps Installations – Pacific (MCIPAC)			
H&HS Futenma 'Magic'	Futenma, Japan	UC-12W	
H&HS Iwakuni 'Torii'	Iwakuni, Japan	UC-12W	
H&HS Kaneohe Bay 'Ghost'	Kaneohe, Hawaii	C-20G	

USMC overseas bases and operating locations

1. HQ Camp Foster, Okinawa, Japan (HQ 1st MAW)
2. MCAS Futenma, Japan
3. MCAS Iwakuni, Japan
4. Morón AB, Spain (SPMAGTF-CR-AF)
5. NAS Sigonella, Italy (SP-MAGTF-CR-AF)
6. Vaernes Air Station, Norway (Marine Rotational Force – Europe)
7. Stuttgart AAF, Germany (SP-MAGTF-CR-AF)
8. Ahmed al Jaber AB, Kuwait (SPMAGTF-CR-CC)
9. RAAF Base Darwin, Australia (Marine Rotational Force)
10. Soto Cano AB, Honduras (SP-MAGTF-S)

USMC air stations and operating locations in the United States

1. Andrews AFB, Washington DC
2. MCAS Beaufort, South Carolina
3. MCAS Camp Pendleton, Oceanside, California
4. MCAS Cherry Point, Havelock, North Carolina (HQ 2nd MAW and base)
5. NAS Fort Worth, Texas
6. MCB Hawaii
7. JB McGuire-Dix-Lakehurst, New Jersey
8. MCAS Miramar, San Diego, California (HQ 3rd MAW)
9. MCAS New River, Jacksonville, North Carolina
10. NAS JRB New Orleans, Louisiana
11. NS Norfolk, Virginia
12. Quantico MCAF, Virginia
13. Stewart ANGB, New York
14. MCAS Yuma, Arizona
15. JB Anacostia-Bolling, Washington DC
16. Edwards AFB, California
17. MCCS Twentynine Palms, California

▶ ▶ Map of the world.
(Drawing by James Lawrence)

▶ Map of the United States, including Alaska and Hawaii.
(Drawing by James Lawrence)

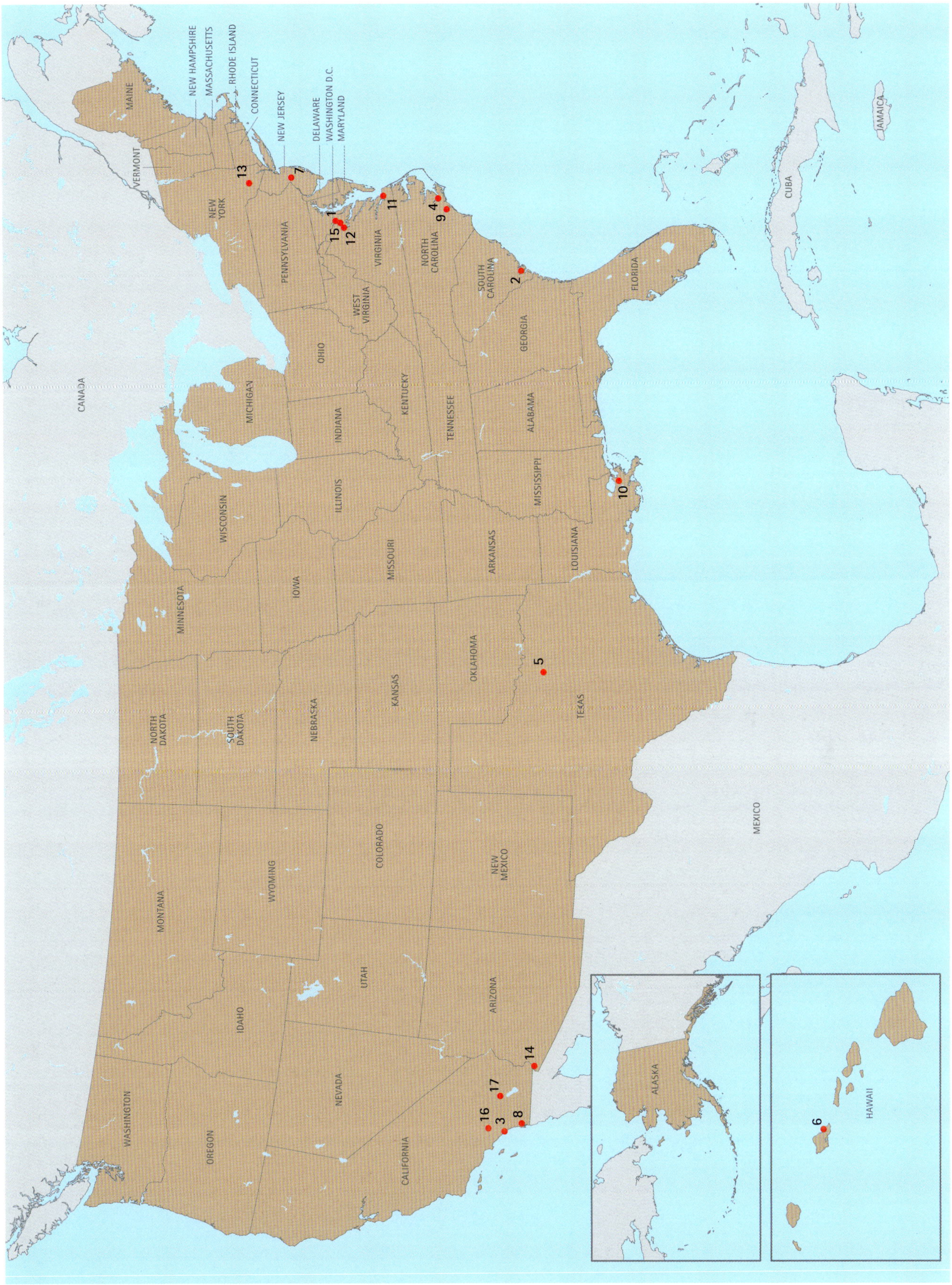
CANADA
MAINE
VERMONT
NEW HAMPSHIRE
MASSACHUSETTS
RHODE ISLAND
CONNECTICUT
NEW YORK
NEW JERSEY
DELAWARE
WASHINGTON D.C.
MARYLAND
PENNSYLVANIA
VIRGINIA
WEST VIRGINIA
NORTH CAROLINA
SOUTH CAROLINA
GEORGIA
FLORIDA
OHIO
MICHIGAN
INDIANA
KENTUCKY
TENNESSEE
ALABAMA
MISSISSIPPI
ILLINOIS
WISCONSIN
MISSOURI
ARKANSAS
LOUISIANA
IOWA
MINNESOTA
OKLAHOMA
KANSAS
NEBRASKA
SOUTH DAKOTA
NORTH DAKOTA
TEXAS
COLORADO
NEW MEXICO
WYOMING
MONTANA
UTAH
ARIZONA
IDAHO
NEVADA
WASHINGTON
OREGON
CALIFORNIA
MEXICO
CUBA
JAMAICA
ALASKA
HAWAII
1
2
3
4
5
6
7
8
9
10
11
12
13
14
15
16
17

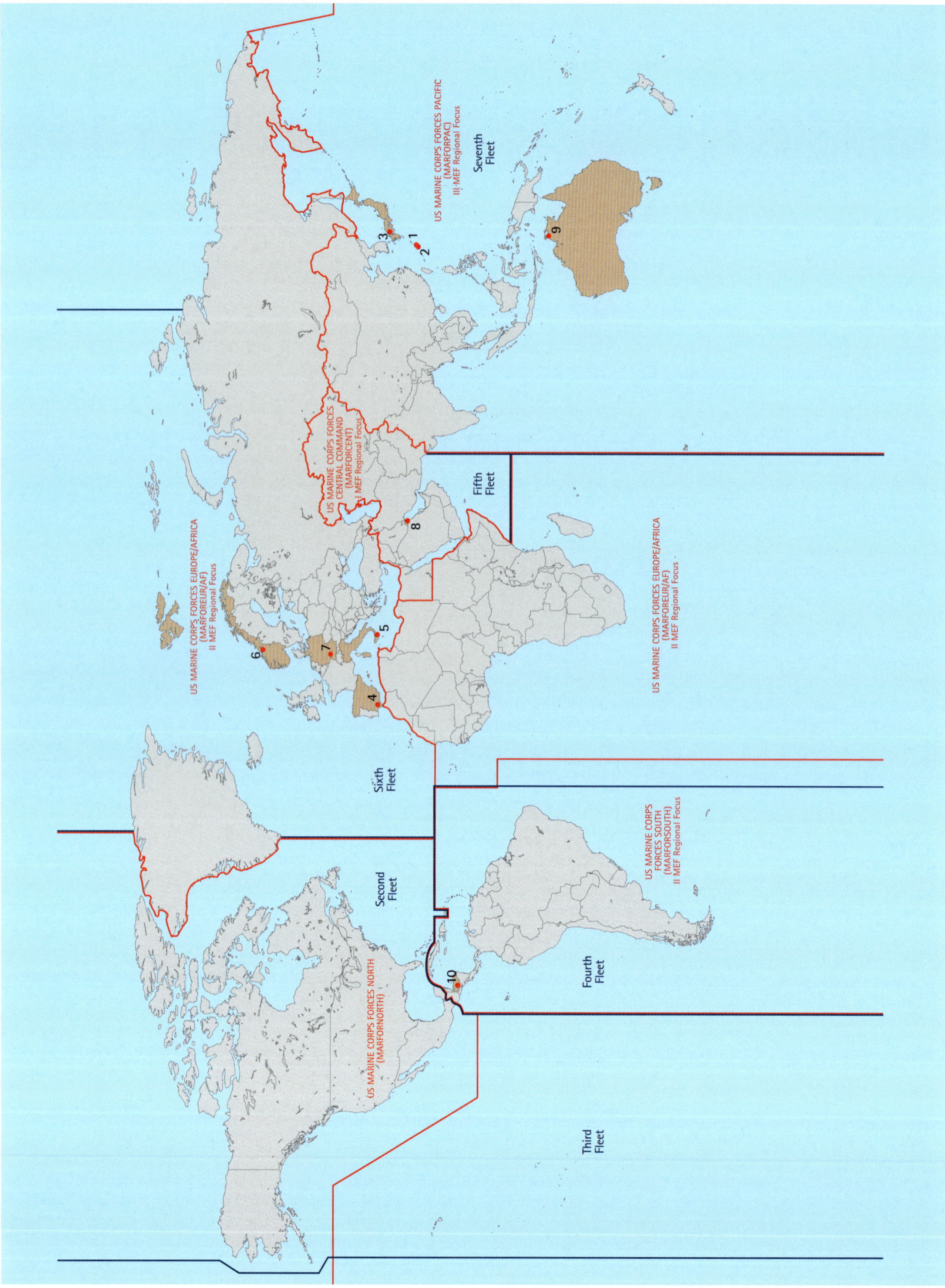
US MARINE CORPS FORCES PACIFIC
(MARFORPAC)
III MEF Regional Focus
Seventh Fleet
US MARINE CORPS FORCES CENTRAL COMMAND
(MARFORCENT)
I MEF Regional Focus
Fifth Fleet
US MARINE CORPS FORCES EUROPE/AFRICA
(MARFOREUR/AF)
II MEF Regional Focus
US MARINE CORPS FORCES EUROPE/AFRICA
(MARFOREUR/AF)
II MEF Regional Focus
Sixth Fleet
Second Fleet
US MARINE CORPS FORCES SOUTH
(MARFORSOUTH)
II MEF Regional Focus
Fourth Fleet
US MARINE CORPS FORCES NORTH
(MARFORNORTH)
Third Fleet
1
2
3
4
5
6
7
8
9
10

USMC AVIATION TRAINING

From its inception, Marine aviation has been tied to US naval aviation. Nearly every Marine aviator flying today went through the US Navy's aviation training pipeline – just like Alfred Cunningham did back in 1912. For a Marine to become an aviator, he or she must first earn a commission as an officer. This happens though a number of ways – through naval Reserve Officer Training Corps (ROTC) programmes at universities throughout the United States, through USMC Officer Candidate School in Quantico, Virginia for those who earned their bachelor's degrees outside of an ROTC programme, or through graduating from the United States Naval Academy in Annapolis, Maryland.

Once commissioned as a 2nd Lieutenant, new Marine officers attend The Basic School (TBS) at Quantico, where they learn how to lead a Marine rifle platoon. Aside from aligning with the service's core ethos of 'every Marine a rifleman', this training is critical for prospective Marine aviators, as it reinforces for them the primary purpose of Marine air – to support the infantryman on the ground. After six months at TBS, prospective aviators report to Naval Air Station (NAS) Pensacola in the Florida panhandle for Aviation Preflight Indoctrination, a six-week introduction to the basics of naval aviation.

Flight training – from primary to pipeline

Students who graduate from API advance to Primary Flight Training where they fly the T-6B Texan II (which replaced the T-34C Mentor in 2011) with Training Wing Four (TW-4) at NAS Corpus Christi in Texas, or TW-5 at Florida's NAS Whiting Field. Primary is where students learn the aircraft systems and capabilities and the operating and emergency procedures for the T-6, engage in flight fundamentals like take-offs, landings and basic manoeuvres, as well as navigation, formation, instrument and night flying. Upon graduation from primary, students continue on to either Intermediate Flight Training or directly to Advanced Flight Training based on which track they are on. The four tracks available to Marine aviators are strike fighter (AV-8B, F/A-18 and F-35), multi-engine (KC-130), tiltrotor (MV-22) and helicopter (AH-1/UH-1 and CH-53). A student's performance has considerable bearing on the course their career will take. While personal preference and the needs of the military factor in as well, lower-performing graduates desiring fighters may instead be offered KC-130s or MV-22s.

After graduating from primary, students assigned to the strike pipeline report to either Training Wing One (TW-1) at NAS Meridian in Mississippi or Training Wing Two (TW-2) at NAS Kingsville in southern Texas for approximately 27 weeks of intermedi-

The Raytheon/Beech T-6B Texan II replaced the long-serving T-34C Turbo Mentor as the US Navy's primary trainer. (Scott Youman)

ate jet training in the McDonnell-Douglas T-45C Goshawk. Introduced in 1991, the T-45 replaced both the TA-4J Skyhawk and T-2 Buckeye in the Naval Air Training Command. Intermediate jet training introduces students to flying high-performance jet aircraft. Once strike pipeline students graduate from Intermediate Jet Training, they spend approximately 25 weeks in Advanced Strike Training, again at Meridian or Kingsville, learning to employ a jet as a weapons system. Cumulatively, the strike syllabus covers advanced instrument flying, tactical formations, low-level navigation, air combat manoeuvring, carrier qualification and air-to-surface attack.

Marine aviators destined for service in the VMGR (Marine Aerial Refueling/Cargo) community flying KC-130s report directly to Training Wing Four (TW-4) at NAS Corpus Christi for advanced multi-engine training. Here they fly the Beech T-44C Pegasus, with the 21-week syllabus focusing on single-engine procedures and advanced instrument flying. Students in the tiltrotor pipeline also go through the advanced multi-engine syllabus with TW-4 at Corpus Christi after completing ten weeks of intermediate tilt-rotor training flying the Bell TH-57 SeaRanger helicopter (soon to be replaced by the Leonardo TH-73) with TW-5 at Whiting Field. Whiting Field is also where students destined for the H-1 or H-53 communities complete their advanced training in the TH-57 with TW-5. The advanced rotor-wing syllabus lasts 28 weeks and includes helicopter familiarisation, navigation, instrument and night flying, tactics and formation flying.

FRS – transition to type

Regardless of which pipeline a student aviator is in, completion of advanced training is how they earn their wings of gold, designating them as naval aviators. From advanced, new Marine aviators move on to type conversion at the Fleet Replacement Squadron (FRS) for their specific type. Whereas all their training up to this point has been with Navy training squadrons under Navy training wings, every FRS – with one exception – is a Marine Corps squadron underneath one of the service's two CONUS-based active-duty air wings. Pilots selected to fly the F-35C – the carrier-based, tailhook-equipped

variant of the Lightning II – currently complete their type conversion with VFA-125 'Rough Raiders' at NAS Lemoore in central California.

The two FRS units for Marine F-35B pilots are VMFAT-501 'Warlords' and VMFAT-502 'Nightmares', both at MCAS Beaufort, South Carolina. With no two-seaters for training, F-35 training is simulator-intensive, with perhaps the highest-fidelity simulators available to pilots of any tactical aircraft type in service. Like all Marine FRS units, both F-35 VMFATs offer different training tracks. Students entering training as 'Category 1' pilots are those with no experience in the aircraft, coming straight from the training pipeline. The remaining categories – 2 through 5 – are for those who have prior F-35 flight experience, but need refresher training after coming back to the jet after time away, whether due to injury, an instructor tour with one of the Navy Training Wings, a ground tour as a forward air controller, or any other reason pilot may be away from the cockpit. As FRS units, both squadrons teach students the basics of flying the aircraft and operating its systems. Though graduates are qualified as F-35B pilots, there remains significant training to be completed at their gaining unit, where a training officer is responsible for moving new pilots through an in-house syllabus where they learn to fight the aircraft and operate as a wingman in multi-ship formations.

The other strike-pipeline FRS units in the Marine Corps are VMFAT-101 'Sharpshooters' at MCAS Miramar in California for F/A-18 pilots (and Weapons Systems Officers – WSOs – for the two-seat F/A-18D) and VMAT-203 'Hawks' at MCAS Cherry Point, North Carolina for AV-8B Harrier pilots. With two-seat, dual-control variants assigned, both the 'Shooters' and the 'Hawks' incorporate more flying events into their respective syllabi. Simulators still factor prominently into this training, especially for emergency

Beginning in 1991, the Navy began replacing the Rockwell T-2C Buckeye and McDonnell-Douglas TA-4J Skyhawk in the intermediate and advanced training role with the BAe/McDonnell-Douglas T-45A Goshawk.
(Joe Copalman)

The Marine Corps operates 13 two-seat TAV-8B Harrier IIs for transition-to-type training for new pilots assigned to fly the AV-8B. All 13 are assigned to VMAT-203, the Marine Corps' Harrier Fleet Replacement Squadron. (Joe Copalman)

procedures training. A student F/A-18 pilot with VMFAT-101 completes sixty simulator events over the course of the approximately 44-week syllabus. Whereas carrier qualification used to be a component of the Hornet syllabus at -101, the last students to 'hit the boat' with the 'Sharpshooters' did so in July 2019, as the Marine Hornet community's last carrier deployment begins in late summer 2020. In place of carrier qualification, VMFAT-101 is introducing a phase called fleet transition, in which instructors will take some of the burden off squadron training officers at the gaining units of new pilots by doing that training in-house. With the Marines phasing out the WSO position in the F/A-18D community, the service is training far fewer Naval Flight Officers (NFOs), though as of January 2020, VMFAT-101 at MCAS Miramar was still responsible for training WSOs for the two-seat Hornets.

Graduates of the Navy's multi-engine training pipeline do not have a dedicated training squadron for KC-130J transition, as the service's sole 'Herk' FRS, VMGRT-253 'Titans' disestablished in 2006. Instead, new KC-130J pilots and crewmasters train at Cherry Point with the KC-130J Fleet Replacement Detachment, collocated with VMGR-252 'Otis' and using the squadron's aircraft for flight training events. Tiltrotor pilots and crew chiefs report to Marine Medium Tiltrotor Training Squadron 204 (VMMT-204) at MCAS New River in North Carolina. As with the other pipelines, learning to fly the MV-22 Osprey involves extensive classroom instruction, many hours of simulator time practicing tactics, techniques and procedures (TTPs), and dozens of actual flight events putting it all together. Lastly, pilots on track to fly either the AH-1Z or UH-1Y report to HMLAT-303 'Atlas' at Camp Pendleton. While a few reserve squadrons continue to fly the AH-1W SuperCobra as of this writing, HMLAT-303 trained its last 'Whiskey' pilots back in February 2018.

Pilots assigned to fly the F-35B Lightning II complete their transition training with VMFAT-501 'Warlords' (pictured) or VMFAT-502 'Nightmares' at MCAS Beaufort. (USMC/WO Bobby Yarbrough)

Marine Unmanned Aerial Systems (UAS) operators go through an entirely different training pipeline, which until recently, included divergent pathways depending on which Unmanned Aerial Vehicle (UAV) a student was assigned. When the Marines operated the RQ-2 Pioneer, enlisted UAS operators trained in a combined Navy/USMC schoolhouse at Whiting Field. When the RQ-7B Shadow – a US Army UAV purchased by the Marines – entered service, Marines trained alongside army RQ-7 operators at Fort Huachuca in Arizona. With the introduction of RQ-21 Blackjack, the Marine Corps took control of UAS training, initially with a mobile training team, but now by a formal FRD at MCAS New River for RQ-21 training. Since 2012, the UAS community has had officers permanently assigned, instead of having aviators on temporary tours. With the establishment of the UAS Mission Commander position in 2012, officers assigned to Marine UAV Squadrons (VMUs) go through the Air Force's Remotely Piloted Aircraft course at Randolph Air Force Base in Texas before moving on to the RQ-21 FRD at New River.

Additional training

Additionally, several communities in Marine Corps aviation – namely those performing adversary, operational support airlift, and (until recently) search and rescue – only accept second-tour aviators, and as such, lack any formal FRS units. Rather, type conversion in each of these units is managed by each individual squadron in accordance with a Naval Air Training and Operating Procedures Standardisation (NATOPS)-approved syllabus.

In January 2020, the Navy signed a deal with Leonardo Helicopters to replace its Bell TH-57 Sea Rangers with the TH-73A, a development of the company's AW119, for intermediate tiltrotor and advanced helicopter training for Navy, Marine Corps and Coast Guard pilots.
(Leonardo)

Beyond entry-level and squadron-level training, pilots and aircrew can earn advanced qualifications though Marine Aviation Weapons and Tactics Squadron One (MAWTS-1). Based at MCAS Yuma, MAWTS-1 is the USMC's aviation centre of excellence, administering instructor qualifications for skills like night systems instructor, air combat manoeuvring instructor, low-altitude tactics, instructor, and the pinnacle qualification in any community, the Weapons and Tactics Instructor (WTI) qualification.

Student aviators in the KC-130J and MV-22B pipelines complete their multi-engine training with Training Wing Four at NAS Corpus Christi flying the Beech T-44C Pegasus.
(Joe Copalman)

HMH | MARINE HEAVY HELICOPTER

A heavy-lift workhorse – the CH-53E Super Stallion

Among heavy-lift helicopters within the American military, the Sikorsky CH-53E Super Stallion is the current king of the hill. With the capability to lift payloads up to 36,000lb (16,363kg) the 'Echo' has been the Marine Corps' go-to aircraft for moving large numbers of Marines and outsized materiel like artillery pieces, Humvees, and even light armoured vehicles over long distances or from ship-to-shore since entering service in 1981.

Explaining what the CH-53E brings to the Marine Air-Ground Task Force (MAGTF), Major Andrew Baxter from Marine Aviation Weapons and Tactics Squadron One (MAWTS-1) said, '*It gives a lot of flexibility to the MAGTF commander, especially the capability of moving mass amounts of people, combat supplies and heavy equipment. We have a very robust external capability – that's a really important capability, as we can move things out of austere sites like smaller vehicles and downed aircraft. It also gives your infantry battalion commander the ability to mass combat power quickly in a single wave. It would be simple for us to fly a flight of four -53s and insert almost an entire company in one wave.*'

The CH-53E entered the 21st century as a proven workhorse, with 20 years of operational service – and all the normal wear and tear expected of an aircraft at that point in its lifespan. The most significant upgrade to the 'Echo' up to that point was the addition of a Hughes AN/AAQ-16B forward-looking infrared (FLIR) turret. This provided an increased night capability and was especially useful for low-level navigation and identifying landing zones from a distance in the dark – both capabilities CH-53E crews would need in the conflicts in Afghanistan and Iraq.

From the sea – Super Stallions in Afghanistan

On 26 November 2001, the Marines joined the fight against al-Qaeda and the Taliban in Afghanistan as part of Operation Enduring Freedom (OEF), with a flight of six CH-53Es being the primary ship-to-shore connector. Flying 371.5 nautical miles from the USS *Peleliu* (LHA 5) and USS *Bataan* (LHD 5) steaming off the coast of Pakistan to an abandoned airfield the Marines called Camp Rhino, the aircraft – three from the 15th MEU's Aviation Combat Element and three from the 26th MEU's ACE – executed the longest amphibious airfield seizure in the Corps' history.

The six CH-53s – flying as two flights of three – rendezvoused with two KC-130s south of the Afghan border for aerial refuelling. While four of the six made successful 'plugs' and had enough fuel to land at Rhino, offload their Marines and cargo, then fly on to a FARP (forward arming and refuelling point) in Pakistan for more fuel before heading back to their respective ships, the two 'Echoes' that could not aerial refuel landed at Rhino and awaited a KC-130 for rapid ground refuelling before returning to their ships as well. The six 'Echoes' carried 161 marines in that first wave, establishing a foothold to enable the site to start functioning as an effective forward operating base, with hundreds more Marines coming to Rhino aboard KC-130s that same day.

From the outset of Marine operations in Afghanistan, the limitations of the Boeing-Vertol CH-46 Sea Knight in hot and high conditions made it clear that the CH-53E would be shouldering most of the MEUs' assault support burden there. Super Stallions transported not only Marines in Afghanistan, but Army and other special operations forces as well. On 5 March 2002, CH-53Es attached to HMM-165(REIN) flew 730 nautical miles from the USS *Bonhomme Richard* (LHD 6) off the coast of Pakistan to the Shah-i-Kot Valley in northeast Afghanistan to support American and Australian troops during Operation Anaconda, aimed at decimating a large force of al-Qaeda and Taliban fighters. Over the next two weeks, the CH-53Es helped the army's CH-47 Chinook transport helicopters stay in the fight by providing aviation-delivered ground refuelling (ADGR). When tasked for ADGR missions, the 'Echo' is outfitted with the Tactical Bulk Fuel Delivery System (TBFDS), which consists of three 800-gal (3,028-lit) self-sealing and crashworthy auxiliary fuel tanks in the CH-53E's cargo hold. Utilising fuel from both the TBFDS tanks and the aircraft's own external drop tanks, the CH-53E can transfer up to 16,800 gallons (63,959 lit) of fuel, allowing other aircraft or vehicles to continue their missions. The system is set up to enable the TBFDS tanks to be re-filled through aerial refuelling, allowing a single 'Echo' to make several rotations through a FARP to keep fuel moving to units that need it. During Operation Anaconda, the CH-53Es utilised this set-up, tanking from orbiting KC-130s overhead, landing at the FARP, and dispensing that fuel to Chinooks and other helicopters.

The CH-53E is currently the most capable heavy-lift helicopter operated in the US Department of Defense. (USMC/CWO Jorge Dimmer)

Desert warhorses: CH-53E in Iraq

The invasion of Iraq in March 2003 pushed all Marine air and ground communities to their limits, sustaining a rapid advance over long distances through hostile territory and a dusty environment that is notoriously hard on mechanised vehicles – especially helicopters. Amphibious shipping played a role in Operation Iraqi Freedom (OIF), with two complete HMH squadrons – HMH-464 'Condors' and HMH-465 'Warhorse' having 16 aircraft each based on ships in the Northern Arabian Gulf. A third squadron, HMH-462 'Heavy Haulers', operated from Ali Al Salem Air Base in Kuwait. Throughout the initial push on Baghdad, all three squadrons provided critical heavy lift support, transporting food and water, ammunition and spare parts for ground vehicles. The 'Echoes' also hauled bulk fuel blivets to FARP sites to keep ground vehicles and aircraft topped off and able to take the fight deeper into Iraq and inserted and extracted reconnaissance teams ahead of the advancing US forces. While the CH-46 was the primary vehicle for casualty evacuation, Marine CH-53Es occasionally fulfilled 'CASEVAC' taskings. Super Stallions from HMH-465 even inserted Army Rangers during the rescue of captured army PFC Jessica Lynch.

As OIF evolved from conventional operations to a counterinsurgency, Marine CH-53 squadrons routinely deployed to Al Asad Air Base in Al Anbar province west of Baghdad to support the Marines operating there from 2004 through withdrawal in 2010. Though the overall mission changed, the CH-53E's role remained largely the same – moving people, supplies and mail wherever they needed to go. With the proliferation of the improvised explosive device (IED) threat making ground transportation increasingly dangerous, Marine CH-53Es provided a means of transportation that avoided IEDs entirely.

While most general support missions occurred at night to reduce vulnerability to ground fire, the potential threat in various areas dictated where the Super Stallions could and could not go. As former CH-53 pilot Major Brian Friestman (USMC, retired) explained, '*There were areas you wanted to avoid because of surface to air fire or just concentrations of . . . you just don't want to be there. We were not cleared into black zones. There were different threat levels, and black was the highest threat level. You'd need an escort. And then the green zones were like free flight. You could be a commercial guy flying a Cessna 172 and you'd be fine. Then red zones, you're going to get shot at, there's going to be some action, but you're going to get through there, and we can use tactics to mitigate the risk.*'

In addition to general support, HMH squadrons in Iraq also participated in VIP transport, recovery of downed aircraft, refuelling of aircraft and ground vehicles at FARPs, raid force insertion and extraction, CASEVAC, and the unfortunate but necessary execution of 'angel flights' – transporting Marines and others killed in action to mortuary affairs troops. Towards the end of OIF, CH-53s participated in 'aeroscout' missions, which were effectively armed presence patrols that could cover much wider areas than foot or mechanised patrols on the ground.

During these daylight missions, CH-53s carrying teams of infantry or reconnaissance Marines would be inserted to investigate suspicious activity on the ground. While some questioned the efficacy of the mission, several aeroscout operations resulted in the apprehension of insurgents, the destruction of IED factories, and the seizure of hundreds of weapons that could have potentially been used against coalition troops.

The other Stallion in the stable – CH-53D Sea Stallion

While the CH-53E was firmly established as the Marines' heavy-lift programme of record, another Sikorsky 'Stallion' soldiered on in USMC service. The stalwart CH-53D Sea Stallion – more commonly known as the 'Delta' – remained active with five squadrons, all assigned to Marine Aircraft Group 24 (MAG-24) at MCB Kaneohe Bay, Hawaii. By the year 2000, the overall number of serviceable CH-53Ds dropped low enough for the Marines to deactivate a 'Delta' squadron.

The 'Hammerheads' of HMH-366 stood down on 1 October 2000, with the squadron's eight aircraft being redistributed, bringing the primary authorised aircraft figure from eight to ten for the Delta-equipped HMHs.

The CH-53D formed the basis for the CH-53E, with the longer tail boom and canted vertical stabiliser of the 'Echo' being a result of a third engine being added and a 79ft (24.1m) seven-bladed main rotor replacing the CH-53D's 72ft (21.9m) six-bladed rotor. Internally, the two aircraft were identical, with the exception of the controls and gauges for the third engine added to the CH-53E's cockpit. With only two General Electric T64-GE-413 3,925shp turboshafts versus the CH-53E's three T64-GE-416s rated at 4,380shp each, the Delta carried less, but burned fuel less prodigiously than the Echo. Colonel Allen Broughton (USMC, Ret) commanded HMH-363 'Red Lions' through most of 2005 and 2006. Regarding the range differences between the two variants, Broughton said, '*The great thing about the Echo is that they could aerial refuel. But if aerial refuelling is not available, the Deltas actually had longer legs. They could fly for six hours, but you're at 120 knots, whereas the Echo, you're flying at 130 knots, but you can only really fly for four hours.*' In terms of lift, the CH-53D could reliably carry up to 8,000lb (3,629kg), but could also carry up to just under 13,000lb (5,897kg) in a heavier configuration yielding slower speeds over a reduced range. During its final decade of operation, the CH-53D was considered a 'medium-heavy-lift' helicopter, placing it between the CH-46 and CH-53E.

The CH-53D at war

As the Global War on Terror gathered steam following the 11 September 2001 attacks, the USMC kept the 'Delta' squadrons on the sidelines, committing the more powerful 'Echoes' to combat in Afghanistan and Iraq. This relegated the CH-53D units to providing heavy lift for the Okinawa-based 31st MEU, supporting Rim of the Pacific (RIMPAC) exercises in Hawaii, or providing lift assets for the Weapons and Tactics Instructor course at MCAS Yuma.

The 'Delta' community's first taste of combat came in fall 2004 when HMH-463 'Pegasus' provided a detachment to the 31st MEU aboard the USS *Essex* (LHD 2), which steamed west towards the Northern Arabian Gulf to support OIF. After ferrying five of the detachment's six CH-53Ds to Al Asad, the Marines of HMH-463 (attached to HMM-263 'Red Dragons' as part of the 31st MEU's ACE) flew very little, as the 'Delta' community had a lower logistical priority than that of the CH-53E up to that point. Further, the squadron deployed in the midst of a fleet-wide stand-down following the loss of an HMH-463 'Delta', which crashed on the campus of Ginowan University in Okinawa when its tail folded in flight, a result of maintainer negligence.

The Marines kept the Vietnam-era CH-53D in service through November 2012. The 'Ugly Angels' of HMH-362 took the 'Delta' on its final deployment, with a six-month tour to Afghanistan in the summer of 2012.
(USMC/Cpl Isaac Lamberth)

The 'Pegasus' Marines received a second chance to prove the CH-53D in combat, deploying to Al Asad as a full squadron in March 2006. With as thinly spread as the CH-53E squadrons were due to concurrent combat operations in Afghanistan and Iraq as well as all the other commitments around the globe, the Marine Corps decided to insert the Hawaii-based 'Delta' squadrons into the Iraq rotation. In contrast to the 2004 MEU detachment, this deployment went very well for HMH-463. Then-Captain Brian Friestman, who flew CH-53Ds with 'Pegasus' on both deployments attributes this to logistics and leadership. '*We had figured out the logistical side of it, which made all the difference in the world*', he recalled. Friestman also credited this success to the proactive leadership of squadron commander Lieutenant Colonel Randy Parker and the maintenance management prowess of Chief Warrant Officer 4 Bill Lennox, the squadron's maintenance material control officer. In contrast to the 2004 MEU detachment, 'Pegasus' enjoyed high readiness rates and an operational tempo to match. '*Our readiness numbers for that deployment with 463, we were hovering around 90 to 92 per cent readiness the whole time,*' Friestman said. '*We flew a lot. Most guys, if they didn't have a month where they busted 100 hours and had to get a waiver to keep flying, they were pretty close.*'

While in Iraq, HMH-463 took on all the heavy-lift missions of the CH-53E, with the exception of downed aircraft recovery. While most of the flying was night logistics movement, HMH-463 occasionally participated in named operations, inserting Marines or Navy SEALs to capture or kill known insurgents. It was on such a mission that a 'Pegasus' Delta (reported to be BuNo 157146) suffered a hard landing on 7 September

2006, resulting in the aircraft needing to be recovered on a flatbed truck and hauled back to Al Asad. This mishap led to the squadron that relieved 'Pegasus', HMH-363, flying fewer raids during their deployment, which began in October 2006. While HMH-363 flew fewer tactical insertions, the squadron flew between 800 and 1,000 hours a month, more than any HMH squadron up to that point. As Broughton recalls, *'The normal peacetime utilisation rate per aircraft was about 20 hours per month, and that's in a good month. In Iraq we were averaging utilisation rates over 100 hours a month.'*

The 'Ugly Angels' of HMH-362 had an even more eventful deployment when they replaced HMH-363 in April 2007. In addition to the cargo and passenger flights flown every night and the occasional hard-hit raids, the 'Uglies' were the first HMH tasked with the aeroscout mission. Crews from HMH-362 helped develop the tactics, techniques and procedures (TTPs) used by the 'Echo' and MV-22 Osprey squadrons that took up the mission after the squadron left Iraq in November 2007.

The 'Uglies' returned to Iraq once more in January 2009, finding the country far less volatile than when they left in 2007. With stabilisation operations having been largely successful in the wake of the 2007 'surge', there was little work for HMH-362 to do. As CH-53D crew chief Sergeant Matthew Crooks recalls, *'We didn't have a mission. It was pretty much wrapped up by that time in 2009. It was really weird on that second deployment, we actually flew to Baghdad during the day. It was like 'Okay, I think we're good here. There's really not a lot happening.'*

The lull in operations gave HMH-362 time to perform engine upgrades on the 11 CH-53Ds the squadron had in-country, the most significant upgrade to the CH-53D fleet in the 21st century. With the Marine CH-53E fleet having upgraded to the same

Marines board a CH-53D in Afghanistan at the conclusion of an Aero Hunter operation to disrupt suspicious activity and counteract enemy drug and weapons trafficking in support of Operation Enduring Freedom. (USMC/Robert Carrasco)

T64-GE-419 engine used by the Navy's MH-53Es, the remaining Marine Deltas received the Echo community's hand-me-down T64-GE-416s. With nothing to do in Iraq, and with the engine swaps completed, the 'Uglies' were re-tasked mid-deployment and sent to Afghanistan.

Arriving at Kandahar on 15 April 2009, the 'Uglies' reassembled their aircraft and began flying missions in support of ISAF (International Stabilisation and Assistance Force) operations. The squadron assumed the same role it performed in Iraq, transporting people, necessities like food and water and equipment. Whereas Deltas rarely lifted any external loads in Iraq, they were an almost daily occurrence in Afghanistan. Given the dispersal of ground units in remote locations throughout the Marines' area of operations, underslung loads were often the best means of delivering supplies. As Crooks explained, '*That happened because they were in the middle of fields everywhere. There was nowhere to go, so we would just drop a load to them, whether it was water, ammo, food, anything. I'd say almost every day we did one external mission.*'

Though not as capable as the CH-53E, much longer in the tooth, and harder to support, the CH-53D covered a crucial gap in combat capability for the Corps' battle-worn fleet of 'Echoes'. With the drawdown of combat operations in Iraq and Afghanistan, the Marines finally retired the Delta, with HMH-362 standing down as the last CH-53D operator on 30 November 2012.

The Super Stallion soldiers on – back to Afghanistan

Marine CH-53Es were the go-to asset for downed or disabled aircraft recovery in Afghanistan. Here an HMH-461 'Echo' lifts a Canadian Chinook in May 2007. (USMC/Sgt Thomas W. Dowd)

The mid-deployment move of HMH-362 from Iraq to Afghanistan in 2009 reflected a larger shift of focus throughout the US military. During the years between 2003 and 2009, the HMH squadrons that deployed to Afghanistan largely supported the Provincial Reconstruction Teams operating in remote areas of the country helping local authorities rebuild their communities after decades of war and to establish stronger ties to the country's new national government. With the renewed focus on defeating the Taliban, the Marines accepted responsibility for Helmand Province in southern Afghanistan, initially operating from Kandahar, later expanding to Camp Bastion (also known as Camp Leatherneck) northwest of Lashkar Gah and Forward Operating Base (FOB) Dwyer near Garmsir. Marine CH-53D and CH-53E squadrons operated alongside one another, hauling Marines and other ISAF troops and supplies throughout Helmand Province. The Super Stallions also transported artillery pieces and ammunition to firebases throughout the region as well.

One of the most important missions flown by Marine CH-53Es in Afghanistan was aircraft recovery, part of a broader mission set called tactical recovery of aircraft and personnel. Afghanistan's altitude, climate and extremely dusty conditions presented operational challenges for all aircraft, but especially for helicopters, which made frequent emergency landings due to mechanical issues, suffered hard landings due to insufficient power, or were downed by enemy ground fire. Given the vast distances and poor road conditions in Afghanistan, externally lifting downed or disabled helicopters proved the safest, most economical way of recovering these aircraft, which needed to be kept out of the hands of the Taliban at all costs. As Major Baxter at MAWTS-1 explained, '*We did a lot of lifts in Afghanistan where another helicopter would go down and externally lifting that helicopter out of wherever it went down so it couldn't be used as a propaganda tool. The enemy could say 'Look at us, we did this, this, and this to this aircraft', when really it was just a maintenance issue that put it down in a field, but we could go in and pull it out of there.'*

Doing the most good

The Super Stallion's size, lift capacity, range and aerial refuelling capability make it an ideal platform for humanitarian assistance and disaster relief (HA/DR) missions. Marine CH-53 crews are just as likely to haul food and water to a remote island village in the aftermath of an earthquake, hurricane, or other natural disaster as they are to transport a load of combat-ready Marines to a landing zone near an active firefight.

While HMH detachments assigned to MEUs are the most likely to perform HA/DR missions, the Marines sometimes task HMHs directly to humanitarian operations. One such commitment is Operation Continuing Promise, a humanitarian mission in Central and South America aimed at providing medical care to people in communities so deeply impoverished that they would otherwise never receive such care. Major Eric Rodriguez made a Continuing Promise deployment aboard the USS *Kearsarge* with HMH-464 in August 2008. Recalling this deployment, Rodriquez said, '*It was basically a Central and South American deployment where we transitioned a full amphib, the USS* Kearsarge *into almost a hospital ship. We were off the coast of Nicaragua, and we flew -53s ashore with medical equipment. We did some testing to make sure we could support and help this community. We ended up finding children that needed cleft palette surgeries. We'd fly them aboard the ship, do the surgery, flew in their parents. Being able to do that is a unique experience that this aircraft allows to happen.*'

A CH-53E demonstrates humanitarian assistance and disaster relief (HADR) techniques for the Peruvian armed forces as part of a US Southern Command initiative to strengthen military cooperation in the region. (USMC/Sgt Marimar M. Morales)

Continuing Promise would not be the last time Rodriguez would have an opportunity to fly humanitarian missions in Central America. Between March and December 2016, reserve squadron HMH-772 'The Hustlers' operated four aircraft as the ACE for Special Purpose MAGTF – Southern Command (SPMAGTF-SC), with Rodriguez serving as the detachment operations officer. Operating out of Soto Cano air base in Honduras, the 'Hustlers' supported numerous civil engineering projects throughout the region, with the SP-MAGTF involved in projects in not just Honduras, El Salvador, Guatemala and Nicaragua.

Additionally, the four CH-53s assigned to SPMAGTF-SC during that time served as a prepositioned response force for the Caribbean region during the 2016 summer hurricane season. When Hurricane Matthew tore through Haiti in early October, two CH-53s committed to the MAGTF travelled to Haiti to provide heavy lift for the relief and recovery efforts. Explaining the mission of CH-53s in Haiti, Rodriguez recalled, '*It was mainly hauling relief supplies around for us. We worked out of Port-Au-Prince, the national airport in Haiti. Basically, 747s would land and drop off a ton of supplies, and we had a team there from McGuire AFB, the 612th Contingency Response Squadron. They went in and sorted all of the supplies and told us where to go. Joint Task Force Matthew was created, headed up by a Navy admiral, and we just fell into that JTF for that couple of weeks, flying supplies all over the place.*'

In addition to facilitating delivery of aid and relief supplies to disaster areas, the cavernous CH-53 cargo hold allows for mass movement of people in situations warranting evacuation. The standard passenger capacity of the 'Echo' – 30 combat-loaded Marines strapped into crash-resistant seats – can be expanded in extreme situations such as evacuations. As Major Baxter at MAWTS-1 explained, '*You can get a waiver for the number of pax we can carry, so you can throw 50 to 100 pax in an aircraft to get them to safety. In 2010, -53s did Pakistan flood relief, basically getting Pakistani people out of harm's way. They were loading about 80 or 90 people up in the aircraft at a time just to get them to safety.*' The CH-53E's external lift capability has humanitarian applications as well. Speaking in October 2017 while relief operations were underway throughout the Caribbean after a rough hurricane season, Baxter said: '*There's a dam that ruptured down in Puerto Rico, and we've got -53s that are taking concrete slabs and externally lifting them, just dropping them in this canal right now just to stop the water flow.*'

While the bulk of HA/DR missions flown by HMH squadrons tend to be overseas, CH-53Es occasionally support civil authorities responding to natural disasters in the US. When Hurricane Katrina ravaged the Gulf Coast in August 2005, leaving much of New Orleans, Louisiana and the surrounding communities underwater, crews and aircraft from HMH-461, HMH-464 and HMH-772(-) deployed to the region to support rescue, relief and recovery efforts. For three weeks, the Marines used CH-53Es to transport thousands of relief workers, evacuate hundreds of civilians from areas hardest-hit by the storm, and haul food, water, construction materials and other critical supplies throughout the region.

Like the CH-46 and CH-53D, the CH-53E possesses the capability to employ 'Bambi buckets' for aerial wildfire suppression. While not a core CH-53 mission, California-based crews train to use Bambi buckets to give MCAS Miramar and MCB Camp Pendleton an organic aerial firefighting platform, and to assist civil authorities during particularly severe wildfire seasons. One of the most notable call-ups for this mission occurred in July 2008, when California Governor Arnold Schwarzenegger formally requested military support to fight several wildfires raging throughout central and northern California. Miramar-based HMH-465 'Warhorse' answered the call, deploying three aircraft to Naval Air Station Lemoore near Hanford and later to McClellan Airfield near Sacramento to assist in firefighting efforts for almost a month.

Upgrades – keeping the 'Echo' relevant

Marine CH-53s received a firepower upgrade in April 2003, with the addition of a third XM218 .50-caliber machine gunun on the rear ramp. This gave crew chiefs the ability to provide rear-quarter suppressive fire during egresses from contested LZs or to engage point targets when a source of ground-fire could be identified. The CH-53 fleet received a further upgrade when the Marines replaced the old XM218, which had a cyclic rate around 750 rounds per minute, with the GAU-21, which has a roughly 1,200 rounds per minute cyclic rate. The GAU-21 also has a more robust barrel, with an average barrel life of 10,000 rounds.

In 2005, the USMC awarded a contract to Raytheon to provide the AN/AAQ-29A mid-wavelength infra-red turret system for its CH-53E. The 'Q-29' represented a significant upgrade over the AAQ-16 in terms of image quality and resolution, and helped improve the situational awareness of H-53 crews at night. The 'Echo' fleet also received a major self-protection upgrade beginning in June 2007, with the addition of the Northrop-Grumman Directional Infrared Countermeasures (DIRCM) system. This system was in turn replaced by the Department of the Navy Large Aircraft Infrared Countermeasure (DoN LAIRCM) missile warning system beginning in December 2014. According to Naval Air Systems Command's Advanced Tactical Aircraft Protection Systems programme office, '*The DoN LAIRCM system consists of five major components: five Infrared (IR) MWS sensors; a dedicated Central Processor; a Control Indicator Unit (CIU) for cockpit display; two Pointer-Tracker/Jamming Subsystems or Guardian Laser Tracker Assemblies (GLTA) consisting of four-axis stabilised gimbaled system, a Fine Track Sensor (FTS) and a ViperTM laser.*'

As new systems are developed for the CH-53K King Stallion, the Marines are finding ways of adapting them for use in the 'Echo' to keep it tactically relevant throughout the programmed E-to-K transition phase. One such system under consideration for CH-53E integration is a brownout symbology upgrade to assist 'Echo' pilots while making reduced visibility landings in dusty conditions. As Major Baxter explained, '*We've had additions to our heads-up display that we use when we fly at night. What we've been trying to do is incorporate a near-brownout symbology for when we land in the desert. It's a work in progress. Really what it's trying to do is condition the current generation of Echo pilots to what they're going to see in the Kilo as far as that brownout symbology. In the Kilo, you're basically going to have a multi-function colour display right in front of your face that's going to have that symbology in there, and with that fly-by-wire capability in the Kilo, pretty much you don't have to look outside anymore when you're landing in the dust, you just look at that display, and you've got a tangible system to get down in the dust.*' The system Baxter refers to is the Smart Multifunction Color Display kit with Brown Out Symbology Set, programmed for implementation in the Marine CH-53E fleet by 2024. The CH-53E is also set to receive software reprogrammable radios with a Link 16 network capability and embedded satellite communication abilities by 2024 as well.

War-weary Stallions and the reset

The demands of concurrent conflicts in Iraq and Afghanistan resulted in CH-53E utilisation rates nearly 400 per cent above standard programmed usage. While engine and airframe fatigue were issues as early as 2005-2006, CH-53E readiness deficiencies were dire and systemic by 2014. In the wake of the drawdown of US forces in Afghanistan, and in the face of the forced fiscal austerity of the 2013 budget sequester, some HMH squadrons had mission-capable rates in the mid-20-per-cent range. With fewer 'up' aircraft to fly, pilots flew considerably less, sometimes logging fewer than ten flight hours per month. Along with diminishing basic pilot proficiency, this also slowed down pilot progression, resulting in fewer qualified aircraft commanders and fewer instructor qualifications being earned. With development of the CH-53K encountering delays, and the Marine Corps still needing heavy-lift support, the situation for the HMH community in the post-Afghanistan timeframe was truly grim. Further, with over 50 fewer CH-53Es in service than the 220 required to fully equip all active, reserve, training and test CH-53 squadrons, the Marines reduced the primary mission aircraft inventory (PMAI) for the deployable, active-duty HMH squadrons from 16 aircraft to 12, with the two (later one) reserve squadrons being reduced from eight aircraft to six each.

While the CH-53E maintenance and readiness struggles were well-known at the time, it was the January 2014 crash of a Navy MH-53E Sea Dragon that drove home just how poor a state the 'Echo' community was in. While the cause of that mishap was

The Marines pride themselves on being able to fight and win in any clime and place. Here, a pair of CH-53Es from HMH-464 'Condors' conduct an extraction of NATO troops during COLD RESPONSE 2016 in Norway. (USMC/MSgt Chad McMeen)

chafed electrical wiring breaching a fuel line, it drew attention to a general degradation of CH-53E readiness and the costs of mission-focused maintenance where minor 'gripes' are overlooked in order to have mission-ready aircraft to meet operational demands. In response to the poor state of CH-53E readiness, one of Lieutenant General Jon Davis' first directives after becoming Deputy Commandant for Aviation (DCA) in June 2014 was commissioning a readiness review board to assess the driving factors impacting the poor readiness of the 'Echo' fleet and to recommend ways to improve it. Known as the Super Stallion Independent Readiness Review (SSIRR), the board's report recommended a multi-prong approach to solving the readiness problem.

The first component of restoring Super Stallion readiness is the CH-53E Reset Program. When the US Army withdrew from Afghanistan, it spent more than USD1.2 million inspecting and rehabilitating its CH-47 Chinook fleet to full readiness, a process that demanded about 6,000 man-hours per aircraft. By contrast, the Marines put their CH-53Es through a comparatively low-impact tune-up process that only took about a month per airframe. Seeking to achieve the same success as the army, the CH-53E Reset Program will put all 142 CH-53Es remaining in service through a roughly 110-day process in which each aircraft is stripped down to its bare metal airframe for inspection and completely rebuilt. Any worn components are either restored or replaced during the rebuild.

The Reset Program has been a resounding success, bringing squadron readiness rates up significantly, enabling more flight hours, increasing pilot proficiency, and rebuilding a pool of instructors. While the CH-53E community still has 142 aircraft doing the job of 220, the Reset has given the community some breathing room, with commanders far more confident their aircraft will be able to cover the gap until the transition to the CH-53K – the completion of which remains a potential moving target. Once the CH-53K transition begins, transitioning squadrons will divest of their 'Echoes', allowing remaining CH-53E squadrons to restore their PMAI from 12 aircraft to the programmed allotment of 16, further increasing CH-53 readiness and enabling more simultaneous detachments.

In addition to the Reset, the SSIRR recommended significant changes in how Marines maintain the CH-53E fleet. During the wars in Afghanistan and Iraq, the primary focus of maintenance efforts was ensuring each squadron had enough 'up' aircraft to meet current mission requirements. While this often yielded the aircraft necessary to support ongoing operations, it resulted in a growing backlog of deferred maintenance items across the fleet. An outcome of this mission-centred focus was a generation of maintainers skilled in doing whatever it takes to get aircraft mission-ready, but deficient in performing the troubleshooting and deep maintenance required to ensure aircraft operate to the full extent of their capabilities. The remedy to this has been a renewed focus on total aircraft maintenance, versus simply on getting CH-53s in the air. The Reset, in turn, is making it easier for squadrons to reorient their maintenance efforts in this direction.

Additionally, the SSIRR recommended other changes, like functional check flight training standardisation, distribution of more portable electronic maintenance aids, and correcting over 1,600 discrepancies found throughout all Super Stallion maintenance publications. Lastly, the Marines are working closely with Sikorsky to ensure that it has the spare parts inventory to sustain the CH-53E fleet through full transition to the 'K', and the logistics system to distribute those parts effectively and efficiently.

As the Marine Corps' dedicated heavy-lift asset, the CH-53E is regularly tasked with carrying underslung loads like fuel bladders, artillery and vehicles. Here an 'Echo' takes fuel from a KC 130T while carrying an underslung High Mobility Multipurpose Wheeled Vehicle. (USMC)

Digital interoperability

As with all other tactical communities in Marine aviation, for the HMH squadrons, digital interoperability (DI) has progressed from an acquisition buzzword to being an operationally effective tool enabling more reliable delivery of precision fires and enhancing the situational awareness of commanders across the MAGTF. At the moment, the primary means of accessing DI is the Marine Air-Ground Tablet, or MAGTAB, which allows all parties within a network to monitor and update one another on the progress of missions involving multiple types of aircraft, ground forces, and even amphibious shipping.

Discussing how the HMH community utilises DI, Major Baxter at MAWTS-1 said, '*We're using different waveforms to communicate with each other over the tablets, mainly to streamline our communications process. We're using that in an objective area with multiple assets, so it's a very useful tool to be able to communicate when we use our execution checklist. We built this checklist in planning, now all I have to do is go into the app in the tablet and I can just hold down that line number to say 'the raid force has been inserted.' I just hold that down. In planning we identified that I'm the assault flight lead, I was responsible for making that call, so I just hold down that line number, it populates, and everybody who's in the network, it will populate instantly on their tablet.*' Digital Interoperability can also be used for threat identification and avoidance. As Baxter explained, '*If a threat pops up in the battlespace, on my moving map I can drop that threat on the map and say 'Here is*

A CH-53K King Stallion conducting aerial refuelling over Chesapeake Bay. The 'Kilo' promises improved capability over the CH-53E, designed to carry loads up to 27,000lb (12,247kg) over 110nm to landing zones up to 3,000ft (914m) above sea level. Under the same conditions, the CH-53E can carry a maximum load of 9,654lb (4,379kg). (Dane Wiedmann)

an enemy whatever, we just spotted this,' and then everybody in the network, once I drop it on the moving map on the tablet, I can publish it and it will pop up on everybody's tablet.' Pending upgrades like Link 16 and satellite communications capabilities will only broaden the DI capabilities of the CH-53E fleet.

The King

The CH-53K King Stallion dates to an April 2006 USMC contract with Sikorsky to replace the CH-53E. Whereas the CH-53E is effectively an upgraded and slightly redesigned CH-53D, the CH-53K is a clean-slate design that leverages numerous technological advances and meets emerging Marine heavy-left requirements. While similar in layout to the 'Echo', including engine placement, tail design, and general front and side profile lines, significant differences clearly distinguish the King Stallion from the legacy CH-53s it will replace.

Up front, the CH-53K boasts much larger windows on the front windscreen and on either side of the cockpit, improving visibility. Another change up front is the integrated mount for the AN/AAQ-29A EO/IR sensor turret in the centre of the aircraft's nose, vice the cantilevered offset mount for the same sensor on the CH-53E. Inside the cockpit, the vast array of analogue 'steam' gauges has been replaced by five Collins 6in by 8in (15.2 × 20.3cm) multi-function display screens. Pilots control the aircraft with a triple-redundant digital fly-by-wire system that includes an automatic flight control system that offers a considerable upgrade in reduced-visibility landing capability over the CH-53E. The 'Kilo' also comes equipped with an Integrated Vehicle Health Monitoring System – developed with extensive input from crew chiefs and maintainers – to ease troubleshooting and identify components in need of repair before their scheduled maintenance or replacement dates. Maintenance overall has been eased significantly by a far more intuitive aircraft design, with easy access to components that are much harder to reach on the CH-53E. The three General Electric T408 turboshaft engines yield 7,500shp each, which the Marines claim is 57 per cent more horsepower over the CH-53E's engines. With a goal of easing engine maintenance and reducing the logistical footprint of the 'Kilo', the new engines have 63 per cent fewer parts.

Compared to the CH-53E, the 'K' comes equipped with significantly larger sponsons, utilising more space along the side of the fuselage to eliminate the need for external fuel tanks. This keeps the CH-53K's footprint similar to that of the 'Echo' for shipboard operations, as the CH-53K was designed with a fuselage 12 per cent wider than that of the CH-53E to accommodate full Transcom 463C cargo pallets and vehicles as large as the HMMMV internally. The blade-fold mechanism – required for shipboard stowage – is automated, able to fold all seven blades into 'hangar' configuration in under two minutes. While the CH-53K retains the Echo's seven-bladed main rotor and four-bladed tail rotor configuration, the blades are composite, making them both lighter and far more resistant to corrosion than the metal blades on the CH-53E. Like the CH-53E, the Kilo comes equipped with 32 crashworthy seats in the rear cabin, can carry up to 24 litters for CASEVAC, and can provide ground refuelling with the tactical bulk fuel delivery system.

The most common claim in Lockheed Martin-Sikorsky and Marine Corps literature regarding the CH-53K is that it can carry three times the load a CH-53E can. While both the CH-53E and CH-53K can carry a maximum payload of 36,000lb (16,329kg), that represents the absolute heaviest weight the aircraft can lift vertically, the same way a competitive weightlifter lifts a barbell over the head, holds it there, then puts it back on the ground. Requiring the weightlifter to walk several hundred feet holding the barbell above his or her head and to put it down somewhere else is something entirely different, and is essentially how the CH-53K's performance is measured against that of the 'Echo' – how much can it carry over a certain distance? One of the primary design requirements of the CH-53K is that it can carry up to 27,000lb (12,247kg) externally over a distance of 110 nautical miles with an ambient temperature of 95°F (35°C) to a landing zone at an elevation of 3,000ft (914m) above sea level. While the Integrated Test Team has not yet validated this capability under all of these conditions at the time of this writing, results of individual tests at high altitude and in extreme heat fuel their optimism that the King Stallion will easily meet this goal. By contrast, the CH-53E can only carry a load of 9,654lb (4,379kg) under those same conditions. While not quite three times the CH-53E's maximum load under those conditions, the Kilo's 27,000lb loadout still represents an enormous gain in lift capability, one that reduces the overall trips from ship to shore currently demanded of the 'Echo'. The CH-53K can further expedite ship-to-shore logistics using its three independent cargo hooks. In addition to the central hook stressed for the maximum 36,000lb (16,329kg) load, the front and rear hooks are stressed for 25,200lb (11,431kg).

The CH-53K developmental test programme has advanced by fits and starts, with bursts of significant progress interrupted by the discovery of new issues that need to be remedied before testing can resume apace. 2018 proved to be a very productive year for the programme. On 18 January 2018, a CH-53K test aircraft lifted a Joint Light

Tactical Vehicle (JLTV) weighing 18,870lb (8,559kg) as an underslung load. Less than a month later, on 10 February, a test 'Kilo' lifted the type's maximum load of 36,000lb (16,329kg). In June, test crews brought an aircraft to Gunnison, Colorado – situated at 7,700ft (2,347m) above sea level – to test the CH-53K's performance at high altitude.

2018 also saw the Marine Corps take delivery of the first low-rate initial production aircraft on 16 May, the validation of the CH-53K's air transportability aboard US Air Force C-5s and C-17s, and the first in a series of degraded visual environment tests in September at the Yuma Proving Grounds (YPG) in Arizona. For these tests, the CH-53K involved flew at an operating weight of 60,000lb (27,216kg) in temperatures as high as 108°F (42°C). These tests further validated the abilities of the automatic flight control system (AFCS), which flew by-the-numbers approaches to a stable, drift-resistant hover, allowing pilots to use the CH-53K's advanced hover symbology to lower the aircraft through a complete brownout to a successful landing.

The AFCS can also be used during external load operations, holding a drift-resistant digitally-controlled hover and using micro-adjustment inputs from the pilot (per verbal cues from the crew chief looking down through the 'hell hole' in back) to place the aircraft precisely where it needs to be for the external load to be secured to the cargo hook(s). The tests at Yuma also validated the reliability of the GE T408 engines in dusty conditions, enabling the test pilots to extend the amount of time they kept the aircraft hovering in the massive dust clouds churned up by the rotors. In summer 2020, a test CH-53K will return to YPG to repeat these tests at the aircraft's full 82,000lb (37,195kg) maximum gross weight.

Developmental test by the Integrated Test Team (comprised of personnel from Sikorsky, Naval Air Systems Command and HX-21) has identified numerous issues that require remedy, some significant enough to delay the type's programmed initial operating capability from December 2019 to early 2021. Among the most significant issues facing the CH-53K is the ingestion of hot exhaust gas into the No. 2 engine and resultant high temperatures in the No. 2 engine bay. Other serious issues include fuel systems and airspeed indication anomalies, main rotor damper overheating, suboptimal main rotor gearbox reliability, tail boom inadequacies, and hot gas impingement on external structures.

As with the F-35 and MV-22 test programmes, the lag between when items requiring rework or redesign are identified and when the mandatory test reports documenting those issues are published often means that the issues brought to the public's attention in those reports have already been solved. Whether this is the case with the King Stallion at the time of this writing is unclear, but what is clear is that the Integrated Test Team is making every effort to have enough CH-53Ks on the ramp at HMH-366 'Hammerheads' in time for the squadron to make the type's first deployment in the 2023–2024 timeframe.

Chapter 5

HMLA | MARINE HELICOPTER LIGHT ATTACK

The Marine Light Attack Helicopter Squadrons (HMLAs) bring a broad set of capabilities to the Marine Air-Ground Task Force (MAGTF), ranging from assault support to forward air control (airborne) to reconnaissance to close air support, electronic warfare, and even a limited counter-air capability. Comprised of seven active-duty and two reserve squadrons, the HMLA community currently operates the Bell UH-1Y Venom, and two variants of the Bell 'Cobra' gunship – the AH-1W SuperCobra and the AH-1Z Viper. Transition from the AH-1W to the AH-1Z is nearing completion, with only a detachment from reserve squadron HMLA-773 'Red Dogs' still operating the AH-1W as of late 2020. While the Marine Cobras have been upgraded numerous times since the late 1960s, the UH-1Y represents the first upgrade for the Marine Hueys since the introduction of the UH-1N Twin Huey (also known as the 'November') towards the end of the Vietnam War.

The November

Having served throughout the 1970s, 1980s and 1990s, by the beginning of the 21st century, the service's UH-1Ns were showing their age. Various upgrades over 30 years of service impacted performance, as each new black box or bolt-on system added weight. These gains went unanswered by any significant powerplant upgrades. As a result, operating the 'November' became a study in compromise. While the UH-1N remained capable of performing a broad array of assault support and attack missions, weight restrictions meant Marine 'November' crews could only perform one or two of those missions on any given flight. As Lieutenant Colonel Andrew Turner, a prior UH-1N pilot recalls, '*Let's say you wanted to take personnel from point A to point B. In the 'November' I probably would have had to have limited or been very careful about how much gas I had to take or how much ammunition I had to take. Operating in Iraq, if I wanted to take personnel on my aircraft, I may have had to give something up in order to make that happen depending on the length of that trip.*'

The November's power limitations also impacted how crews conducted basic flight operations. Retired Lt Col Steve Mount, who flew the November from 1999 through 2004, observed, '*It was always about range and weight. That's the struggle we always had as November pilots. We took off from the boat probably 1,500 pounds, sometimes 2000 pounds overweight. We had to get 25 knots across the deck (to take off). We'd have the ship point into the wind, make about 17 or 18 knots, then it wouldn't be that typical take-off from the boat where you slide off the side and then go forward.*

We would just go forward and use our ground effect; it was called a deck run. That was the only way we could get off the boat because we were so power-limited. Those old Novembers were tired and underpowered.'

Into Afghanistan – the 'November' at war

Tired or not, Marine UH-1Ns still had a job to do. In the wake of the 11 September 2001 terror attacks, three Hueys from HMLA-169 'Vipers', detached to HMM-163 (Reinforced) 'Ridge Runners', the aviation combat element (ACE) for the 15th MEU aboard the USS *Peleliu* (LHA 5), were among the first USMC aircraft into Afghanistan. On 25 November, the MEU's three Novembers, with four HMLA-169 AH-1Ws, departed *Peleliu* for a Forward Arming and Refuelling Point (FARP) in southern Pakistan en route to what became known as Camp Rhino, the Marines' first foothold in southern Afghanistan. Given the limited range of Marine 'Skids', for UH-1Ns (and Cobras) to provide observation and threat suppression for the CH-53s in the landing zone, they departed ahead of the other helicopters and stopped at a FARP to top off their fuel tanks before continuing on to join up with the rest of the assault force near the objective area. With Camp Rhino being over 370 miles (595km) inland, the distance was longer than any such mission the Marines had performed up to that point.

While at Camp Rhino, the UH-1Ns stood up to southern Afghanistan's ubiquitous 'moon dust' surprisingly well. Explaining how the Novembers fared in Afghanistan, Lt Col Mount said, '*In the Huey, we had an intake cover that had particle separators, then we had covers that we would put on when we put the birds to bed at night. We also did engine washes, but water was at a premium – we had to ship all of our water in. I don't think we had to replace an engine the whole time we were there. The November was a good, old, simple, reliable aircraft. It was simple, and stuff didn't break. Our readiness rates were fantastic.*'

The 'Vipers' deployment to Camp Rhino lasted only five weeks, and was relatively uneventful, with the squadron flying mostly armed reconnaissance and convoy escort missions. For his part, Mount never employed ordnance in Afghanistan, though he noted that the Cobras occasionally fired on some 'angry bushes'. The Camp Rhino deployment taught the November community valuable lessons about operating from austere locations in the desert for extended periods of time.

Into Iraq – Operation Iraqi Freedom

From the first day of Operation Iraqi Freedom (OIF) on 20 March 2003 through the departure of the final HMLA to leave Iraq in December 2009, Marine 'skids' factored heavily into USMC ground operations in Iraq. Whether fighting uniformed Iraqi troops, Shiite militiamen, or al-Qaeda 'foreign fighters', the HMLA's mix of capabilities remained relevant through six years of sustained combat. Marine UH-1Ns entered Iraq with the same disadvantages the type brought to Afghanistan – it was overweight, underpowered, under-gunned and slow. Despite these handicaps, the 'November' still brought critical capabilities to the fight.

During the initial phase of OIF – known as OIF 1 – Marine Huey and Cobra crews flew as combat crew – set teams of personnel matched for experience and qualifications. In addition to spreading each squadrons' experience and 'quals' evenly, combat crews allowed pilots and crew chiefs to get to know each other well in a combat environment, able to understand one another's non-verbal cues and vocal inflections, and to anticipate what each crew member will do in certain situations. In addition to combat crews, the HMLA squadrons flew as pure sections in OIF 1 – Cobras flew with Cobras in divisions of four, while the Hueys operated in sections of two. The rationale for this was that the Cobras performed deep air support missions against Iraqi tanks and artillery, destroying them with TOW and Hellfire missiles long before ground forces encountered them. The Hueys, meanwhile, provided route reconnaissance, overwatch, transport for general officers, and command and control closer to the convoys pushing towards Baghdad. With some convoys stretching out over 20 miles (32km), UH-1Ns provided communications relay, orbiting above and helping the regimental commander maintain communications with the entire convoy. Additionally, having Hueys overhead offered near-immediate visual reconnaissance or aerial fire support when needed.

From 'Shock and Awe' to static counterinsurgency

After Baghdad fell on 9 April 2003, OIF shifted from combat operations against Iraqi troops to stability operations in which the Coalition Provisional Authority worked with Iraqis to rebuild the nation's government and infrastructure. As early as May 2003, US and coalition forces faced minor ambushes and 'pot-shot' attacks that intensified over time, but the USMC avoided much of this as most Marine units left Iraq by summer 2003. As lawlessness and a widespread lack of basic services created hostility towards US and coalition troops, disaffection blossomed into a full-blown insurgency in parts of the country in spring 2004. Marines returned to Iraq to meet these challenges, assigned responsibility for al-Anbar province, a large region west of Baghdad that proved a hotbed of insurgent activity. Additionally, the 11th MEU deployed to Najaf to meet the challenge presented by Shiite Cleric Muqtada al-Sadr's increasingly belligerent Madhi Army militia. (It was during the Battle for Najaf when Steve Mount took a round through his right eye while searching for a mortar position – his co-pilot

Since the late 1980s, the HMLAs operated the UH-1N Twin Huey (foreground) and AH-1W Super Cobra (background), a combination the Marines took to war in Afghanistan and Iraq throughout the first decade of the 21st century. (USMC/Cpl Theodore Ritchie)

– Andrew Turner, took the controls and made a hard landing, resulting in all four crew aboard the UH-1N surviving with no major injuries beyond the loss of Mount's eye).

During this period, HMLAs rotated in and out of Iraq on six- to seven-month deployments, typically flying from Al Asad Air Base and providing overwatch for Marine infantry units in places like Fallujah, Haditha and Ramadi. While local and regional militia groups continued to attack American and coalition troops, tensions between Shiite and Sunni Muslim militias grew considerably, with open sectarian violence becoming a bigger problem. By early 2006, many observers classified the situation as civil war. Committed to stabilising Iraq and helping re-establish government control over the country, the US waged a counterinsurgency campaign, while simultaneously training and equipping Iraqi military and police forces to take on increasing responsibility for ending the violence.

Demand for air support remained high, and with HMLAs being the among the best-equipped units to provide armed reconnaissance and close air support over urban areas, the operational and deployment tempo remained exceptionally high for Marine H-1s. The 'Warriors' of HMLA-167 based at MCAS New River, North Carolina, for example, deployed to Iraq five times between March 2003 and October 2008, sometimes with as little as six months of 'dwell' time in the US before deploying again.

'November' weapons

Though not primarily an attack platform, the UH-1N possessed modest offensive and defensive weapons capabilities. The most potent weapons available to Marine November crews were 2.75-inch (70mm) rockets. Due to weight restrictions, Novembers typically carried a single seven-shot LAU-68 rocket pod. The rockets could carry a variety of warheads depending on the desired effects, including M255A1 flechette warheads carrying 1,179 steel darts, M257 or M278 illumination flares, or a variety of smoke warheads, but high explosive warheads like the 9.3lb (4.2kg) M151 or 17lb (7.7kg) M229 were the most common for UH-1Ns in Iraq. Having flown the UH-1N in mixed sections with AH-1Ws over Najaf, Lt Col Mount said of rockets: '*Honestly, we didn't really need pods anyway. I had big brother Cobra there next to me and he was loaded for bear. The minigun and the fifty were my weapons of choice for pretty much everything. I would mark stuff with tracer, pull off, and then protect him when he pulled off. Then he'd come in with either PGMs or rockets.*'

In addition to rockets, UH-1Ns carried a pair of machine guns, one on either side in flexible mounts manned by crew chiefs and aerial observers. The lightest gun the November carried was the M240G 7.62mm (0.3in) light machine gun, with a variable rate of fire between 650 and 950 rounds per minute. Marine UH-1Ns also carried the GAU-17/A six-barrelled Gatling-type 7.62mm minigun, a very effective weapon against infantry and unarmoured targets with a devastating 3,000 rounds-per-minute rate of fire. Lastly, the .50-caliber GAU-16 heavy machine gun offered Huey crews a more powerful punch for lightly armoured targets or targets under cover, with a 750-round cyclic rate.

'November' tactics

With the shift from fighting a conventional army in OIF 1 to supporting Marines fighting an insurgency from May 2003 onward, HMLAs in Iraq switched from pure sections of Cobras or Hueys to mixed sections. Explaining this change, Lt Col Turner said, '*There are benefits of having mixed sections. The Cobra gives you that punch if you need it. They've got the Hellfire missile, at that time (summer 2004) they were carrying TOW missiles too. They're also packing that 20mm cannon. The benefit of the Huey is that you get that 360-degree weapons engagement. I can shoot to the side, I can shoot to the front, I can shoot behind myself. When you don't know where the enemy is at, there's the benefit of having that protection aspect, of having a Huey and a Cobra fighting together, instead of just a Cobra where the pilots are just focused off the nose. Another aspect is that I've got four sets of eyeballs in the Huey. I've got crew chiefs. Those crew chiefs are phenomenal. A lot of the time, they were pointing stuff out that otherwise would have been missed.'*

For the first three years of OIF, HMLA crews employed low-altitude tactics, operating at 300ft (91m) and below to mitigate the threat of man-portable air defence systems, or MANPADS. In 2006 this was raised to between 1,500 and 3,000ft (457 and 914m) to avoid small arms fire. Despite this shift, the increased need for route reconnaissance ahead of ground convoys to detect possible IEDs or ambushes routinely drove November crews to lower altitudes. At Lt Col Turner explained, '*We'd go down to 100 feet and parallel the road, and I'm using my crew chiefs more so than a sensor to see if there is disturbed dirt or bundles of wires or something that might indicate somebody planted an IED. We did that a lot.*'

The UH-1N was an integral part of each Marine Expeditionary Unit's Aviation Combat Element, used for utility, reconnaissance and light attack missions. (US Navy/MC2 Greg Johnson)

'November' upgrades

For all the performance penalties new systems and equipment imposed on the November, they also enhanced the type's survivability, lethality, reliability and overall combat effectiveness. The 1990s saw the addition of a GPS navigation system, night-vision-compatible displays and a FLIR systems Navigational Thermal Imaging System (NTIS) turret with a laser rangefinder. By 2003, this was replaced by the FLIR Systems AN/AAQ-22C Star SAFIRE sensor. While accurate navigation systems and the ability to fly, fight and find targets at night made the UH-1N more lethal, the addition and/or upgrade of defensive systems like the AN/APR-39(v)2 radar warning receiver, AN/AAR-47 missile approach warning system, chaff and flare dispensers and an AN/AVR-2 laser warning system increased the type's survivability.

New sensor

For its time, the Star SAFIRE was a good sensor. The upgrade to the BRITE Star – another FLIR Systems product – beginning in 2004 brought an even better sensor with a targeting capability as well. Regarding this upgrade, Lt Col Turner said, '*That was somewhat of a gamechanger, because you now have a laser designator. Whether it's bombs for fixed-wing or Hellfire missiles coming off of Cobras, or even a Predator or Reaper, now the Huey can be a designator, and it's not just a sensor piece.*' This represented a true evolution to a 21st-century FAC(A) capability, being able to guide precision munitions directly to targets without relying on a third party.

The first operational use of the new laser designator occurred in August 2004 during the battle of Najaf. HMLA-169 received a single BRITE Star system while deployed as part of HMM-166(REIN) attached to the 11th MEU. During the fight against the Mahdi Army, 11th MEU Marines were taking fire from a building adjacent to the Imam Ali Mosque. A November crew used the designator to guide a Hellfire from a Predator UAV, successfully silencing that specific threat.

Marine Novembers received upgraded guns and feed systems as well. The first upgrade occurred between the start of OEF in late 2001 and OIF in March 2003. The feed system for the Huey's minigun proved prone to jamming. Mount expressed his frustration with the GAU-17 feed system, '*especially when it's quiet in the back and you look back and you're yelling at the crew chief to get their gun up, and there's parts all over the floor. When you're trying to break down the minigun in flight and it's night-time, the crew chief's not very happy back there.*' Equipping the GAU-17 with a new feed system made a tremendous difference. As Mount recalls, '*We got new feeders from Dillon Aero for our miniguns, and those things would sing. They would never jam, whereas previously, they jammed all the time.*'

Though the GAU-21 0.5in (12.7mm) calibre machine gun was tested on UH-1Ns in 2002, the HMLAs did not replace the older GAU-16 until 2010. Whereas the GAU-16 fired 750 rounds per minute, the GAU-21 put out an impressive 1,200 rounds per minute. The new gun also relied on a larger magazine mounted on the wall inside the November's cabin. Crash-rated for 600 rounds but capable of carrying more if needed, the GAU-21's magazine eliminated the need for crew chiefs to swap out World War II-style ammunition cans every 100 rounds. The GAU-21 also featured a mechanical feed system that improved reliability.

With some UH-1Ns being 15 or more years older than their AH-1Ws hangar-mates, and with the operational limitations of the November, the Marines prioritised Novem-

Entering service in 2008, the UH-1Y brought speed and payload advantages over the UH-1N, able to keep up with (and even outpace) the AH-1W and to carry troops as well as fuel and a full weapons load, something the 'November' could never do. (Joe Copalman)

ber-to-Yankee transition ahead of replacing the AH-1W with the AH-1Z. The Marines accepted the first production UH-1Y on 8 August 2008, initiating a six-year transition. The final Marine UH-1N deployment occurred in late 2013, when reserve squadron HMLA-773 'Red Dogs' detached two Novembers along with aircrew and maintainers aboard the Royal Netherlands Navy Landing Platform Dock Ship HNLMS *Rotterdam* (L800). During this deployment, the 'Red Dogs' formed the aviation component of the Security Co-Operation Task Force operating off the West African coast, with the primary mission being helping African Partnership nations refine their military capabilities. The 'Red Dogs' were the last HMLA squadron to retire the November, bringing 43 years of UH-1N service to a close on 28 August 2014.

UH-1Y

The successor for the UH-1N came as part of a combined AH-1/UH-1 package known as the H-1 Upgrade Program. Initiated in 1996 through a contract between the Marine Corps and Bell Helicopter, the upgrade programme initially included a plan to remanufacture 100 UH-1Ns as UH-1Ys, with new tail booms, engines, avionics and a composite four-bladed rotor system. In 2005, the remanufacture requirement was dropped in favour of an all new-build Huey fleet. At the core of the UH-1Y's performance advantages over the UH-1N is a pair of General Electric T700-GE-401C turboshaft engines, each providing 1,546 continuous shp, versus the 1,134 continuous shp of the Pratt &

Whitney T400-CP-400 turboshafts on the UH-1N. Paired with the four-bladed composite main rotor, the new engine gave the Yankee a maximum take-off weight of 18,500lb (8,391kg), versus the 10,50lb (4,763kg) maximum of the November.

When the USMC received its first operational UH-1Ys in 2008, it represented not just an evolution in capabilities, but a quantum leap. Whereas the AH-1Z was three variants removed from the AH-1J of the early 1970s, the November was of the same vintage as the AH-1J, with no intermediate variants before the introduction of the Yankee. Having transitioned to the UH-1Y in 2011, Lt Col Turner quickly appreciated just how much more capable it was. *'There were significant changes, things that are impressive like airspeed. That aircraft is faster than an AH-1W. We can go up to 170 knots. In the November, we were typically operating at about 100 knots. A hundred knots is comfortable, 110 you're pushing it, anything past that, the aircraft is shaking. In the Yankee, you don't even realise it, but you're going 120 knots, and you're not even pulling a lot of pitch. And 130, 140 knots, not unheard of if you're trying to get from point A to point B. You could go up to 170, but I don't think I've done that all that often.'*

In addition to speed, the lift capability of the UH-1Y exceeds that of the November. Explaining the advantages of this, Lt Col Turner said, *'Now I can carry a full tank of gas. I can load up with two rocket pods and as much ammunition as is reasonable, and I can take a full load of Marines in the back of my aircraft. We couldn't do that in the November. We'd have to give something up.'* This enables a single Yankee to perform a much broader range of tasks than the November could. Regarding the expanded capabilities of the Yankee, Captain Mike Harper, a UH-1Y instructor pilot at MAWTS-1 observed, *'The HMLA mission has not changed. What has changed is our ability to provide the capability in the form of additional power, airspeed, and range. We're a jack-of-all-trades platform – offensive air support, assault support, escort, supporting arms coordination, FAC(A) – we can do a little bit of just about everything. It gives the MAGTF commander a lot of flexibility.'*

Every community in Marine Corps aviation has embraced digital interoperability. Here a UH-1Y crew chief monitors mission progress on a networked handheld device during a deep air support training event. (Joe Copalman)

'Yankee' at war

Having entered the fleet too late for OIF, Marine UH-1Ys supported ongoing combat operations in Afghanistan, where its improved hot, high and heavy performance better matched the altitude and weather in Helmand Province, and enabled a true attack/utility capability, often in a single mission. The Yankee's first combat deployment came in October 2009 when HMLA-367 'Scarface' deployed to Afghanistan. 'Scarface' flew their Yankees in support of Operation Moshtarak in February and March 2010, an operation intended to clear Taliban insurgents from the town of Marjah. After providing attached escort for the CH-53D Sea Stallions and CH-53E Super Stallions transporting the bulk of the Marines into Marjah, HMLA-367 continued to provide overwatch and CAS over the next two months.

Digital interoperability

As with nearly every other Marine aviation community, UH-1Y crews are integrating digital interoperability (DI) technologies into how they communicate and coordinate during missions. The primary means of accessing DI is currently the Marine Air-Ground TABLet (MAGTAB), a ruggedised tablet supporting the numerous apps used to push and receive information digitally. However accessed, DI is not platform, system,

Whereas the UH-1N had mostly analogue gauges and instruments, the UH-1Y features a 'glass' cockpit with multiple digital displays. (Joe Copalman)

or application-specific, but rather a means of increasing situational awareness across multiple air and ground platforms, keeping all connected parties updated on mission progress, weather changes, threat locations and any emergencies or contingencies. In the UH-1Y, DI is often managed by the crew chiefs, who can monitor communications on a tablet and push any information useful to the pilots as it is presented.

For all the advantages DI brings to the Huey, Captain Harper emphasises the importance of staying rooted in the fundamentals. '*We still teach that they need to stick to the basics and not become reliant on the technology. Pen and paper is still going to be the primary means to catalogue things. That's the way we've been doing it for years and it's a tried and trusted method. What we're trying to do is teach them to use this technology to enhance their existing procedures, not replace them. We're not going to always be able to operate with digital interoperability and electronic signals, and with battery life and things like that, there's just a host of things where we can't become reliant on it.*'

Top Owl

In another sign of just how much of a leap forward the UH-1Y is from the UH-1N, the Top Owl helmet-mounted sight display (HMSD) system replaced the 'grease pencil mark on the windscreen' targeting method utilised by November crews. Describing what Top Owl offers, Captain Harper explained, '*It allows us to wear this monocle over our right eye that gives us essentially a heads-up display that we can just look around anywhere and have relevant information to us such as flight instruments or target information. It's like having a HUD where you can look around and carry with your field of view. It gives us the ability to look heads-up and conduct target handovers and keeps our heads outside for reduced-visibility landings. In low-light-level conditions, we want to keep our heads out as much as possible when we're flying in formation. It's a really good capability, and really, the Marine Corps as a whole is working toward equipping that technology with every platform, we're just one of them.'*

'Yankee' weapons

The Yankee largely carries the same weapons as its predecessor – 7.62mm (0.3in) and 0.5in (12.7mm) flex-mount machine gununs and 2.75in (70mm) rocket pods. The primary difference is that the Yankee can carry two fully loaded guns and two full rocket pods no matter how much fuel it is carrying or how many passengers are aboard. Giving an overview of the weapons carried by the UH-1Y, Captain Harper said, *'One of the great things about the Yankee is our ability to mix ordnance configurations. Each of our weapons systems can provide a different capability. Starting with our crew-served weapons, the GAU-21 .50-caliber machine gun obviously packs a bigger punch, it can reach out a little bit further, it can be used for light armoured vehicles, etc. The other main crucial weapon we use is the GAU-17, the minigun, at 7.62mm, with a much higher rate of fire. Smaller calibre, but for smaller target sets, lower collateral damage, personnel, it just provides a different weapons engagement envelope. We also have the M240, which is obviously a smaller 7.62 variant if we need*

A UH-1Y crew chief fires a GAU-17 7.62mm (0.3in) minigun on a rocket pass over the Chocolate Mountain Aerial Gunnery Range. (Joe Copalman)

more space or we need to carry more troops in the back, then we can lighten that load a little bit. For our rockets, the 2.75in rocket has a bunch of different variants. We typically carry high explosive. We also have the APKWS, advanced precision-kill weapons system that essentially takes a normal 2.75in rocket and a guidance section, so it becomes a laser-guided weapon. It's great right now for low collateral damage, a very small warhead, yet very precise, so it allows us to have some standoff vice having to employ it in a dive like we normally would. There's also a number of other warheads that we can put on those rockets. We have flechette, we have smoke, we have illumination, etc. Between all of those different combinations, that gives us a bunch of different capabilities depending on what's out there and what's necessary.'

Loss in Nepal

Over more than 10 years of flight operations, combat deployments and MEU cruises, the UH-1Y has maintained a good safety record. The worst mishap to date occurred on 12 May 2015 near Charikot, Nepal while two UH-1Ys from HMLA-469 'Vengeance' flew disaster relief following a 7.8 magnitude earthquake. Yankee crews supported relief and recovery efforts in the rugged mountain communities of Nepal. At the time of the mishap, the crew of UH-1Y BuNo 168792 was transporting five Nepali civilians from a remote village to a medical facility in Kathmandu for treatment, when other aircraft operating in the area lost contact with it. Nepalese troops discovered the wreckage three days later in rugged terrain at 11,200ft (3,414m), charred and mangled, with no survivors. Among the dead were six Marines, two Nepalese troops, and the five villagers being transported to Kathmandu. A subsequent investigation attributed the crash to the crew's decision to take the most direct route to Kathmandu, which took them over unfamiliar terrain in unfavourable weather, losing visual reference in thick clouds and manoeuvring into terrain.

On 25 April 2018, HMLA-469 took delivery of the final UH-1Y produced for the Marines, the last of 160 delivered over a ten-year span. Within that decade, the Marine Huey transformed from a overweight, underpowered, jack-of-one-or-two-trades-at-a-time study in forced compromise to a jack-of-all-trades that will run out of cargo space before it runs out of power, capable of precision fires and electronic warfare.

In 2016, Marine UH-1Ys began operating with the Intrepid Tiger II (V)3 electronic warfare (EW) pod. Intrepid Tiger II is a component of the Marine Corps' new electronic warfare construct, MAGTF-EW. (USMC/Koby Saunders)

Fangs out – Marine Corps Cobras

Still in service as of this writing, the Bell AH-1W SuperCobra – known as simply the 'Cobra' or the 'Whiskey' – is at the end of its 35-year USMC service life. Whereas the UH-1N left USMC service in a state of perpetual compromise, after numerous upgrades, the AH-1W is being retired at the top of its game.

Keeping the 'Whiskey' venomous

For as potent an air support platform as the Whiskey has been for the Marines, it is a 1980s refinement of a 1970s update of a 1960s design. With the introduction of the AH-1Z Viper (also known as the 'Zulu', 'Cobra', or simply the 'Z') in 2010, the Whiskey has ceded its position as the HMLA community's gunship programme of record. Throughout this decade-long transition, however, the Marines have continued to deploy the AH-1W for combat. This continued presence at the tip of America's expeditionary spear necessitated numerous modifications and upgrades to keep the AH-1W tactically relevant, providing the lethality and survivability needed to meet ever-evolving threats.

At the onset of OEF in 2001, AH-1Ws operated the same sensor – the Night Targeting System (NTS) – that the aircraft carried during Operation Desert Storm ten years prior. The NTS was a generation or more behind those fielded by other helicopters, including the UH-1N. The one technological advantage the Novembers had over the Whiskey was a better sensor in the form of the BRITE Star turret.

By 2003, the limitations of the NTS resulted in a programme to improve its fidelity and extend the range at which targets could be identified, tracked and engaged. Development of the upgrade – called the Night Targeting System Upgrade, or NTSU – was accelerated due to strong demand, with a functional protype produced in April 2004 ahead of a planned July 2004 delivery date. Lt Col Dave Fitzsimmons is a Cobra pilot with over 2,000 hours and four combat deployments in the Whiskey. Regarding the sensor upgrade, he said, '*Technically you went from a first-generation FLIR, which was eight-to-twelve micron (waveform) on a small green and black screen in the front of the aircraft to the NTSU, which was a third-generation FLIR with a three-to-five micron, just a different spectral field. But then they also made the MFD (multi-function display) in the cockpit two inches bigger, and colour. You had a few things working for you, where the FLIR quality itself was much better, and then the representation in the aircraft was much better.*'

Another significant AH-1W upgrade was the Elbit Systems tactical video datalink (TVDL), introduced in 2010. The TVDL enables pilots to share full-motion video from the NTSU with JTACs, ground commanders and other aircraft equipped to receive it. The ability for a JTAC to see the AH-1W's sensor feed and either confirm a target is the one he wants struck, or to talk the sensor onto the correct target proved critical in shortening the 'kill chain', increasing combat effectiveness and minimising civilian casualties. The high-definition signal broadcast by the TVDL further enabled ground commanders to discern and validate targets at a resolution unavailable to the pilots in the AH-1W sharing its sensor feed. Major Rob Dugan, a career AH-1W pilot with HMLA-773(-) 'Red Dogs' recalled, '*I've used that system very effectively in combat. A guy sitting in a COC is looking at an HDTV screen the size of my whiteboard, and I'm looking at a seven-inch by seven-inch little monitor. I'm broadcasting HD, I just can't see it that clearly. I've had them where they literally said 'Move your cursor*

A colorful AH-1W at high speed and low level over the ranges near MCAS Yuma. After nearly 35 years of service, the 'Whiskey' has been almost completely replaced by the AH-1Z. (Joe Copalman)

left – stop – up – stop – that's the target. Zoom in real close and click it.' Okay, got it, that's the one. Then it was missile off the rail, and it was a direct hit.' Additionally, TVDL allows Whiskey crews to receive video from unmanned aerial systems, which can be critical in giving AH-1W pilots situational awareness on the location of a target, disposition of friendly forces, and any civilian concerns before arriving on station.

The situational awareness afforded by the TVDL has been enhanced by the introduction of digital interoperability. Like Yankee crews, Whiskey pilots utilise MAGTABS to access digital communications networks for enhanced situational awareness. Explaining one particularly useful function of DI, Major Lynn Larson, an AH-1W instructor pilot at MAWTS-1 said, *'The software that we use includes mapping tools, so if there are things we want to point out on the map, instead of reading off lists of grids, we can plot it, publish it, and push it over digitally.'*

The most visible modification is the turned exhaust nozzles in place of the Whiskey's original exhaust. Developed by Bell's XWorX for the UH-1Y/AH-1Z in 2004, Naval Air Systems Command approved retrofit of the new nozzles to all AH-1Ws beginning in 2005. In addition to reducing the infrared (IR) signature of the engines, and with it, the likelihood of being successfully engaged by an IR-seeking missile – the new nozzles direct hot engine exhaust away from the tail boom, reducing heat-induced airframe fatigue while also reducing temperatures in the engine compartment itself.

Another major upgrade to the Whiskey was the Helmet Display and Tracker System (HDTS), which replaced the Helmet Sight System (HSS) the AH-1W inherited from its predecessor, the AH-1T. Explaining the significance of this upgrade, Major Larson said, *'When I first got on the Cobra, we were still using the Helmet Sight System, which were rails with an actual mechanical linkage to your helmet, and as you moved your head around, this arm is moving with your head, and that's how it tells where your head is. You'd use that to slew the gun and the sensor. By the time I got to the Whiskey in 2011, none of those things worked, they were so old and decrepit. They replaced that with the HDTS. It takes all the mechanical junk out, puts in a couple of computers and magnetic trackers. They fit your helmet with a device, and it uses magnetic fields to track where you're looking instead.'*

In addition to freeing pilots from having their heads mechanically linked to the aircraft and a system that no longer worked, HDTS solved another problem that had long frustrated AH-1W crews. As Larson explained, '*Up until that point, for the front and rear seat pilots, if they see something outside and look at a target, the only way for me to tell the other guy where it's at is to start describing the area to him. With HDTS, I look around, I've got a reticule in my right eye, he's got a reticule in his right eye, and we can see where each other are looking. Additionally, it allows either pilot to slew the turret to their line of sight. That was one of the biggest cockpit enhancements that came along while I was flying the aircraft.*'

'Whiskey' weapons

The Whiskey offers ground commanders tremendous flexibility, with three major weapons systems providing varying levels of lethality against a broad range of targets. The only weapon integral to the AH-1W is the M197 20mm three-barrelled, Gatling-type cannon. The primary ammunition used by the AH-1W is semi-armour-penetrating high-explosive incendiary rounds, which are effective against everything from infantry to lightly armoured vehicles. Major Dugan at HMLA-773 spoke highly of the M197, saying: '*For precision fires with the gun – it's not guided, but it's a pretty precise gun – you're only talking about a seven-meter dispersion at 1,000m. It's a 7.5-mil gun with exploding rounds of 5m explosions, so she'll do a lot of damage with the 20. But you can zoom in, you can get very precise, you can hit specific targets and avoid other ones by looking through the FLIR at night.*'

Introduced in 2004, the Night Targeting System Upgrade significantly increased the range at which AH-1W pilots could detect targets and the fidelity with which they could view them. The M197 20mm cannon dates from earlier Cobra variants and is so effective it equips the new AH-1Z as well. (Joe Copalman)

The M197's linked ammunition feed system proved vulnerable to fouling, leading to jamming issues that could not be resolved in flight. To increase gun reliability, the Marines approved the installation of a new, linkless feed system developed by Meggitt Defense Systems into its Cobra fleet beginning in 2011. Though the new feed mechanism reduced the maximum ammunition capacity from 750 to 650 rounds of 20mm, it has increased the reliability of the gun and reduced the time required to reload it.

One rung up the lethality ladder from the gun is the Hydra 2.75in/70mm rocket system. Rockets offer the greatest flexibility, with numerous warheads for the common Mk 66 rocket motor. Describing the range of warheads, Major Larson at MAWTS-1 stated, '*We've got an inert training round, we've got four different high-explosive rounds, we've got flechette rockets filled with anti-personnel darts, but we've had limited success with those. We've got smoke – red phosphorous and white phosphorous. Those are so small you're not putting a smokescreen down with them, you're mainly marking targets when you're doing FAC-A. We also have illumination rockets. There are covert ones that burn primarily in the IR spectrum, then there are overt ones that are super-bright.*'

While rockets have historically been unguided weapons, the development of the Advanced Precision Kill Weapons System (APKWS) has given the Whiskey a stand-off precision weapons capability for a fraction of the cost of a Hellfire missile, with the added flexibility of multiple warhead options. The APKWS consists of a Mk 66 motor, 2.75in (70mm) warhead and a guidance section between the motor and the warhead containing pop-out control surfaces with small laser seekers in the leading edges. Explaining the advantages of the APKWS, Larson said, *'Formerly in the Whiskey, you'd get in close, tip into a dive, and you're shooting from within a thousand meters. With APKWS, you can bullseye a target from four or five kilometres out. You just have to be able to see it.'*

In addition to 2.75in (70mm) rockets, AH-1Ws can also fire the 5in (127mm) 'Zuni' rocket. Describing the Zuni employed by Marine Cobras, Larson said: *'The fixed-wing Zunis in Vietnam were literally telephone poles, like twelve feet long. These are less than half that length, around five feet long. They're still monsters though. The warhead is equivalent to a 155mm shell from an artillery piece. Both the warhead and the motor of the five-inchers are significantly more powerful than their 2.75in cousins.'* As Larson explained, *'You're not supposed to get any closer than 500m (to the target) when firing them. Even shooting at 800m and pulling off target, you can feel the explosion in the aircraft. It's pretty intense. It's awesome to shoot, but it's also slightly terrifying, because when that thing comes off, you really hear it. Unfortunately, those rockets are so old and so heavy that we don't carry them all that often. It's more like a fun thing to do in training.'*

While the AH-1W was designed to carry the AGM-114 Hellfire missile from the outset, the type retained the AH-1T's capability to fire the BGM-71 TOW (tube-launched, optically tracked, wire-guided) missile as well. The TOW trailed a thin fibre-optic wire behind it after launch allowing a Cobra's front-seat pilot to guide the missile through the telescopic sight unit (replaced in the 1990s by the NTS) from launch through impact. The TOW was a remarkably effective weapon against tanks, bunkers and other fortifications, buildings and unarmoured or lightly armoured vehicles. For as effective as it could be, wire guidance proved to be the TOW's Achilles' heel, limiting its maximum range to between 3,750m (2.33mi) and 4,500m (2.8mi). During OIF, AH-1Ws often carried a mix of TOWs and Hellfires. While the Hellfire had longer range, higher speed and a more lethal warhead, it relied on laser energy for guidance. In cases where battlefield obscurants like smoke or dust degraded the Hellfire's ability to 'see' a laser mark, the TOW remained an effective option, with the front-seat pilot in a 'Whiskey' able to visually guide the missile to the target.

The introduction of the AH-1Z into the USMC inventory in 2010 signalled the beginning of the end for the TOW in the HMLA community. Unlike the 'Whiskey', the 'Zulu' was designed without the capability to fire the TOW, instead relying exclusively on Hellfire as its primary air-to-surface missile, at least until the AGM-179 Joint Air-to-Ground Missile (JAGM) enters service. The Marines ceased using the TOW in 2013, with HMLA-467 'Sabers' being the final HMLA to fire the missile on a weapons detachment to NAF El Centro.

At the top of the Whiskey's lethality pyramid is the AGM-114 Hellfire. Developed as a laser-homing antitank missile in the 1980s, the Hellfire gives the AH-1W a credible capability to defeat heavily-armoured threats from as far away as 11km (6.8mi). Detailing the Hellfire variants employed by the AH-1W, Major Larson stated, *'The three primary ones we shoot are the Kilo 2, the Mike, and the November, with the Kilo 2 having the anti-armour warhead, Mike being an HE warhead, and November being a thermobaric warhead, so bigger overpressure effects, mostly an antipersonnel urban weapon.'*

To defend against air-to-air threats, the AH-1W can fire the AIM-9 Sidewinder air-to-air missile, though this is not commonly carried. Non-lethal stores carried by Whiskeys include auxiliary fuel tanks and pods of rear-release parachute flares for the battlefield illumination mission. The latter are hardly carried due to the unrealistically high minimum altitude required to safely release them.

'Whiskey' at war

Marine Cobras played a major role in OIF, both during the opening drive towards Baghdad, and in the long counterinsurgency fight that followed. AH-1Ws fired some of the first shots of OIF, attacking and destroying observation posts along Iraq's border with Kuwait, effectively blinding Iraqi artillery batteries, which war planners worried could inflict excessive casualties on US forces crossing into Iraq. Once US forces breached the berms along the Iraqi border, Cobras ranged out ahead of the convoys seeking out the two most worrisome threats – tanks and artillery. As Regimental Combat Teams (RCTs) 1, 5 and 7 made their way northwest towards Baghdad, AH-1W crews responded to an increasing number of troops in contact calls, utilising all weapons at their disposal to engage Iraqi troops, artillery and armour still engaged against coalition forces.

Like the UH-1Ns, Marine AH-1Ws relied heavily on FARPs. These remote sites enabled Cobras to maximise time on station with heavy weapons loads while keeping them close to the fight instead of returning to Kuwait every time they expended

An AH-1W engages an enemy mortar position inside the Wadi-us-Salaam cemetery with 2.75in (70mm) rockets during the Battle of Najaf in summer 2004. Mahdi Army militants loyal to Shia cleric Moqtada al-Sadr were using the cemetery to stage attacks on Iraqi police and US Marine positions in the city. (USMC/Capt Jason Grogan)

their ordnance. This resulted in some particularly long missions for Cobra crews from HMLA-169 'Venom' and HMLA-267 'Stingers'. The pattern for these missions was for a four-ship AH-1W division to launch from Ali Al Salem Air Base in Kuwait, check in with a Direct Air Support Center for tasking while en route into Iraq, flying that tasking, then landing at a FARP to rearm and refuel, checking in with the DASC while on the ground for the next mission. The taskings varied, from simple calls to get a sensor on a suspected enemy position to attacking Iraqi troops in trenches to CASEVAC escort, to finding and destroying tanks hidden in palm groves. With all three RCTs and Task Force Tarawa making contact with Iraqi troops committed to defending Saddam Hussein's regime, there was no shortage of missions. In cases where the ground situation demanded the Cobras remain on station, the sections sometimes could not make the nearest FARP, and would simply set down alongside a ground convoy. As UH-1N pilot Steve Mount recalls, '*There were some Cobra guys who ran themselves out of gas doing CAS, and couldn't make it home and landed on a road randomly and got fuel from a truck wherever.*'

The AH-1W proved its toughness in Iraq, able to take significant hits and remain in the fight. On a 19-hour mission spanning 22 to 23 March, Captains Dan Sheehan and Brad Lagaski from HMLA-267 took two rounds through their tail boom over An Nasiriyah. After assessing the damage as inconsequential during a FARP stop they returned to An Nasiriyah to continue providing CAS for the Marines engaged with a determined enemy there. The Cobra's ruggedness was not lost on others, as Huey pilot Steve Mount observed, '*Guys were landing in Cobras with a fist-sized chuck out of their driveshaft and barely noticing a little vibration. The mechanical reliability of these aircraft is just fantastic.*'

An AH-1W from HMLA-269 receives fuel from a passing convoy after making an emergency landing along a highway in Iraq. (USMC/LCpl Nicholous Radloff)

Following President Bush's declaration of the 'end of major combat operations in Iraq' in May 2003, the Marines left Iraq – only to return less than a year later to deal with the growing insurgency in al-Anbar province. With the negotiated end to the first Battle of Fallujah in May 2004 resulting in the US-appointed Iraqi security force dissolving and giving its weapons to the insurgency, the Marines made a second attempt to rid Fallujah of insurgents starting on 7 November 2004. Known as Operation Phantom Fury, the battle involved AH-1Ws from HMLA-367 'Scarface' and a detachment from HMLA-167 'Warriors' providing overwatch and CAS for the Marines and soldiers in Fallujah. Prior to Phantom Fury, 3rd MAW planners began applying lessons learned from OIF as well as the earlier Battles for Najaf and Fallujah, resulting in more efficient employment of aircraft. For the opening hours of Phantom Fury, the Whiskeys held positions 0.6 miles (1km) outside the city, with pre-established lanes of fire into the city. All AH-1Ws assigned to the operation carried a standard weapons load of four Hellfires, two TOWs, one pod of rockets, and 300 to 400 rounds of 20mm ammunition. Marine AH-1Ws provided critical support to the infantry, destroying enemy positions impeding their movement through the city. One Cobra was lost during Phantom Fury, an HMLA-169 machine that succumbed to intense small arms and RPG fire, though the crew survived and was recovered.

Though Phantom Fury represented perhaps the most intense concentration of insurgent activity throughout OIF, the pattern established for the HMLA employment held over the next several years as the insurgency gave way to sectarian civil war. Following the 2007 troop 'surge' that played a role in ending much of the violence in Iraq, US forces began to leave the country under the terms of a withdrawal agreement negotiated by President George W. Bush. The 'Gunrunners' of HMLA-269 were the last HMLA squadron to leave Iraq, departing Al Asad on 15 December 2009.

Afghanistan operations

The first AH-1Ws to enter Afghanistan after 9/11 came – appropriately for the Marines – from the sea. On 25 November 2001, four Whiskeys from HMLA-169 attached to the 15th MEU lifted of the deck of the USS *Peleliu* off the Pakistani coast and headed north for a FARP site in Pakistan before continuing to an abandoned air base near Kandahar called Camp Rhino. Four more AH-1Ws from HMLA-269, detached to the 26th MEU aboard the USS *Bataan*, arrived at Camp Rhino a few days later. While at Rhino, the eight Whiskeys flew armed reconnaissance and convoy escort missions, with no major engagements before both detachments returned to their respective ships.

The next Cobras in Afghanistan – a four-ship detachment from HMLA-369 – flew in support of Operation Anaconda, a massive multi-national effort to clear the Shah-i-Kot Valley of Taliban and al-Qaeda fighters. Over a period of 22 days, the Cobras established a reputation for aggression and effectiveness, employing run-and-gun tactics. The Whiskeys provided attached escort for Army transport helicopters ferrying troops into the valley, as well as conducting armed reconnaissance, FAC(A) and CAS – sometimes all in the same mission. The first full-squadron HMLA deployment to Afghanistan came in October 2003, when reserve squadron HMLA-773 deployed to Afghanistan flying in support of several Army-led combined joint task forces.

With combat operations in Iraq taking priority, HMLA deployments to Afghanistan over the next five years remained modest, typically comprising a MEU's 'skid' detachment operating from Bagram or Kandahar for a limited time. Afghanistan once again became a major focus of effort for the HMLA squadrons once the Marines left Iraq and President Obama initiated a 'surge' in 2009. The first HMLA to deploy in support of the surge was HMLA-169 in spring 2009, kicking off a consistent rotation to Camp Leatherneck/Bastion that lasted through 2014.

'Whiskey' over Libya

More recently, Marine AH-1Ws saw combat over Libya during Operation Odyssey Lightning, a combined US, French and British operation aimed at assisting militias aligned with the Government of National Accord in retaking the coastal city of Sirte from Islamic State militants. Beginning on 1 August 2016, Cobras from HMLA-467 'Sabers', attached to VMM-264(REIN) assigned to the 22nd MEU aboard the USS *Wasp* (LHD 1) joined in air operations with the MEU's Harriers and several Air Force MQ-1 Predator and MQ-9 Reaper armed unmanned aerial vehicles.

Working with US special operations forces assisting the pro-government forces, the 'Sabers' targeted Islamic State fighting positions, tanks, 'technical' trucks, artillery and bulldozers. Early strikes during Odyssey Lightning pushed the militants into even more built-up areas deeper in the city, an environment in which the Cobra excelled. By the end of Odyssey Lightning, the 22nd MEU's four Cobras and six Harriers had flown a combined 600 CAS and strike missions in Sirte, with the Cobras firing 164 Hellfire missiles and the Harriers dropping 290 precision-guided bombs. Among the targets destroyed by the MEU were 197 defensive positions and 25 tactical targets, including tanks, 'technicals' and artillery.

HMLA-773 'Red Dogs' are one of two Marine reserve light attack squadrons, and will be the last to complete the transition from the AH-1W to the AH-1Z. (Joe Copalman)

Coyotes and Sabers – squadron changes & reserve reorganisation

In addition to the active-duty 'skid' squadrons, the Marines began the 21st century with two reserve HMLAs – HMLA-773 'Red Dogs' on the east coast and HMLA-775 'Coyotes' on the west coast. Comprised primarily of reservists drilling one weekend a month and two weeks per year, both squadrons received mobilisation orders for Iraq and Afghanistan. The first reserve HMLA to deploy was HMLA-773, which spent 18 months in Afghanistan starting in October 2003. HMLA-775 deployed to Iraq twice, once in early 2004 and again just a few months after returning to the US, departing for Iraq in early 2005. In September 2007, HMLA-773 deployed to Al Asad, Iraq for seven months. As part of a total force restructuring initiative, HMLA-775 stood down in September 2008.

The decommissioning of HMLA-775 freed up the aircraft needed to establish a new active-component HMLA. That same month, former 'Coyotes' UH-1Ns and AH-1Ws began arriving at MCAS New River to outfit newly-established HMLA-467 'Sabers', which activated on 23 October 2008. The addition of another HMLA provided flexibility that a reserve squadron, being on a five-year deployment cycle, could not provide. Within HMLA-467's first year of existence, the squadron supported several exercises, including an Enhanced Mojave Viper at Marine Corps Air-Ground Combat Center Twentynine Palms in September and October 2009. As American troops left Iraq, and operational commitments in Afghanistan eased following the 'surge' of 2009-2011, the need – and funding – for an additional active-duty HMLA faded. The 2013 budget sequester further compounded this, and on 16 June 2016 – with aircraft still deployed as part of the 26th MEU's ACE – the Marine Corps deactivated HMLA-467 after less than six years of existence.

The disestablishment of the 'Sabers' was not a total loss, as it enabled re-establishment of HMLA-775 as a reserve HMLA to ease pressure on HMLA-773, which during the period HMLA-467 existed, remained the sole Marine reserve H-1 squadron. Concurrent with the reactivation of HMLA-775 at Camp Pendleton, HMLA-773 consolidated from three operating locations to two, moving the squadron's 'flag' from Warner-Robins Air Force Base in Georgia to Joint Base McGuire-Dix-Lakehurst in New Jersey on 17 June 2016 – the day after HMLA-467 stood down. As part of a March 2020 force design initiative aligned with Commandant David Berger's planning guidance, HMLA-469 'Vengeance' will stand down by 2030.

The AH-1Z

Shortly after the AH-1W entered service in 1986, Bell experimented with a four-bladed main rotor system on the 'Whiskey', the goal being increased lift and speed. Impressed with the performance of the 'four-bladed Whiskey', and intent on upgrading both AH-1W and UH-1N fleets, the Marines partnered with Bell on the H-1 Upgrade Program beginning in 1996. With new Huey and Cobra variants on the drawing board, the upgrade programme prioritised commonality of parts to ease maintenance and supply concerns, especially for detachments operating at sea with MEUs. The resulting Cobra

This AH-1Z assigned to the 11th Marine Expeditionary Unit carries a loadout to meet virtually any air or ground threat as the USS *Boxer* (LHD 4) passes through the Strait of Hormuz in August 2019. (USMC/LCpl Dalton Swanbeck)

upgrade, the AH-1Z Viper (commonly known as 'The Z', 'Upgrade', or simply 'Cobra') shares 84 per cent parts commonality with the new UH-1Y, with common tail booms, rotor systems and cockpit displays.

Making its first flight on 7 December 2000, the AH-1Z is powered by a pair of General Electric T700-GE-401C turboshaft engines, which are an upgraded version of the same T700-GE-401 that powered the AH-1W. The engine features a digital fuel control system, resulting in greater efficiency and improved ability to coax additional power from the engine. Paired with the new composite four-bladed rotor system, the -401C gives the AH-1Z a maximum take-off weight of 18,500lb (8,391kg), versus the 14,750lb (6,690kg) maximum of the AH-1W. The new engine and rotor system combination also enables a greater maximum speed of 222kts (411km/h), vice the AH-1W maximum speed of 190kts (352km/h). Whereas the Whiskey required hands-on flying from lift-off to landing, a new automatic flight control system, which allows the pilot to program things like altitude or heading holds to ease some of the burden of flying, can make a difference should the HMLA community find itself flying 19-hour combat missions again.

For as much as the AH-1W was loved by the pilots who flew it and the Marines they supported with it, the 'Z' is a holistically more capable aircraft. The Lockheed Martin Target Sight System (TSS) outperforms the NTSU on the 'Whiskey' in several key areas. As Lt Col Dave Fitzsimmons, a Cobra pilot with over 2,000 hours in the AH-1W and almost 600 in the AH-1Z explained, '*An NTS, if you were looking at a tank-sized target at night that was hot, you're looking at maybe 1,500m to be able to tell that's a tank. With an NTSU, you could probably push that out to 5,000m to be able to tell that's a tank. Then with the TSS, you're talking probably 20km or better in some cases. It's just got exponentially better fidelity and zoom capability.'* In addition to enhanced view range over the Whiskey's NTSU, the TSS offers increased stability, enabling weapons engagements from greater distances than if the same weapons were fired from an AH-1W. This increased stability is further enhanced by the AH-1Z's four-bladed rotor system. As Lt Col Fitzsimmons explained, *'A Whiskey with a two-bladed system bounces around a lot more than the four-bladed system, which is much smoother. Not only is the system better stabilised, but the aircraft is more stable, so you've got much better laser stabilisation at range.'*

Helmet-Mounted Sight Display – the good and the bad

As in the Whiskey, both AH-1Z crew members are pilots. However, with the front and rear cockpit stations being identical in the Z, the Whiskey's front seat/back seat dynamic no longer applies. The placement of the NTS scope in the Whiskey demanded that the non-flying pilot sit up front to operate the TOW missiles and to fire the 20mm cannon off-axis. With rockets aimed through a reticule in the heads-up display (HUD) in the Whiskey's rear cockpit, only the flying pilot could aim and fire the rockets. With identical displays and the analogue scope of the NTS/NTSU replaced with all-digital optics in the TSS, pilots in both positions in the AH-1Z can operate the sensor, lase targets, launch Hellfires and fire the cannon.

Additionally, the Optimized Top Owl (OTO) Helmet-Mounted Sight Display (HMSD) projects rocket aiming symbology onto the monocle in both pilots' helmets, giving AH-1Z crews the ability to accurately fire unguided rockets from the front or rear cockpit. The rocket symbology in the HMSD offers multiple modes, including fixed reticule, constantly computed impact point (CCIP) and constantly-computed release point (CCRP). Describing the latter mode, Lt Col Fitzsimmons said, *'Constantly-calculated release point gives me a diamond and a plus, and if I put the plus in the middle of the diamond, the rocket is going to land where the computer wants it to land. That can be based off a GPS grid or a laser spot or whatever it is you're using as your source. Practicality-wise it just means that from range we can shoot unguided rockets with much better precision than anything the Whiskey could ever do.'* The enhanced symbology options available to 'Z' pilots also increases accuracy within shorter ranges, dramatically increasing the likelihood of a first-shot kill with unguided rockets.

For all the capabilities the HMSD offers, the system is not without drawbacks. As Lt Col Fitzsimmons explains, *'It mounts onto the side of the helmet instead of the centreline, so we get a lot of people with neck pain now, because you have an asymmetric weight on your head as you're flying around, which over time is going to cause some physical stress.'* Compounding the asymmetrical ergonomics of the new helmet, the monocle system is heavier than that used in the AH-1W, and the power pack for the system is heavy, unwieldy, and connected to the cord itself, which can 'tug' on the helmet unless the pilot secures it to his or her vest or something else nearby. In addition to increased weight, the HMSD used in the Z is far less customisable than the Whiskey's HDTS. Whereas the HDTS allowed pilots to individually customise the 25 or so symbols utilised in the monocle like the horizon bar or targeting reticule, the HMDS only

Upon the type's introduction into the HMLA squadrons, the UH-1Y brought enhanced capabilities over the UH-1N it replaced, and it enhanced the lethality of the AH-1W, able to see farther than the Cobra with its BRITE Star sensor turret and designated targets for Hellfire missiles from longer range. (Joe Copalman)

offers three global presets. Despite these drawbacks to the new system, it remains a benefit to AH-1Z crews, particularly while flying at night.

Another change in the front-seat/back-seat dynamic in the AH-1Z is driven by aerodynamics. The AH-1W naturally flew between seven degrees and nine degrees nose-down, giving the pilot in the rear excellent forward visibility. The design of the AH-1Z puts its neutral position with the nose more or less level to the horizon in forward flight, and slightly nose-high in a hover, restricting the rear-seat pilot's forward vision. For this reason, the handling pilot in the 'Z' more often than not sits up front, while the pilot operating the weapons systems sits in back.

Evolution of the HMLA mixed fleet

Marine HMLA squadrons treat their mixed AH-1 and UH-1 fleets as a unified weapons system offering complementary capabilities to execute every task in the HMLA mission statement. Since the beginning of Operation Enduring Freedom in 2001, the HMLA squadrons have operated three distinct pairings of the AH-1 and UH-1: the all-legacy

AH-1W and UH-1N, the transitional AH-1W and UH-1Y, and the all-upgrade AH-1Z and UH-1Y team. Lt Col Fitzsimmons, who flew Cobras in all three pairings, offered the following insights into the efficacy of each: '*In Iraq in the early days, the Whiskey and the November were a bad match for endurance and speed. The Whiskey had much better time on station and it was much faster. Flying around with a November was kind of a pain. The upside was that they could see more because they had crew chiefs and crew-served weapons for close-in section defence. So there were benefits to it, but the two platforms were definitely not well-paired.*' Regarding the synergy between the AH-1W and UH-1Y, Fitzsimmons continued, '*I flew the Whiskey with the Yankee in Afghanistan, and I would say the Yankee definitely had the advantage because it had a longer loiter time and it was technically faster. Their sensor was way better – the BRITE Star was better than the NTSU, but they didn't have the video downlink. The video downlink made a big different in Afghanistan with JTACs and getting clearance to shoot. But a lot of times, you'd have the JTAC telling the Cobra where to look, the Cobra telling the Huey where to look, the Huey lasing, and the Cobra shooting. It was a pretty good team. The Yankee and the Z, we've kind of gone back to the other end of the spectrum. The Z sees farther than the Yankee, the Z can host its own missiles (at range), it is technically a bit faster, and you get back into where there's not as many complimentary systems on the aircraft to make it as good of a pair. The Z shoots from much further back, so now that the gun is much more accurate, I can shoot it at two kilometres. For a Yankee to shoot, he needs to be back around a klick, or even inside of that, 700m, because they're shooting .50-cal and 7.62. So if I can shoot effective 20mm from 2km and then turn off-target, I don't have to get into small arms range, and that's where being with the Yankee is no longer cooperative. I would have to go into small arms range with him so he can shoot, or he doesn't shoot, and we just turn around after I'm done.*' Despite this divergence in effective weapons engagement distances, the pairing of the AH-1Z and UH-1Y represents – by far – the most potent manifestation of the Huey/Cobra team over the 50-year operational history of this dynamic duo.

The AH-1W earned a reputation for being an effective CAS platform with enough loiter time to make a difference over nearly three decades of combat in Afghanistan, Iraq, Libya and Somalia. Numerous upgrades kept it lethal and survivable through what is now the twilight of its career. But for those who transitioned from the Whiskey to the Z, the advantages are clear. As Lt Col Fitzsimmons explained, '*I've never done anything operational in the Z, but one of my friends who flies and who had done my conversion, I asked him 'If the bell went off and you had to run off to a troops-in-contact, which aircraft would you rather fly?', and he said 'The Z every day and twice on Sundays.' Now that I've done the conversion, I would absolutely agree. For the capability that that aircraft brings, there's no comparison. It is that much better, and that is from somebody who absolutely loved flying the Whiskey over 2,000 hours and four combat deployments. It brought me home safe more times than I care to remember. But the Z is better.*'

Looking forward

With all UH-1Ys delivered and AH-1W to AH-1Z transition scheduled for completion by 2022, the Corps' focus has shifted from H-1 acquisition to sustainment. Current plans call for the Marines to fly the Yankee and Zulu well into the 2040s. In addition to ensuring the 'skid' fleet remains serviceable and healthy through its projected lifespan, the Marines are already seeking ways to make the H-1 more lethal and survivable.

In terms of overall upgrades, the Marines are seeking ways to coax more speed out of the Yankee and Zulu, and to increase the range of both. Range and speed are common 'want list' items as the service seeks solutions to the 'tyranny of distance' that characterises operations in the Asia-Pacific region and in Africa. Though the UH-1Y easily bests its predecessor in terms of carrying capacity, the Marines are looking into ways of strengthening the aircraft's floor and external hardpoints to allow it to carry even more. Given the proven operational need for operating from austere desert environments and the increasing focus on winter operations, the Marines are also seeking enhanced symbology for degraded visual environment operations. Further, the AH-1Z is set to gain the same electronic attack capability as the UH-1Y with the integration of the AN/ALQ-231(v)3 Intrepid Tiger II jamming pod.

To meet and defeat current and emerging air defence threats like those being developed by Russia and China, new aircraft survival equipment must be developed and upgraded to keep pace. In March 2015, the Department of Defense issued a joint urgent operational needs statement for new countermeasures that could defeat advanced infrared-guided missiles. For Marine H-1s, the system currently being tested to meet this need is the AN/AAQ-45 Distributed Aperture Infrared Countermeasures (DAIRCM) system developed by Leonardo and intended to replace the AAR-47 Missile Warning System. Comprised of an integrated network of sensors, DAIRCM detects, identifies and tracks incoming missile threats, then defeats those threats through use of laser-based IR countermeasures. Spring 2019 saw HX-21 'Blackjack' – the Navy and Marine Corps helicopter and tiltrotor developmental test squadron – fitting the DAIRCM system to an AH-1Z for compatibility trials ahead of any prospective decision on fielding the system.

Offensively, the AH-1Z is set to receive a major weapons upgrade. The Lockheed Martin AGM-179 Joint Air-to-Ground Missile (JAGM) will replace the Hellfire in the near future. The JAGM has its origins in the unsuccessful AGM-169 Joint Common Missile which was a US Army-led programme intended to replace the Hellfire, but was cancelled in May 2007. Only a month after the cancelation, the Department of Defense initiated a competition for the JAGM contract with a draft request for proposals to fulfil Army, Navy and USMC needs for an improved missile. The Navy and Marines withdrew from the JAGM programme in February 2012, but re-entered in March 2014 with the stated intent of arming the AH-1Z with the new missile. The AGM-179 utilises a dual-mode guidance system, which employs both millimetre-wave radar and a laser seeker to provide flexibility in targeting while ensuring precision in either mode.

Beyond the H-1

The most significant factor handicapping the H-1 in USMC service is the type's inability to keep pace with the tiltrotor MV-22B. While detached escort tactics are the solution *du jour* for this mismatch in performance, they do nothing to address the challenges presented by the distances Marines face in both the AFRICOM and INDOPACCOM areas of responsibility. Even if planned upgrades are successful in squeezing more range and speed out of the Yankee and the Zulu, the gap between tiltrotor and con-

The Bell 360 Invictus is a light attack and reconnaissance proposal for the US Army's Future Vertical Lift system, which will likely inform or influence the Marine Corps' replacement for the H-1 family of aircraft.
(Bell)

ventional rotorcraft performance is still too vast for such upgrades to have much of an impact.

To close this gap, the Marines are partnering with the Army and US Special Operations Command on a joint effort called Future Vertical Lift (FVL). Planned as a family of systems, FVL is divided into five capability sets linked to the lift performance of current platforms slated to be replaced. The planned H-1 replacement is Capability Set 3 (FVL CS 3), expected to enter service in the 2030s. At the time of this writing, no specific system has been selected to replace the H-1, though it is likely that with FVL being a joint programme, the Army's decisions on which FVL platform(s) to pursue will have a strong influence on that. Current competitors for the Army's FVL CS 3 replacement for the UH-60 Black Hawk utility helicopter and AH-64 Apache attack helicopter are the Boeing-Sikorsky composite-rotor SB-1 Defiant and Bell's V-280 Valor tiltrotor. Both layouts offer significant speed and range advantages over conventional rotorcraft like the H-1, though ultimately, the overall footprint of each aircraft will likely drive the Marine Corps' decision, as deck space considerations factored greatly into the acquisition of the F-35B, CH-53K and MV-22B.

Whatever form the Marines' H-1 replacement takes, it will have to clear a high-performance bar compared to conventional rotorcraft. Per the 2019 Aviation Plan, '*The Marine Corps' driving requirement is attached escort in tomorrow's battlespace during distributed expeditionary operations from the sea. Speed, manoeuvre envelope, all-weather capability, and survivability will facilitate full integration of this aircraft into the MAGTF. To meet these goals, the Marine Corps FVL CS 3 rotorcraft will operate above legacy rotor-wing aircraft performance attributes like airspeed, combat range, altitude, and endurance with a full payload. FVL CS 3 rotorcraft will require a comparable mission radius and loiter time to match the MV-22B, time on station to support distributed ACE operations; and G-force limitations and service ceilings higher than legacy rotor-wing airframes.*'

HMM TO VMM | THE EVOLUTION OF MARINE MEDIUM LIFT

The CH-46 Sea Knight

The Boeing-Vertol CH-46 Sea Knight – popularly known as the 'Phrog' on account of its decidedly amphibian appearance – served the Marine Corps for more than 50 years before the final example was retired in 2015. During its USMC career, the CH-46 saw combat in Vietnam, Grenada, Iraq, Somalia, the Balkans and Afghanistan.

Though designed in the late 1950s with the ability to transport 24 combat-loaded infantrymen from ship to shore, Marine Phrogs began sacrificing lift capacity for protection during the Vietnam War. By the start of Operation Iraqi Freedom (OIF) in March 2003, enough armour, armament and aircraft survival equipment (ASE) had been added to the CH-46 that the Corps restricted the type to carrying 12 combat-loaded Marines. The additional weight also restricted the Phrog's flight envelope. Once noted for its ability to rapidly decelerate using a manoeuvre known as a 'side flare' – which allowed for quick ingress into a landing zone – additional total mass increased the risk of structural fatigue on these already-tired airframes.

Despite the Phrog's age and the limitations on it towards the end of its service life, it remained immensely popular with pilots and aircrew though its retirement. Addressing what made the CH-46 a good assault support aircraft, retired Phrog pilot Major Seth Goldstein told the author, '*It was just a very stable platform, especially when you start talking about SPIE rigging or fast-roping for inserts. It was kind of the best well-rounded machine out there. It wasn't the fastest, but it was fast enough. It couldn't lift the most, but it lifted enough. It was small enough to get into smaller zones, it was small enough to not beat up troops with rotor wash when they're sliding down a rope.*'

Desert Phrogs – into Iraq

Over the course of multiple Marine Expeditionary Unit (MEU) detachments into Afghanistan between late 2001 and early 2003, the Marines found the Phrog's performance in 'hot and high' operating environments a poor match for the mission. As a result, MEUs operating in Afghanistan primarily relied on Sikorsky CH-53Es for assault support transport, as the Super Stallion's ample power proved equal to the challenges of Afghanistan's altitude and heat. By contrast, when American and coalition forces invaded Iraq in March 2003, Marine CH-46s played a major role.

Marine CH-46s participated in one of the first movements of troops into Iraq ahead of the scheduled 23 March invasion date. At 551ft (168m), Safwan Hill served as an observation post (OP) for Iraqi troops, who could observe the movements of ground forces crossing into Kuwait and direct artillery fire against them. Together with a force of ten AH-1W SuperCobras from HMLA-269, six Phrogs from HMM-162 'Golden Eagles' attempted to insert a Marine reconnaissance platoon on top of Safwan Hill on 19 March after artillery and precision-guided bombs dropped by F/A-18 Hornets killed most of the OP's defenders. Poor visibility from blowing dust and smoke from nearby oil well fires forced the assault force to abort the landings, but they returned the next day and successfully inserted the reconnaissance force atop Safwan, denying its use to the Iraqis and giving the coalition its own OP to detect the approach of enemy reinforcements.

The Marines crossed into Iraq on 20 March 2003, with the primary effort being the movement of Regimental Combat Teams (RCTs) 1, 5 and 7 and the 2nd Marine Expeditionary Brigade (known as Task Force Tarawa) via massive ground convoys northwest towards Baghdad. During this period, Marine CH-46s primarily served as casualty evacuation (CASEVAC) aircraft, following the convoys as they advanced through numerous towns on the drive towards Baghdad, ready to transport wounded Marines or other coalition troops to medical facilities in Kuwait for treatment. Phrogs tasked with CASEVAC operated in pairs, both for mutual support and for additional lift in case the number of casualties on a mission exceeded a single aircraft's capacity.

Sea Knights flown on CASEVAC missions had a slightly different cabin configuration than that used for the transport mission. As Goldstein recalls, '*We carried six litters whenever we were doing CASEVAC. Facing the front of the helicopter, we left the right-side seats down, and then the left side was two-long by three-high with stanchions (for litters).*' The Navy corpsmen who flew along on CASEVAC missions to tend to the wounded were assigned directly to the HMM squadrons, with augments occasionally joining units during heightened periods of need.

Some HMM squadrons served as the aviation element of dedicated 'TRAP' forces, tasked with tactical recovery of aircraft and personnel should it be required. In this role, the 'Blue Knights' of HMM-365 supported a multinational operation involving US,

Soldiers from the US Army's 1st Cavalry Division carry a wounded soldier to a waiting CH-46E from HMM-268 'Red Dragons' during the second battle of Fallujah in November 2004.
(US Army/SFC Johancharles Van Boer)

British and Polish forces aimed at seizing and securing oil and gas terminals and harbour facilities on Iraq's al-Faw Peninsula along the Arabian Gulf. This operation served two purposes – to prevent Iraqi forces from creating an environmental catastrophe like they had in 1991, and to secure a port for humanitarian aid to flow into. While the main force of Navy SEALs, Polish GROM commandos and Royal Marines inserted via Royal Air Force Chinook and Royal Navy Sea King helicopters, the CH-46s carried the TRAP force and the command element of the Royal Marines Brigade Reconnaissance Force. As with the initial attempt to land Marines on top of Safwan Hill the day before, poor visibility complicated the insertion, during which the Marines lost the first aircraft of OIF, a 'Blue Knights' CH-46. All four aircrew and all eight British troops were killed in the crash.

Though CASEVAC remained the primary focus of the HMMs, Marine Phrogs provided assault support transport for the RCTs moving northwest on the ground. This included hauling equipment, ammunition, food and water, and personnel to forward positions, as well as inserting reconnaissance teams and conducting raids. As an example of how busy the HMM squadrons were during this period, over just two months in combat and initial stability operations, HMM-162 transported more than 2,200 troops and delivered more than 500,000lb (226,796kg) of cargo. Phrogs from HMM-165 participated in one of the highest-profile missions of OIF, the rescue of US Army PFC Jessica Lynch, successfully inserting and extracting 280 Army rangers as a blocking force on the periphery of the hospital in An Nasiriyah where Lynch was being held.

Post 'Mission Accomplished'

As the clear-cut victory of American and coalition forces over Saddam Hussein's Ba'athist regime and military gave way to the confusing ambiguity of post-'Mission Accomplished' Iraq, stability operations and counterinsurgency took precedence. Marine CH-46 operations stabilised beginning in 2004 with rotating deployments to Al Asad Air Base and Al Taqqadum Air Base between Fallujah and Ramadi. As the insurgency grew in both size and complexity, and as the scourge of improvised explosive devices (IEDs) proliferated, the HMM community once again began flying more CASEVAC missions. One of the most trying days was 11 May 2005, during Operation Matador, an effort to clear al-Qaim of insurgents. Marines from Lima Co, 3rd Battalion/25th Marines, a reserve infantry company from Ohio, took heavy casualties after an AAV-P7A1 amphibious assault vehicle sustained a direct hit from an IED buried in the road, killing nine Marines and wounding 40. Though not all encounters with the enemy were so costly, day-to-day operations resulted in enough wounded Marines, sailors and soldiers to keep the CASEVAC-tasked HMMs busy

As an example of how the HMM squadrons supported Marines amid an escalating insurgency, during its March through August 2004 deployment to Al Taqqadum, HMM-161 'Greyhawks' logged 3,072.8 combat flight hours and transported 328 wounded troops to higher levels of care. By contrast, when the Greyhawks returned to Al Taqqadum in August 2005, the squadron logged 5,199 combat flight hours, evacuating 2,100 casualties from locations all over al-Anbar province before leaving Iraq in February 2006. When not flying CASEVAC missions or sitting CASEVAC alert, Phrog crews flew people, equipment, mail and supplies between air bases and forward operating bases (FOBs), flying at night to avoid being easy targets for insurgents. During the squadron's July 2004 through February 2005 deployment to Al Taqqadum, HMM-263 logged 4,669.9

of its total 7,472.5 combat flight hours at night on night vision goggles. On that particular deployment, the 'Thunder Chickens' flew a diverse array of missions, ranging from CASEVAC to general support to 'hard-hit' raids with Marines and special operators fast-roping onto roofs and extracting any high-value individuals who had been captured. Marine Phrogs also transported Iraqi poll workers to polling stations throughout the region during Iraq's first democratic election on 30 January 2005.

Humanitarian Assistance and Disaster Relief

Humanitarian Assistance and Disaster Relief (HADR) is a core mission for MEUs, and with the CH-46 having comprised the core of every MEU's aviation combat element prior to the introduction of the MV-22, Phrogs routinely participated in relief and recovery operations worldwide. In the wake of Tropical Cyclone Sidr in Bangladesh in mid-November 2007, over 3,100 Bangladeshis died. The storm rendered hundreds of thousands homeless, destroyed crops and contaminated water sources. Infrastructure such as roads and bridges were devastated as well, complicating aid distribution and reconstruction efforts. Following a request from the Bangladeshi government for assistance, the Marines diverted the 11th and 22nd MEUs from their patrols to conduct HADR operations in Bangladesh as part of Operation Sea Angel II. The 22nd MEU arrived first, commencing operations on 23 November. Over the next seven days, the MEU's ACE – HMM-261(REIN) – delivered over 12,000 gallons of water and 73,000lb of food and relief supplies with its CH-46Es and CH-53Es. On 4 November, HMM-166 'Sea Elk' began flying Sea Angel II missions with its Phrogs and attached -53Es, working with personnel from the State Department and US Agency for International Development, delivering 54,165lb (24,569kg) of food and 1,875 gallons (7,098 litres) of water to remote villages. Additionally, the helicopters transported US Navy medical teams to treat sick and injured villagers in otherwise inaccessible areas of Bangladesh. The medical teams brought by HMM-166 and HMM-261 treated over 1,000 patients.

Humanitarian Assistance and Disaster Relief is a core capability of Marine Expeditionary Units (MEUs). Here a crew from HMM-165(REIN), the aviation combat element for the 15th MEU, delivers relief supplies to a remote village in the wake of massive flooding in Pakistan in 2010. (USMC/Capt Paul Duncan)

Over a ten-week period spanning most of August, September and October 2010, HMM-165(REIN) flew HADR missions in the wake of devastating floods in Pakistan. In addition to transporting food, water and medical teams to remote villages along the flooded Indus River, the 'White Knights' – attached to the 15th MEU aboard the USS *Peleliu* – evacuated over 9,000 Pakistanis from flood-ravaged areas to safer places utilising the MEU's CH-46s and CH-53s.

In addition to providing humanitarian assistance all around the world, the Marines occasionally put the Phrog to work on US soil. In the wake of Hurricane Katrina in late August 2005, HMM-264 'Black Knights' at MCAS New River sent two Phrogs to assist in relief and recovery efforts in New Orleans and the surrounding areas. Then, in July 2008, with summer wildfires spreading rapidly throughout central California, Governor Arnold Schwarzenegger requested firefighting support from the military. Marine Aircraft Group 16 answered the call, sending CH-46s and crews from HMM-268 'Red Dragons' and HMMT-164 'Knightriders' to NAS Lemoore to fly firefighting missions with 'Bambi Buckets'.

Phrog upgrades

Marine CH-46Es received limited upgrades in the years leading up to the type's replacement by the MV-22 Osprey, with most being related to performance or survivability. Under a programme called the H-46 Dynamic Component Upgrade initiated in the late 1990s, the CH-46 fleet received new rotor heads and transmissions that improved handling and reliability. Concurrent with these upgrades, Marine Phrogs received new Rockwell-Collins ARC-210 radios and night vision-compatible heads-up displays. One of the biggest problems facing the Phrog community was the declining reliability of the type's General Electric T58-GE-16 engines. In 2003, the Marines initiated an engine upgrade known as the Engine Reliability Improvement Program (ERIP). At the core of this upgrade were new high-pressure turbines, compressors and combusters, with

During the last year of type's service, the Marine Corps painted BuNo 153369 in a paint scheme representative of the one this same airframe wore during the Vietnam War. (Kevin Whitehead)

Though the CH-46 has faded from active service in the Marine Corps, those who flew and crewed the 'Phrog' retain a strong, unshakeable affection for the type. (USMC/LCpl Lauren Falk)

the compressor blades being coated with titanium nitride to reduce blade erosion and increase reliability. Delivery of all 446 modified engines – known as T58-GE-16As – occurred between April 2003 and March 2007, giving the CH-46 fleet the safety and reliability it needed to keep the type flying through the MV-22 transition.

Survivability upgrades in 2006 included crash-attenuating seats for pilots and crew chiefs and composite armour to replace the original steel armour, cutting down on weight while still offering protection. Early 2007 saw an expansion of the Phrog's aircraft survivability equipment, as the chaff/flare dispensers mounted atop the rear sponsons were augmented with dispensers positioned under the forward fuselage, just aft of the nose gear.

End of the road for H-46

On 1 August 2015, a crew from Marine Medium Helicopter Squadron 774 (HMM-774) 'Wild Goose', a reserve squadron based at NAS Norfolk, Virginia, flew the final CH-46E in USMC service – bureau number 153369 – to the National Air and Space Museum's Steven F. Udvar-Hazy annex in Chantilly, Virginia. While this was technically not the last 'Phrog' in USMC service – MCAS Cherry Point's 'Pedro' Search and Rescue detachment still flew four HH-46Es at that time – it represented the end of the CH-46 as a combat-deployable medium lift asset for the Marine Corps. Looking back on his time flying the CH-46, Seth Goldstein told the author, '*It was just incredible that we were using Vietnam-era machines and getting every bit we could out of them. They worked their butts off and kept flying until the last day.*'

The MV-22B Osprey

The term 'revolutionary' tends to be overused with regard to military technology, but using any other term to describe the impact of the Bell-Boeing MV-22B Osprey on Marine Corps aviation would arguably be an exercise in understatement. Though the aircraft it replaced, the undeniably charismatic CH-46 served with distinction for over 50 years, the Osprey has expanded the speed and range envelope of the MAGTF orders of magnitude beyond what the beloved Phrog could provide. Whereas the CH-46 topped out around 165mph (266km/h), the Osprey cruises at 350mph (563km/h). The Phrog's maximum range was 630 miles (1,014km), while the MV-22 can fly over 1,000 miles (1,609km) without refuelling, and considerably further utilising aerial refuelling – something the CH-46 could never do. In terms of lift capacity, the H-46 peaked at 24,300lb (11,022kg) maximum vertical take-off weight, while the MV-22 can lift off vertically weighing as much as 42,500lb (19,278kg). The introduction of the MV-22 into the MEU construct has expanded the reach of the MEU from its old helicopter-centric 200-mile (322km) unrefuelled radius out to over 1,000 miles. The impact of this has been a shift from relying on amphibious fighting vehicles and hovercrafts as the MEU's primary ship-to-shore connector to relying heavily on aviation assets to move Marines and equipment ashore. With the Osprey's range and speed, the MEU can almost bypass the beach entirely.

The introduction of the Osprey into amphibious operations altered the structure of the MEU's aviation combat element. With the MV-22 having a slightly larger footprint than the CH-46, the ACE's medium-lift complement was reduced from 12 to ten aircraft. Though a reduction on paper, this still represents a net gain in capacity. While the Phrog had long been limited to carrying a maximum of 12 passengers, the MV-22 can carry a full load of 24 combat-loaded Marines. At maximum capacity, 12 CH-46Es could move 144 Marines ashore in one wave, while ten Ospreys can transport 240. Further, the increased speed of the Osprey allows it to cycle from ship to shore and back again much more quickly than the CH-46 could.

Tiltrotor challenges

The advantages brought by the Osprey over its predecessor also introduced some new tactical challenges. Historically, CH-46s operated with attached escorts, primarily AH-1 Cobra and UH-1 Huey gunships. In addition to providing overwatch and suppressive fire for the Phrogs coming into landing zones, the H-1s provided en route protection, able to provide top cover should an aircraft go down. With the Osprey cruising at speeds over 300mph (483km/h) and the AH-1Z topping out at 255mph (410km/h), that divergence forced a transition to detached escort, where the 'skids' fly well ahead of the MV-22s, timed to arrive over the landing zone shortly before the Ospreys do.

One disadvantage to this arrangement is that the Osprey far outranges the H-1s, a gap widened further by the MV-22's air-to-air refuelling capability. One solution is the establishment of forward arming and refuelling points (FARPs) along the route. This is something Marine HMLA and VMM communities train for, with both the MV-22 and KC-130 being capable of aviation-delivered ground refuelling (ADGR). The Osprey's advantage for ADGR is that it can land virtually anywhere, negating the need for a runway. Lacking the capacity for aerial refuelling, H-1s have long required the use of FARPs to take on fuel to extend their combat radius. During the 15th MEU's move-

Initially plagued by the developmental problems one would expect of a revolutionary new aircraft, the Bell-Boeing MV-22B Osprey has proven to be an improvement over the CH-46 in terms of range, speed and lift capacity. (Kevin Whitehead)

ment from the USS *Peleliu* deep into Afghanistan in November 2001, the H-1s provided detached escort, routing through a FARP in Pakistan before continuing on and meeting the MEU's CH-53Es (which refuelled en route from KC-130s) just outside the objective area of what became known as Camp Rhino.

To compensate for the loss of attached rotor-wing escort, Marine Osprey crews train with fixed-wing assets providing a modified form of attached escort. Osprey pilot Major Tommy Keech said, '*We've gone to being escorted by jets. With Harrier escort, you can get fairly similar airspeeds. Then to a lesser degree, F-18s and F-35s, but obviously they don't fly 240 knots. They fly faster than that, but they can set up a flight profile to support the package en route, and they use their sensors to support us as well. And with them, there may be a much quicker response time.*' Additionally, the Marines recently started attached escort training in both the joint and coalition environment, working with USAF A-10 'Warthogs' and Royal Australian Air Force Pilatus PC-9 light turboprop aircraft.

Another challenge presented by the Osprey's extended range is that traditional electronic-line-of-sight communications degrade the further an MV-22 is from headquarters or 'the boat' or friendly radio relay. Given the vast distances involved in the AFRICOM and INDOPACCOM theatres, Marine Ospreys routinely operate over the horizon, and require reliable communications with headquarters, Marines in the field/

objective area, and other aircraft. To this end, the Marines have been evaluating various satellite communication (SATCOM) systems to keep assault support forces connected to headquarters and to build situational awareness en route to an objective that might be thousands of miles from 'home plate'.

One of the most frustrating challenges for the Osprey community had nothing to do with the aircraft itself, but rather how many in the public and in government perceived the aircraft. Developmental delays, cost overruns, and a handful of deadly crashes early in the programme earned the V-22 an army of committed, seemingly unswayable critics, many of whom wished to see the programme cancelled. Some of the most vocal critics relied on data several months or even years out of date to sustain scepticism as to whether the speed, range and lift capabilities of the Osprey were worth the money and lives spent on the programme. Another frustration early Osprey pilots had to manage was a lack of education about the aircraft's capabilities throughout the Marine Corps. With over 40 years of CH-46 employment having set expectations for medium-lift support, ground and aviation commanders treated the MV-22 as a 'Phrog' surrogate, rather than leveraging its enhanced speed and lift capabilities. While aggressive outreach efforts and capabilities briefings raised awareness of what the Osprey brought to the Corps, the best way to spread the word about what the MV-22 could do was to put it to work for Marines in combat.

Into combat – Osprey makes its debut

On 4 October 2007, ten MV-22Bs from VMM-263 'Thunder Chickens' arrived at Al Asad Air Base in Iraq, beginning the first ever Osprey combat deployment. For as much bad press – warranted or not – as the Osprey received over the years, no capabilities briefing, no reassurances of the type's readiness for combat, no praise of the aircraft from career CH-46 pilots who transitioned to the MV-22 could convince the sceptics and critics that the Osprey was a safe, capable and effective assault support platform. The only thing that could do that was a successful deployment, followed by another successful deployment, followed by another one.

Under the leadership of Lieutenant Colonel Paul Rock – one of the Corps' highest-hour Osprey pilots by that time – the 'Thunder Chickens' hit the ground running, taking the same assault support taskings as the H-46 squadron they replaced at Al Asad. While this was in many ways a trial by fire for the Osprey, Rock's focus remained on providing seamless support for the Marines in al-Anbar province, wanting to prove the Osprey's capabilities to them far more than to anyone on the outside. In addition to moving people and cargo between bases and FOBs, VMM-263 began flying missions the H-46 typically did not. The 'Thunder Chickens' took on the aeroscout mission, which was effectively a form of airmobile presence patrols. Aeroscout involved placing infantry or reconnaissance Marines aboard a transport like the CH-53E or the Osprey, escorted by UH-1Ns and AH-1Ws for reconnaissance and fire support, with an F/A-18D or AV-8B overhead utilising a LITENING pod to seek out areas of interest and provide enhanced situational awareness to the rest of the 'package'. Within the first year of aeroscout operations, Marines seized four tons of homemade explosives, destroyed several terrorist training camps and bomb factories, and captured dozens of insurgents. Iraqi troops also benefited from the Osprey's speed and mobility. With the Iraqi Army growing in size and sophistication, the 'Thunder Chickens' flew multiple raids transporting Iraqi troops on hard-hit missions against insurgents. On one such mission in December

2007, VMM-263 transported Iraqi troops on a raid with the target area being over 150 miles (241km) away.

Though all combat aircraft occasionally struggle with maintenance issues, especially in the desert with dust and heat challenges, the Osprey had such a bright spotlight on it that critics saw any teething problems common to new aircraft on a first deployment as fatal flaws, irrefutable evidence of the type's unsuitability for service. Indeed, VMM-263 struggled with some reliability issues, though most of these problems arose early in the deployment, with the Marines learning how to repair or prevent certain faults as they arose. Over the course of VMM-263's deployment, the squadron only dropped five out of 500 missions for maintenance problems.

In the wake of the 'surge' prior to the end of Operation Iraqi Freedom, the Marines only managed three deployments to Iraq with the MV-22. Though reliability remained an issue through all three deployments, the Osprey generally acquitted itself well in combat, with the Marines who flew, crewed and maintained it proving the type as not only a valid replacement for the CH-46, but as an aircraft offering vastly improved capabilities over the Sea Knight. Following the Osprey's success in Iraq, the Marines began deploying VMMs to Afghanistan in November 2009.

Afghanistan and beyond

The arrival of VMM-261 'Raging Bulls' in Afghanistan brought Marine medium-lift assets back to Operation Enduring Freedom. Within a month of arriving at Camp Bastion in Helmand Province, VMM-261 put the Osprey to work in its first named operation in Afghanistan, Operation Cobra's Anger. Aimed at disrupting Taliban lines of communication in the Now Zad Valley, Cobra's Anger included the insertion of an 80-man reconnaissance force with MV-22s at the beginning of the operation on 4 December

Under the leadership of Lt Col Paul Rock, VMM-263 'Thunder Chickens' was the first MV-22 squadron to deploy overseas, operating from Al Asad, Iraq between September 2007 and April 2009.
(US Navy/CPO Joe Kane)

2009. Later during that same deployment, VMM-261 supported Operation Moshtarak, a massive, multi-national effort to drive the Taliban out of their stronghold in Marjah. While the majority of Marine and Afghan National Army troops had been inserted via CH-53s at the beginning of the operation, on 19 February, the 'Raging Bulls' inserted the 3rd Reconnaissance Battalion into Marjah to reinforce Regimental Combat Team 7, which was engaged in a gun battle with tenacious Taliban forces.

In addition to named operations and raid insertions, the 'Raging Bulls' flew general support missions, moving people, mail, supplies and equipment from Camp Bastion to the numerous FOBs throughout the area. The introduction of the MV-22 in this capacity eased the pressure on the Marine CH-53D and -53E squadrons in Afghanistan, freeing them up to focus more on the heavy-lift mission.

General support comprised the majority of sorties flown by Ospreys in Afghanistan. During a seven-month period between July 2010 and January 2011, VMM-365 'Blue Knights' transported 1,073,469lb (486,917kg) of cargo and 22,395 passengers throughout southwestern Afghanistan. In addition to hauling impressive amounts of cargo and passengers, the 'Blue Knights' participated in ten named operations, conducting infiltration and exfiltration of infantry and special operations forces at night. When the 'Blue Knights' returned to Afghanistan in early 2012, the tactical situation had changed to where the squadron flew as many as ten named operations a week for a total of 193 over the course of a six-month deployment. This included three battalion-level inserts, with one such mission involving the insertion of almost 600 Marines. Almost all of these missions involved insertion and extraction of Marine and other ISAF infantry against Taliban targets, and most occurred at night relying on both night vision goggles and battlefield illumination from KC-130s overhead.

Despite MV-22 squadrons operating in Iraq and Afghanistan and having aircraft sustain combat damage on those deployments, the notion that the type could not stand up to battle damage persisted among Osprey critics. 'Blue Knights' Ospreys took fire on 26 separate occasions during the squadron's 2012 deployment. One aircraft sustained 11 hits, another eight, and several more took one or two hits on these missions, with no losses. The blades and fuel system held up particularly well, and the digitally controlled, triple-redundant hydraulics systems effectively isolated battle-damaged components to continue functioning. Though not immune to damage, the Osprey proved capable of taking the proverbial punch. Despite its robust construction and redundant systems, the Ospreys best defences remain speed and altitude – it can get into and out of landing zones quickly, and can climb out of small arms range with a full load of troops faster than the CH-46 could.

While MV-22s performed CASEVAC as a secondary mission in Iraq and Afghanistan, the Osprey had not been committed as a primary CASEVAC in the way the CH-46 had been in Iraq. That changed in early 2014 when VMM-261 deployed to Camp Bastion specifically to provide CASEVAC for ISAF troops in Afghanistan amid the drawdown of forces as OEF wound down. Whereas the typical complement of Navy corpsmen is three per each VMM squadron, the 'Raging Bulls' brought 15 corpsmen plus a flight surgeon to Afghanistan. The Osprey brought a speed advantage to the CASEVAC mission in Afghanistan, as all other CASEVAC or combat rescue units flew conventional rotorcraft like the Chinook or the Black Hawk. Though Ospreys would return to Afghanistan under Operation Freedom's Sentinel just a few years later, VMM-261's CASEVAC deployment proved to be the final one for Ospreys under OEF.

'To the shores of Tripoli' – rescue in Libya

The Osprey's speed and ability to aerial refuel are critical capabilities in the TRAP mission, which the type inherited from the CH-46. These capabilities make the V-22 the ideal rescue vehicle in regions where vast distances separate deployed Marines or other US/allied troops from lifesaving care. The first real-world test of the Osprey's suitability as a TRAP platform came on 21 March 2011 with the rescue of an Air Force pilot forced to eject from his F-15E near Benghazi, Libya. Flying out of Aviano Air Base in Italy, the crew of BOLAR 34 – pilot Major Kenneth Harney and Weapons System Operator Captain Tyler Stark – experienced a weight imbalance after a fuel feed issue and entered a flat spin. Unable to regain control, Harney decided to eject. On the ground at night in a contested area of Libya and separated from one another, Harney shed his equipment and began to run, while Stark sought refuge in a sheep pen.

While Stark was quickly discovered by friendly locals sympathetic to the anti-Gaddafi rebels the US was supporting, Harney remained on the ground and in need of rescue. Steaming 100 miles (161km) off the coast of Libya aboard the USS *Kearsarge*, the 'Fighting Griffins' of VMM-266(REIN) were the closest unit capable of launching an effective rescue. As the ACE for the 26th MEU, VMM-266(REIN) had four MV-22Bs, six AV-8B Harriers, four CH-53E Super Stallions and three UH-1 Hueys at its disposal (the majority of the MEU's Ospreys and the AH-1Ws went ashore in Afghanistan earlier in the deployment). The MEU sent a section of Harriers ahead of the Ospreys to take the on-scene command hand-off from a pair of Air Force F-16s maintaining an orbit over Major Harney and keeping him apprised of vehicle and personnel movements on the ground. Once established overhead, the lead Harrier pilot – Major Eric Grunke

Force Reconnaissance Marines await extraction from a training site in New Mexico during Angel Thunder 2015, a joint personnel recovery exercise run by the US Air Force. (USAF/TSgt Courtney Richardson)

– guided Harney to an adequate landing zone for the inbound Ospreys and used laser-guided bombs to destroy one advancing vehicle and deter another from coming any further.

The two Ospreys inbound to Harney's position carried 15 reconnaissance Marines and – flying at 300 knots (345mph/556km/h) – covered the distance in considerably less time than a CH-46 would have. At the landing zone, lead pilot Major BJ Debardeleben overflew Harney's position with too much speed to stop and land. At the controls of the second Osprey, Captain Eric Kolle had fallen back into a loose trail position to avoid the brownout from Debardeleben's aircraft, putting him into position to decelerate and land just 50 yards (46m) from Harney's position. Once on the deck, the crew chief dropped the ramp and the recon marines stormed out, fanning into defensive positions as Harney ran towards the aircraft, hands in the air to demonstrate he was not a threat. After what only felt like seconds to Kolle, his crew chief notified him the survivor was aboard. It took several minutes to get the recon marines back aboard the aircraft – but once all had been counted and re-counted, the aircraft lifted off and headed back towards the *Kearsarge*.

Going the distance

Over the past decade, the Marines put the MV-22's long-range capabilities to the test with a series of flights in which Ospreys self-deployed from the continental United States to Europe and South America, and from Hawaii to Australia. In November 2015, VMM-764 'Moonlighters' flew three MV-22s from MCAS Miramar to Rio de Janeiro, Brazil, 6,165 miles (9,922km) away, supported by three KC-130Js from VMGR-234 'Ranger' out of Texas and a single KC-130T from VMGR-452 'Yankees' out of New York. Poor weather along much of the route extended the trip to five days, but even with extended ground stops to wait the weather out, aerial refuelling proved critical to covering the distance. Once in Brazil, the 'Moonlighters' engaged in a robust flying schedule as participants in the UNITAS amphibious warfare exercise for nine days. In May 2017, the 'Red Dragons' of Hawaii-based VMM-268 executed the first trans-Pacific (TRANSPAC) flight for the MV-22, with four Ospreys covering the 6,000 miles (9,656km) between Marine Corps Base Kaneohe Bay and Darwin, Australia. While aerial refuelling allowed the Osprey crews to cover most of that distance, the aircraft stopped in Wake Island and Guam for fuel and to allow the crews to stretch out. By self-deploying, the Marines saved up to six weeks and considerable expense moving the aircraft via commercial shipping. The 'Red Dragons' deployed to Australia as the aviation combat element (ACE) for Marine Rotational Force – Darwin, a standing six-month deployment commitment that began in 2012 to strengthen alliances in the Australasian region of the INDOPACCOM area of responsibility.

In addition to validating the Osprey's ability to self-deploy, the Marines have been putting the type's long-range capabilities to work in real-world operations. In the wake of lethal terror attacks on a US diplomatic compound and a CIA annex in Benghazi, Libya on 11 September 2012, the Marine Corps established Special Purpose Marine Air-Ground Task Force – Crisis Response – Africa (SPMAGTF-CR-AF) to stand ready to respond to similar incidents in the future. Based at Morón Air Base in Spain, the Marines have maintained a steady deployment rotation for SPMAGTF-CR-AF, with a contingent of 500 Marines, supported by an ACE consisting of six MV-22Bs and two KC-130Js.

Joint Personnel Recovery

Though the Marine Corps generally does not engage in the same type of combat search and rescue (CSAR) missions as the USAF's rescue forces do, increased personnel recovery commitments like SPMAGTF-CR-AF have created a demand signal for joint force rescue training beyond the Marine-specific TRAP construct. As operators of the Corps' primary personnel recovery vehicle, Marine Osprey crews have increasingly participated in joint personnel recovery (JPR) training with other branches of the military as well as with partner nations. The first major JPR exercise to include Marine MV-22s was Angel Thunder 2015. Initiated as a USAF CSAR exercise in 2006, Angel Thunder quickly grew, with subsequent iterations involving all branches of the US military, government agencies like the US Department of State and Drug Enforcement Administration, and partner nation rescue forces from countries like Colombia, Germany, Israel and Sweden.

During Angel Thunder 2015, VMM-268 sent two aircraft and multiple crews to Creech Air Force Base in Nevada to participate in the exercise as part of the squadron's workup prior to a SPMAGTF-CR-Central Command (CC) deployment to Kuwait. The exercise took the 'Dragons' out of the MEU-centric TRAP construct and plugged them in as an on-call joint-force theatre TRAP asset. With the exercise based out of Davis-Monthan AFB in southern Arizona with training sites ranging from southern New Mexico to several miles off the coast of California, the exercise stressed the long-range rescue capabilities of the Osprey. Further, with one of the primary training sites being Camp Navajo, located near Flagstaff, Arizona and situated 7,000ft (2,134m) above sea level, the Osprey crews gained experience operating in true hot-and-high conditions, with the attendant degradation in both engine and rotor performance. Captain Sean Rafferty, an MV-22B pilot who participated in Angel Thunder explained the training benefit of these scenarios, saying, '*We had to fly two hours to get near the objective area, then we'd have to consider taking fuel and taking pax and then taking that to a landing zone that might be at higher elevation where we'd be power-limited based on the density altitude. There are a lot of good training aspects with that. We had to really crunch down on fuel numbers, the amount of weight we could carry into the zone.*'

As part of a MEU, Osprey crews train with AV-8B Harriers on attached and detached escort for TRAP missions. With no Harriers involved in Angel Thunder, the 'Dragons' worked with Air Force A-10 Warthogs on attached escort tactics. This pairing reflected one of the realities of deploying to the Middle East. As Captain Rafferty explained, '*It came about because we were just working joint with the Air Force, and that's their primary vehicle for rescue escort, going into a rescue mission. We can very well be used if we go for a Special Purpose MAGTF and are requested to respond within CENTCOM, so this gave us the experience that we needed just in case we do work with them in other joint missions in-theatre. It worked out great. It was interesting to see their tactics, techniques and procedures (TTPs) and how they attach to us. Our airspeeds and how we operate within the objective area are very similar. It was a very good experience for myself and I think we greatly benefited from working with them, and in a way that we'd see new TTPs with different aircraft in an objective area, especially for a TRAP mission.*'

In the years following Angel Thunder 2015, USMC-USAF cooperation on joint personnel recovery has grown and evolved considerably. VMM-268 partnered with the

A-10 Thunderbolt IIs from the 442nd Fighter Wing escort MV-22Bs from VMM-268 over Hawaii in February 2019. (USMC/Sgt Alex Kouns)

303rd Fighter Squadron – a reserve A-10 squadron based at Whiteman AFB in Missouri – for an exercise called Tropical Koa Agile Combat Employment in Hawaii in February 2019. During the exercise, the two squadrons practiced attached rescue escort in a maritime environment, similar to what both would encounter during operations in the vast expanse of the western Pacific. Osprey-Warthog integration has become so common that a spokesperson for MAG-24 in Hawaii told the *Marine Corps Times* in March 2019 that the A-10 is the 'preferred escort platform' for USMC Ospreys.

Marine Osprey crews have also trained with partner nation aircraft providing attached escort, again with VMM-268 leading the way. Pitch Black 2018, a multinational exercise conducted in Darwin, Australia, saw Pilatus PC-9s from the Royal Australian Air Force's No. 4 Squadron escorting Ospreys into and out of an objective area, laying the groundwork for coalition TRAP and tactical insertion/extraction missions, possibly even with partner nation infantrymen aboard. As a turboprop light aircraft with a cruise speed of 300kts and a stall speed far below that of any jet, the PC-9 can keep pace with the V-22.

The Osprey community's partnership with joint force and coalition partners extends beyond exercises. In November 2018, SPMAGTF-CR-Africa began integrating USAF pararescue jumpers (PJs) into its operational construct, putting them aboard MV-22s for long-range rescue missions throughout Africa. Additionally, reports indicate that

Air Force A-10s have provided attached escort to Marine Ospreys operationally as part of Operation Inherent Resolve in Iraq and Syria.

Ospreys in Africa – SPMAGTF-CR-AF

The complementary capabilities of the Osprey and the KC-130J give the SPMAGTF commander the ability to task organise along the lines of capability and capacity depending on the mission. A simple example of this is embassy evacuations, where the MV-22s could use the type's vertical landing capabilities to cycle in and out of an embassy compound to evacuate personnel to the nearest friendly (or secure) airfield where they could board waiting KC-130Js to transport them out of the country. In addition to Non-Combatant Evacuation Operations (NEO), SPMAGTF-CR-AF is capable of providing embassy support, humanitarian and disaster relief support (HADR), and TRAP in the AFRICOM area of responsibility, all of which are enabled by the SPMGTF ACE. The stand-up of SPMAGTF-CR-AF itself involved another record-setting flight – a non-stop trans-Atlantic flight of six Ospreys from VMM-365 'Blue Knights' directly from MCAS New River to Morón, supported with aerial refuelling from a pair of KC-130Js from VMGR-252 'Otis'.

In December 2013 an outbreak of political violence put American diplomatic personnel at risk in South Sudan's capital, Juba. In response, SPMAGTF-CR-AF sent 150 Marines and sailors aboard six MV-22s over to Camp Lemonnier, Djibouti to be ready to move into South Sudan to evacuate embassy personnel from Juba. Utilising the

Based at Moron, Spain, SPMAGTF-CR-Africa relies on a squadron of MV-22Bs augmented by a pair of KC-130J Hercules to transport Marines where they are needed in Africa. (USMC/Sgt Kassie L. McDole)

Ospreys at Camp Lemonnier and two KC-130Js operating out of Entebbe, Uganda, SPMAGTF-CR-AF conducted a successful evacuation of US embassy personnel from Juba on 3 January 2014, the first validation of the SPMAGTF-CR-AF concept. Though embassy staff returned to South Sudan after the situation calmed, political tensions persisted, flaring once again in the summer of 2016. In response, US President Barack Obama ordered SPMAGTF-CR-AF to fly 130 Marines and sailors into South Sudan to evacuate non-essential embassy personnel, while a 47-man reinforcement team augmented the embassy's security detail. The US Ambassador to South Sudan, Molly Phee, and her staff remained in Juba attempting to resolve the crisis and continue to coordinate humanitarian relief efforts for those suffering from the chaos and violence between the two warring factions.

In addition to embassy support and evacuations, SPMAGTF-CR-AF has used its Ospreys to support humanitarian missions in Africa. In October 2014 VMM-264 flew four Ospreys to Monrovia, Liberia as part of Operation Unified Assistance, the US military assistance mission help prevent the Ebola virus outbreak in West Africa from spreading. To get from Spain to Liberia, the Ospreys only made three fuel and crew-stretch stops along the way. The SPMAGTF-CR-AF Marines were able to support operations almost immediately after arriving in Liberia, flying relief workers, government personnel, VIPs and 78,000lb (35,380kg) of cargo all throughout the region, helping prevent the spread of Ebola in Africa.

Digital interoperability

One of the biggest innovations in Marine aviation over the past decade has been the introduction of digital interoperability, or DI. As the primary USMC assault support platform, the Osprey has been the central focus of recent DI efforts, with MAWTS-1 at Yuma participating in multiple tactical demonstrations of different DI systems since 2015 and helping develop the TTPs for DI use in the fleet. Since then, MAWTS-1 worked closely with industry developing DI tools to connect air and ground forces for en route situational awareness (SA) and to shorten reaction times when contingencies arise.

Addressing the current status of digital interoperability in the MV-22 community, Captain Kevin O'Malley at MAWTS-1 told the author: '*The ability to build SA, pass information, communicate without actually making a call over the radio is going to kind of change the future of warfare. Everybody thinks of it as the mission commander back hundreds of miles away getting these updates, but also, just think about the ability for me, as just another guy in the flight, to know 'Hey, this aircraft had to go get fuel someplace else, they're not going to be able to come do the extract for another 30 minutes.' That is a huge builder of decisions I'm going to be able to make. That's going to be a huge piece for decisions for that guy who's on deck who is getting ready to do x, y, or z knowing that Dash-2 is going to be a little bit delayed. He's going to change the things he does. The ability to pass that information and get that outside of line-of-sight radio communications is amazing. You have the NOTM-A (Network on the Move – Airborne) system – it's a mod that go into the Osprey, and you're now able to get NIPR (Non-classified Internet Protocol Router), SIPR (Secret Internet Protocol Router), you can make a phone call off the back. That provides amazing capabilities for that mission commander in the back of the aircraft, who as you're flying – and again, taking on that tyranny of distance – and as you're flying six hours, he's able to get up-to-the-minute information on how the situation on the deck is. He's able to tell us 'Hey, the winds have changed.' Simple things like that. Or 'Hey, now we need to do this routing, and there's going to be a tanker located here because it's taking us further.' It's just a real-time decision-making tool. We're very excited about it. It's the future. It changes the way we do things.'*

With DI tools and tactics finally being put to use operationally, Captain O'Malley stressed the need to remain competent in the fundamentals, as advances in GPS jamming and other forms of interference with networked communications have the potential to degrade or disrupt the types of communication DI enables. Addressing how Marines prepare for operating in a communications-degraded environment, O'Malley said, '*It's not lost on us, the capabilities of other countries and the threats that are out there. That's one of our night tactics events (at WTI), we go out into the field. We take off, we land out at Stovall, which is 50 miles east, we shut the planes down, and then it's like 'Okay, start planning. These are going to be paper products, and you don't have a computer. How are we going to do this?' As simple as it sounds to say that, when you are spoiled with having all these tools, that induces a little stress in a new student. So we're still looking at that point of it and not treating it solely as a crutch.*' Beginning in 2019, the Marines are integrating Software-Reprogrammable Payload radios on the 266 Ospreys not already built with them to accommodate most of the DI systems in use.

SPMAGTF-CR-Central Command and Operation Inherent Resolve

With the reduction of US forces in Iraq and Afghanistan, the Marines sought a crisis response capability in the Middle East similar to SPMAGTF-CR-Africa. Established in October 2013, Special Purpose MAGTF – Crisis Response – Central Command fills a crucial gap in MEU coverage in the region, as sea transit times and other obligations like security cooperation exercises tend to occupy much of the time MEUs spend on deployment. As with its AFRICOM counterpart, SPMAGTF-CR-CC provides TRAP, HADR, non-combatant evacuation operations, and embassy relief support for US Central Command (CENTCOM) area of operations, which stretches from Egypt in the west to Afghanistan in the east. While not specifically tied to contingency operations in the region – Marines and aircraft on SPMAGTF-CR-CC rotations routinely support Operation Freedom's Sentinel and Operation Inherent Resolve. Most recently, SPMAGTF-CR-CC utilised its Ospreys (provided by VMM-364 'Purple Foxes') to move 100 Marines to the US Embassy in Baghdad in response to a threat posed by Kata'ib Hezbollah militiamen in the wake of a 3 January 2020 US drone strike that killed Iranian General Qasem Soleimani, leader of Iran's Quds force.

Given the size of the SPMAGTF's area of responsibility, Ospreys assigned to it are typically accompanied by a KC-130J Hercules detachment for aerial refuelling support, allowing the MAGTF to be airmobile throughout the region. Additionally, the task force recently gained a limited maritime operations capability. Though not assigned to ships during SPMAGTF-CR-CC deployments, Ospreys assigned to CENTCOM duty can operate from the expansive flight deck of the USS *Lewis B. Puller* (ESB 3), the US Navy's first Expeditionary Mobile Base ship designed for low-intensity conflicts. Looking remarkably like a civilian oil tanker with the sides cut away for an open-air configuration, the *Puller* can support ship-to-shore operations in cases where a less robust force than a MEU suffices. With the task force's allowable Osprey strength recently scaled up from six to 12 aircraft, SPMAGTF-CR-CC leadership aims to increase the number of locations they have small teams operating in simultaneously.

Armed Osprey

A common criticism when the MV-22 entered the fleet was that it lacked a defensive weapon covering the front hemisphere of the aircraft. While the Osprey was built with a stowable mount for a 0.5in (12.7mm) machine gun on the rear ramp, this only covers the rear of the aircraft. Helicopter gunships like the Corps' AH-1 Cobras have historically helped suppress enemy fire in landing zones as transport helicopters approached, but with the speed differential between the Osprey and even the AH-1Z, attached gunship escort requires more coordination and often the use of FARPs.

The GAU-17 7.62mm (0.3in) Minigun is installed before a flight aboard Kirtland Air Force Base, Albuquerque, New Mexico, 6 April 2015. (USMC/Cpl Andy J. Orozco)

Though numerous proposals for a forward-mounted gun were made before the Osprey entered service, the first real attempt at providing the type with a credible forward-hemisphere defensive capability came in 2015, with the testing of the BAE Systems Defensive Weapon System, or DWS aboard MV-22s. The DWS consists of a gimbaled 7.62mm (0.3in) Gatling-type minigun mounted through the Osprey's 'hell-hole' in the floor of the rear cargo/troop compartment. The gun is controlled by a crew chief in back, sitting at a console with a screen showing the feed from the system's FLIR sensor (which some claim was better than the Osprey's Raytheon AN/AAQ-27 FLIR) and a fire control system.

Having been employed during exercises and by deployed VMM squadrons, the DWS drew mixed responses from Osprey crews. The space taken up by the gun mechanism and the fire control terminal reduces the number of useable seats or cargo area. The Osprey's sensor and the gun's sensor lacked integration, meaning the non-handling pilot up front had to talk the crew chief in the back onto the target and vice-versa. Though presented by BAE as capable of providing fire through a 360-degree arc, personnel at Naval Air Systems Command dispute that claim, citing some restricted zones of fire in order to protect the aircraft. After the 2015 DWS tests, Marines found evidence that the system damaged the fuselages of several aircraft that had it mounted.

Standard weapons fit on Marine MV-22s is a single GAU-21 .50-calibre machine gun mounted on the rear ramp. A swivel mount allows the gun to be stowed against the inside of the troop compartment, allowing easy boarding and egress from the aircraft. (Joe Copalman)

An MV-22 operated as a testbed by Bell-Boeing tests an aerial refuelling system called the V-22 Aerial Refueling System, or VARS in September 2013. Adding an aerial refuelling capability to the MV-22 will give Marine Expeditionary Units an organic tanker capability to extend their reach over the vast expanses of Africa and the Asia-Pacific region. (Bell-Boeing)

In addition to the ramp-mounted gun and the belly-mounted DWS, the Marines are also considering adding forward-firing ordnance in the form of the Advanced Precision Kill Weapons System (APKWS), a system that utilises laser-guided 2.75in (70mm) rockets. This capability – developed by Bell in response to an Air Force Special Operations Command plan to use some CV-22s as gunships – dovetailed seamlessly with an initiative championed by Lieutenant General Jon 'Dog' Davis, the Deputy Commandant for Aviation from June 2014 to July 2017, to make every aircraft in Marine Corps aviation a sensor, a shooter and a sharer. Utilising the company's MV-22 test aircraft with a seven-shot rocket pod on a special mount on the forward fuselage, Bell carried out live-fire tests with both the APKWS and the AGM-176 Griffin air-to-ground missile at the US Army's Yuma Proving Ground in Arizona in November 2014. Though successful, the tests have not yet resulted in operational fielding of such a weapons system.

Aerial refuelling

Unlike the US Navy's carrier air wings that operate from big-deck aircraft carriers, a MEU's aviation combat element lacks an organic shipboard aerial refuelling capability. Historically, this has not presented much of a problem, as MEUs operated close to shore in littoral areas and trips to and from coastal areas in support of amphibious assaults were relatively short-range affairs. Further, MEUs often have a detachment of KC-130s on a 'tether', based in a friendly nation in the region where a MEU is operating.

Operations like the 15th MEU's November 2001 movement to Camp Rhino in Afghanistan, more than 370 miles (595km) inland from where the USS *Peleliu* (LHA 5) was cruising, illustrated the need for MEUs to have an organic aerial refuelling capability. The 'tyranny of distance' accompanying operations in the Pacific only reinforces that need. With the aim of giving MEUs organic aerial refuelling capability, the Marines are acquiring the V-22 Aerial Refuelling System (VARS), a palleted roll-on, roll-off system that can convert any MV-22B into a tanker.

Designed and built by Cobham Mission Systems, VARS was first tested aboard Bell-Boeing's V-22 test aircraft (registration N204TR) in August 2015, successfully extending and retracting the hose while a pair of Marine F/A-18 Hornets closed to within 30 feet (9.14m) of the aircraft, simulating refuelling operations in the skies near Bell's Amarillo, Texas plant. At the time of the tests, the USMC anticipated a two-phase capability evolution, with the initial system sought by the service capable of passing 4,000lb (1,814kg) of fuel to other aircraft, expanding to 10,000lb (4,536kg) shortly thereafter.

The primary drawback of using Ospreys as tankers is that the MEU loses an MV-22 as an assault transport. With the system being roll-on, roll-off, this is not a permanent loss, but during long range movements of large numbers of Marines, having one Osprey committed to refuelling could potentially place greater strain on the aircraft actually flying the assault mission. That said, VARS will be capable of refuelling almost every aircraft in the ACE, with the 'skids' and the two-aircraft Navy MH-60S detachment being the exceptions.

Osprey firefighter?

In addition to performing a broad spectrum of assault and general support functions, the Marines also utilised the CH-46 Sea Knight for domestic firefighting duties aboard bases and in the surrounding communities when civil authorities made the proper request for such support. With the hilly grasslands of southern California being particularly susceptible to wildfires, the west-coast HMM squadrons flew these missions, with Sea Knight crews maintaining 'Bambi Bucket' certifications on top of all the qualifications needed to perform the full range of CH-46 missions.

With the sunset of the CH-46 on the horizon in 2010, the Marines evaluated the MV-22's suitability for firefighting operations. Marine Operational Test and Evaluation Squadron 22 (VMX-22) at MCAS New River, tasked with evaluating the Osprey and all prospective systems for it, initiated testing of the Osprey's compatibility with the 'Bambi Bucket' in July 2010. After testing concluded in March 2011, Bambi Bucket flight clearance was published in the Osprey's Naval Aviation Technical Information Product.

Following a successful February 2016 demonstration of the Osprey's firefighting capabilities to representatives from the California Department of Forestry and Fire Protection (Cal Fire), the Osprey joined to the state's stable of aerial firefighting platforms as an emergency reserve. This means that the Osprey will only be called into action in extreme situations where critical infrastructure is in imminent danger of being damaged or destroyed by wildfires. Within Cal Fire's San Diego zone, Marine MV-22s can respond to firefighting requests within 24 hours.

Mission-capable struggles

Despite its robust construction and proven survivability in the face of the kinds of small arms threat environment Marine helicopters have faced for decades, the Osprey has suffered from low mission capable rates since its introduction into the active inventory. With so many moving parts – including the wing-fold and proprotor blade-fold mechanisms and rotating engine nacelles – the Osprey is a complex machine requiring extensive monitoring and maintenance just to keep it mission-ready. Further, the manufacturer estimates for how long parts would last before requiring repair or replacement proved to be highly optimistic, as the engineers who developed those estimates failed to account for the effects of desert sand and salt air, which drastically reduce the lifespan of certain components. Many of these deficiencies have been mitigated through redesign of components and introduction of improved aircraft blocks (the current standard being Block C), which have reduced the Osprey's cost per flight hour from USD11,651 per hour in 2010 to just over USD9,000 by mid-2015. Still, Marine

MV-22s suffered from a community-wide 50 per cent mission capable rate throughout FY2018, down from a peak rate of about 68 per cent a few years prior. Marine Corps leadership attributed that dip to the increased demand for MV-22s worldwide, with commitments to two additional SPMAGTFs in Africa and the Middle East and a Marine Rotational Force in Australia on top of the needs of three MEUs, two Weapons and Tactics Instructor (WTI) courses, multiple divisional and regimental exercises all demanding VMM support. Though the fleet's mission capable rate appears to be rebounding with a 60 per cent rate for FY2019, the VMM community has a long way to go to meet the Navy's established per-squadron standard of a 75 per cent mission capable rate. The Marines recently instituted the V-22 Readiness Program (VRP), specifically aimed at increasing and sustaining the mission capable rate fleet-wide. Among the initiatives enacted through the VRP are a deepening and widening of the parts supply system, enhanced training for maintainers, contract maintenance support and increased engineering support. Additionally, the VRP includes a nacelle improvement initiative that eases engine maintenance and strengthens wiring harnesses to reduce wear caused by frequent rotation of the nacelles. The most ambitious component of the VRP aims to reduce the number of individual aircraft configurations through a programme called the Common Configuration – Readiness and Modernization (CC-RAM).

Standardising the fleet

Because of the length of the MV-22B acquisition timeline (which began in 2004), older aircraft and newly delivered ones vary considerably in terms of subsystems and configurations. In 2018, there were roughly 70 different configurations among the Corps' 300-plus Osprey fleet. Though some of these differences are minor, they have an impact on overall fleet readiness as these differences can hamper the ability of maintainers to swap components between aircraft. Further, sustaining a fleet comprised of different blocks and variants of aircraft complicates the management of spare parts. These differences impact pilots as well, as the different configurations require the Marines to maintain older systems, and pilots need to stay current on how to use these systems, which vary as one switches from one airframe to another. Captain O'Malley with MAWTS-1 explained one example of these differences, '*When you go out to a plane, the way that we load our mission sets is kind of like having a floppy disk, and then you go into the next plane and it's got a CD, and then the next one has a flash drive. It's kind of like* 'Hey, what plane am I in today? Okay, I need to make sure I have this kind of loading equipment.' *There's a huge change in the way the computers work, having certain types of computers, and then going to a different type of computer, that's an obvious difference. But using it, employing the aircraft, unless you're in a plane that needs a weather radar and you don't have one that day, it doesn't make a big difference. The engine parameters, the way I fly the plane, no difference for me as the user.*'

To remedy this, Naval Air Systems Command initiated the CC-RAM programme in 2017, aimed at reducing the number of different MV-22B configurations from 70 to five. The CC-RAM programme will put 129 older-lot Ospreys through Boeing's Philadelphia plant to be torn down and rebuilt to the same standard configuration as the MV-22Bs still rolling off the production line intended for USMC service. The goal of CC-RAM is to provide consistency from one airframe to the next, simplifying operation and increasing both the readiness rates and safety of the MV-22B fleet. Bell-Boeing deliv-

The Osprey's range and ability to refuel in-flight gives the type a self-deployment capability the CH-46 lacked, enabling the MV-22 to respond much more quickly to crises throughout the world without having to rely on air force airlift or navy sealift assets to get there. (Joe Copalman)

ered the first of 129 Block B MV-22B to be upgraded to Block C under the CC-RAM programme back to the Marine Corps on 10 December 2019. Included in the Block C upgrade are enhanced electronic warfare and defensive countermeasures capabilities, a weather radar, upgraded cockpit displays, updated environmental controls, and a digital display panel in the rear compartment for increased situational awareness among the crew chiefs. Having started in 2017, the CC-RAM programme is expected to run through 2022.

Continuing upgrades and fleet health

In addition to fleet standardisation, the Marines are focused on numerous MV-22 upgrades, including integration of the full range of DI tools like software-reprogrammable payload radios, Network on the Move – Airborne, the MAGTF Agile Network Gateway Link, Link 16 datalink capability, the Common Datalink and Tactical Targeting Network Technology. Upgraded aircraft safety equipment and updated interfaces for reduced visibility landings are also in the Osprey's future. But the primary focus will remain on easing maintenance and continuing to improve reliability, which has been a problem over the course of the Osprey's service life so far. The Marines are considering a future Block D configuration that would leverage technology and engineering developments related to Bell's V-280 tiltrotor for the US Army, namely the elimination of rotating nacelles in favour of a fixed-forward engine with only the front component with the proprotors rotating, which would ease maintenance significantly.

The author had the opportunity to interview two Osprey instructors at MAWTS-1 over four years apart – the first in spring 2015 and the second in late summer 2019. The divergence of opinions on the community's overall health between those two interviews is striking. In 2015, the instructor interviewed told the author, *'I've got 13 squadrons doing the job of 15,'* with attendant problems of strained family lives due to shorter dwell times between deployments, the lack of instructor qualifications within the community due to squadrons focusing on the minimum qualifications to be certified ready to deploy, and concern over proficiency as the expansion of MV-22 mission sets created new boxes for pilots and crew chiefs to check. By contrast, there were 17 operational active-duty and two reserve MV-22 squadrons in 2019. Whereas MAWTS-1 was being asked in 2015 to train Night Systems Instructors in order for squadrons to be certified as deployable, now the squadrons are asking for additional certifications in areas like Defensive Counter-Manoeuvring. Aircraft availability has increased, and should continue to do so as CC-RAM and other reliability initiatives under the V-22 Readiness Program make their way to the fleet.

Pictured on the deck of the USS *America* (LHA 6), this MV-22B from VMM-265(REIN) features a distinctive 'bump' above the rear fuselage. This houses a satellite antenna associated with the Network on the Move – Airborne (NOTM-A), enabling the flight crew and infantrymen or other passengers aboard to utilize digital interoperability tools via a secure WiFi network. (USN/MC1 Rufus Hucks)

VMA | MARINE ATTACK

At the start of the 20th Century, the Marine Corps was already transforming the AV-8B Harrier II from a day-only ground-attack aircraft using unguided weapons to a credible multi-role precision attack platform. The most consequential AV-8B upgrade to this point had been the incorporation of the Raytheon AN/APG-65 pulse-Doppler radar, with both air-to-air and air-to-ground modes. Harriers produced with the APG-65 or modified for it were designated AV-8B Harrier II Plus – the third subvariant of the Harrier II flown by the USMC after the original baseline AV-8B and AV-8B Night Attack models. At the turn of the century, Harriers equipped seven deployable Marine Attack Squadrons (VMAs).

The primary capability the 'II Plus' brought was an organic beyond-visual range (BVR) counter-air capability for Marine Expeditionary Units (MEUs) at sea as part of Amphibious Readiness Groups (ARGs). While the AV-8B already possessed the capability to carry AIM-9 Sidewinders, the Sidewinder is a within-visual range weapon. Marine Harriers at the time also possessed the ability to carry and employ laser-guided weapons, but with no means of self-designating, relied entirely on other aircraft or a forward air controller (FAC) or Joint Terminal Attack Controller (JTAC) to designate targets for these weapons.

Enduring Freedom – Harriers over Afghanistan

The terrorist attacks against the United States on 11 September 2001 initiated military commitments that continue to this day. The Marines typically have three MEUs forward-deployed at all times – one from the west coast, one from the east coast, and the 31st MEU based in Japan and continually manned on a rotational basis. Following the 11 September attacks, the 15th MEU and 26th MEU and their respective ARGs sped to the northern Indian Ocean off the coast of Pakistan to take the fight to al-Qaeda and their Taliban hosts.

The first strike conducted by Marine AV-8Bs was a daylight attack on 3 November 2001, launched from the USS *Peleliu* (LHA 5) against a terrorist training camp in Afghanistan with Mk 82 general-purpose 500lb (227kg) bombs. Conducted by a three-ship formation from VMA-311 'Tomcats' attached to HMM-163(REIN) 'Ridge Runners' as part of the 15th MEU's Aviation Combat Element (ACE), the mission proved to joint force air mission planners that the Harrier could hit targets in Afghanistan from 'L-class' carriers off the Pakistani coast.

While Marine Harrier pilots still train with unguided weapons like CBU-99 cluster bombs seen on stations two and six of this AV-8B Night Attack aircraft, the majority of air-to-ground weapons carried and employed in combat are laser-guided bombs like the GBU-16 seen on station three or GPS-guided bombs like the Joint Direct Attack Munition. (Scott Youmans)

Subsequent to that initial strike, VMA-311's det aboard the *Peleliu* carried a mixed load of Mk 82s and GBU-12 500lb (227kg) laser-guided bombs. Lacking target pods of their own, Harrier pilots dropping GBU-12s relied on special operations Joint Terminal Attack Controllers (JTACs) on the ground to designate targets for them. These early strikes established a pattern the Harrier community employed over the next decade-and-a-half in the permissive air defence environments of Afghanistan and Iraq, flying at altitudes between 15,000 (4,572m) and 20,000 feet (6,096m) and employing laser-guided or GPS-guided munitions on ground targets.

In late November 2001, *Peleliu's* helicopters departed to operate from ground bases in Afghanistan, leaving VMA-311 Det B as the sole flying unit aboard. With *Peleliu*'s deck all to itself, VMA-311 flew two four-ship missions a day, then began alternating day and night operations with VMA-223 'Bulldogs' when they entered the region as part

The first Harriers employed in combat following the 11 September 2001 terror attacks on the United States lifted from the deck of the USS *Peleliu* with unguided 500lb (227kg) bombs. (USMC/Joseph R. Chenelly)

of the 26th MEU aboard the USS *Bataan* (LHD 5). Missions flown by VMA-223 lasted more than five hours and involved close air support (CAS) missions more than 400 nautical miles inland.

LITENING-capable

After over a year in developmental and operational test, the 'Tigers' of VMA-542 flew the first Harrier combat missions with the Northrop-Grumman AN/AAQ-28(V) LITENING II targeting pod when they arrived off the Pakistani coast aboard the USS *Wasp* (LHD 1) as part of the 22nd MEU's ACE in late March 2002. The 'Tigers' established best practices for LITENING employment, providing data that Marine Aviation Weapons and Tactics Squadron One (MAWTS-1) could then translate into official tactics, techniques and procedures (TTPs) for the entire Harrier community.

In October 2002, the 'Flying Nightmares' of VMA-513 became the first land-based Harrier unit in Afghanistan, with a six-aircraft detachment operating from Bagram Air Base north of Kabul. Flying from Bagram put the Harriers much closer to the mountains along the north-eastern border with Pakistan where the greatest concentrations of al-Qaeda and Taliban fighters were than if they flew from a carrier. At 4,895ft (1,492m) above sea level, Bagram's elevation posed significant challenges for flight operations. To keep weight down, the 'Nightmares' brought six radar-less Night Attack Harriers, which weigh 1,000lb (454kg) less than the AV-8B+. The 'Nightmares' flew in pairs, with one LITENING pod per section to designate targets for both aircraft. Standard loadout consisted of the aircraft with a LITENING pod carrying one 1,000lb (454kg) GBU-16 laser-guided bomb (LGB), and another with one 500lb (227kg) GBU-12 LGB and one four-shot pod of 'Zuni' 5in (127mm) rockets, with both aircraft carrying two 300-gal (1,136-lit) external fuel tanks and the GAU-12 'Equalizer' 25mm Gatling-type cannon. As LITENING was a vastly better night sensor than anything the USAF's A-10 'Warthogs' carried at the time, VMA-513 mostly flew at night, while the Bagram-based A-10s flew days. Though deployed for 11 months, VMA-513 rarely employed weapons against the enemy, its Harriers mostly providing overwatch for remote outposts and convoys with the LITENING pod.

The period between late 2003 and spring 2008 saw few Harriers over Afghanistan, as the Marines shifted their focus to fighting insurgents in Iraq's al-Anbar province. VMA-542 deployed to Afghanistan two more times during this period, once in February 2004, and again in June 2006. The 2004 deployment was unique in that while the Harriers carried one LITENING pod per section and could employ laser-guided munitions, the majority of weapons employed by VMA-542 Harriers were 'Zuni' 5in (127mm) rockets and 25mm cannon fire from the GAU-12.

Operation Iraqi Freedom

On the eve of Operation Iraqi Freedom (OIF) in March 2003, 76 AV-8B Harriers stood ready to support the Marines of Task Force Tarawa and Regimental Combat Teams (RCTs) 1, 5 and 7 as they sped from Kuwait northwest to Baghdad. While 16 of those Harriers – belonging to VMA-214 'Blacksheep' – operated out of Ahmed Al Jaber Air Base in Kuwait, the remaining 60 Harriers operated from four amphibious assault ships in the Northern Arabian Gulf (NAG). Two of those ships – the USS *Nassau* (LHA 4) and

USS *Tarawa* (LHA 1) – had only a six-ship Harrier detachment each, the standard complement for a MEU. The other two served as 'Harrier Carriers', each with two nearly full squadrons aboard (a full squadron complement being 16 AV-8Bs). On both 'Harrier Carriers', squadrons combined maintenance shops to maximise effectiveness and efficiency. The two ships rotated 12-hour shifts, providing 24-hour coverage overhead throughout the liberation of Baghdad.

With the *casus belli* in Iraq being the suspicion that Saddam Hussein was operating a WMD production programme, the greatest concern among war planners was the possibility of chemical attacks using artillery. As such, artillery received the highest targeting priority. Harrier pilots flew armed reconnaissance missions searching for Iraqi artillery units to strike, often in response to intelligence reports of cannons or rocket launchers in an area. With the LITENING pods still in short supply – and occupying a wing station that could otherwise carry another weapon – standard practice in Iraq had one AV-8B per section carrying the pod.

The most common loadout during this period was one aircraft carrying a LITENING pod and a GBU-16, and another with a GBU-12 500lb (227kg) LGB under each wing, with two external tanks, two AIM-9Ms, and centreline-mounted ALQ-164 self-protection jammers on both. With the Iraqi Air Force no longer a threat, the Marines de-mounted the AIM-9s and ECM pods, keeping them off for the rest of OIF (aside from a brief period when AIM-9s were reintroduced due to fears hijacked airliners would crash into US bases). For as prevalent as laser-guided bombs were, Marine Har-

The Harrier can carry the ALQ-164 self-protection jammer like the one seen here mounted on the centreline. Also note the LITENING targeting pod and captive AGM-65 Maverick air-to-ground missile. (Joe Copalman)

riers continued to employ unguided free-fall and forward-firing weapons, including Mk 82 and Mk 83 general purpose bombs, CBU-99 cluster bombs, Mk 77 firebombs, Zuni rockets and AGM-65E 'L-Mavs'.

Though the Marines acquired LITENING pods for precision-guided munitions employment, Harrier pilots in OIF frequently flew intelligence, surveillance and reconnaissance (ISR) missions to find targets. At this point, the LITENING II lacked a downlink capability to share its video feed, so pilots recorded areas of interest on 8mm tapes for post-mission intelligence analysis. In 2003, the LITENING had a reputation for producing clear, detailed imagery. While the multifunction displays in the Harrier's cockpit were too small to process the LITENING's feed at full resolution, the large, high-resolution screens used for digital imagery analysis presented the pod's imagery in remarkable detail. In one specific instance, the LITENING's ability to resolve detail led to the destruction of Saddam's last remaining heavy armoured unit, the Republican Guard Baghdad Division. While reviewing a LITENING tape aboard one of the 'Harrier carriers', an astute intelligence Marine noted a large number of tank tracks in the sand. Following the tracks through subsequent images, the analyst found where they led – the Baghdad Division hid its tanks in a village near Al Kut. On a follow-up strike to the area, 12 Harriers destroyed the entire division, eliminating the last Iraqi armour that could threaten coalition forces.

FARPs

While the *Bataan* and *Bonhomme Richard* were validating the Harrier carrier concept on a scale never before attempted, both the sea and shored-based Harriers demonstrated why the Marines invested so heavily in the AV-8. Aside from the weather-induced 'pause' between 25 and 27 March, every day, the lead elements of the RCTs advancing on Baghdad moved further from Kuwait and the NAG. While Ahmed Al Jaber in Kuwait proved useful as a FARP for the AV-8Bs operating from the 'Harrier carriers', as ground forces approached Baghdad, flying all the way back to Kuwait took longer and longer, minimising the time Harriers could spend on station. On 8 April, an Iraqi airfield near Baghdad seized by US forces became operational as a FARP, enabling Harriers to refuel and rearm much closer to the areas where ground forces needed them most. A few days prior to that, pilots from VMA-214 landed at a FARP established on a highway south of Baghdad, taking on fuel and additional weapons, quickly returning to the fight. No other fixed-wing aircraft in the American tactical aviation inventory could do that.

Harriers in post-mission-accomplished Iraq

On 1 May 2003, US President George W. Bush gave a speech aboard the USS *Abraham Lincoln* (CVN 72) announcing the end of major combat operations in Iraq. Baghdad had fallen, the Ba'ath party was removed from power, and Saddam was on the run. With no regime or military targets left to bomb, all Marine Harriers left the region by summer 2003. However, as the insurgency that emerged in the ungoverned lawlessness of post-Ba'athist Iraq grew in size and sophistication, the Marines returned to Iraq, given responsibility for al-Anbar province, stretching from west of Baghdad to the Syrian border. With boots once again on the ground in Iraq, the Marines needed air support, and by May 2004, both VMA-214 and VMA-542 had arrived at Al Asad Air Base to provide it. While the sheer size of Anbar sometimes demanded long flights, it was nothing like Harrier operations at the height of OIF 1, with aircraft flying between the NAG and Central Iraq.

By the time Harriers arrived at Al Asad, the insurgents had learned that direct attacks on Americans typically did not end in their favour. Though ambushes and gun battles still occurred, insurgents turned to improvised explosive devices (IEDs) as their primary weapon against coalition forces. As during OIF 1, convoy escort remained a common mission for AV-8B pilots, but in addition to scanning routes for potential ambushes, they were now using the LITENING pod to search for disturbed dirt or out-of-place objects on or along roads, tell-tale signs of possible IED emplacement. Despite the LITENING being among the best tools for the job of detecting IEDs from the air, roadside bombs continued to menace troops in Iraq (and Afghanistan). Marine Harriers eventually gained a capability to jam IED command detonation signals, though that only came in 2012, four years after the last Harriers left Iraq.

During the summer and autumn of 2004, Harrier weapons loads focused on precision fires and collateral damage mitigation. Though relative scarcity still meant only one AV-8B per section carried a LITENING pod, the aircraft carrying the pods swapped out the standard GBU-16 for the smaller GBU-12, while the other aircraft typically carried a GBU-12 and an AGM-65E. Both aircraft carried the GAU-12, which proved highly accurate and a good choice for reducing collateral damage risks. The most popular weapon during the Battle for Fallujah was the Laser Maverick, as it had a smaller warhead than the 500lb (227kg) GBU-12s and was highly accurate.

Harrier FAC-A

In giving Marine Harriers an organic precision strike capability, the LITENING pod also gave AV-8B pilots the ability to designate targets for other aircraft. Following this, the Marines established a Forward Air Controller – Airborne, or FAC(A) qualification for Harrier pilots. Explaining the genesis of the Harrier as a FAC(A) platform, Major Eric Grunke told the author: *'2005-ish is when we started the push for that. It came about due to the LITENING pods, just the situational awareness that it allows and the precision of fires that it brings to the Harrier. Now I don't have to spend a lot of time from finding a target to generating a game plan to delivering ordnance.'* Describing his role as a FAC(A) in the Harrier, Grunke said, *'We spend a lot of time eyeballs looking out trying to get situational awareness. The first thing we come in looking for is threats, then find the friendly position, because I'm responsible for mitigating the risk of fratricide of any of these fires, so I have to find them, and you do it with your eyeballs, because when you're actually in the attack, you're going to be looking – 'Here's the attacking aircraft, here's me, there's the friendlies, this looks good.'*

Harrier FAC(A) employment brought two advantages to the counterinsurgency fight over Iraq. The first advantage, according to retired Harrier pilot, Colonel Shawn Hermley, was that *'the Harriers in Iraq were the only ones that could create, via the LITENING pod, a JDAM-quality coordinate. Most of the other airframes, the FAC had to produce a high-confidence-level or low-error coordinate to be able to pass to the pilot that they would then punch into their system to employ that GPS weapon.'* These coordinates could also be passed to FACs or JTACs for targeting GPS-guided

In 2009, VMA-231 began receiving the first operational AV-8Bs wired to carry the LITENING pod on the centreline pylon, allowing carriage of another weapon and largely solving the sensor obscuration problem.
(Joe Copalman)

weapons from other aircraft as well. The second advantage – and one of particular interest for Hermley during his 2007 ground tour as Regimental Air Officer (AirO) for RCT 6 in Iraq was that the data embedded in the LITENING's feed was in a format used by infantry units. As Hermley explained, '*Another great thing from a FAC standpoint was on the downlink where we're reviewing what's in the targeting pod, the Harrier was the only one that had MGRS (Military Grid Reference System) grid locations actually written on the video. So as you were trying to figure out where that sensor was looking, it was very easy, because all the guys on the ground have maps that are gridded with MGRS coordinates on them. It was extremely easy from an all-fires standpoint to keep track of where the pilot was looking. Since then, all platforms have upgraded to that, but at the time, the Harrier was well ahead of the game with integration of the aircraft's systems and with the guys on the ground.*'

Expanding precision munitions capabilities

The Battle for Fallujah saw early use of the ROVER (Remote Operational Video Enhanced Receiver) system, which allowed ground FACs, JTACs, AirOs and ground commanders to view LITENING feeds from aircraft overhead in near-real time. This capability proved to be another gamechanger for the AV-8B community. Having FACs and commanders able to see exactly what a pilot's sensor was looking at – in a higher resolution than the pilot could see on his green-and-black screen in the cockpit – resulted in faster approvals to release weapons, as it shortened talk-ons. It also helped in the overwatch role, as having access to a higher-resolution feed than what the pilots could see, a FAC or ground commander could talk the pilot onto areas of interest that the pilot may not have seen on his own screen.

A 2006 software upgrade added another arrow to the Harrier's quiver – the GPS-guided Joint Direct Attack Munition, or JDAM. Like laser-guided bombs, JDAMs consist of Mk 80-series bombs fitted with guidance kits and moveable control surfaces. Rather than employing a 'seeker' that follows a constant beam of laser energy to impact, JDAMs use GPS receivers and inertial guidance systems that adjust the bomb's flight path to ensure it impacts a specific point on the ground, making it a true fire-and-forget weapon. Further, which each JDAM receiving its targeting information though the Harrier's computer, multiple bombs can be dropped simultaneously on different targets. Perhaps most importantly, with no need for a laser, JDAMs can be dropped from inside or above cloud cover (per a FAC or JTAC's authority), giving the Harrier a true all-weather precision attack capability. The addition of the JDAM made the AV-8B one of the most versatile attack platforms in Iraq. The one drawback of the JDAM is that it can only be employed against fixed or static targets and cannot be re-targeted mid-flight. In April 2006, VMA-513 'Flying Nightmares' became the first Harrier squadron to drop JDAMs in combat during a CAS sortie flown from Al Asad.

By 2007, the insurgency in Iraq was on the ropes. Political and economic reconstruction diminished many of the justifications used to take up arms against coalition troops. The Anbar Awakening, in which locals realised that al-Qaeda was more detrimental to the county's future than the Americans, further reduced overall levels of violence. While these gains signified precisely the type of changes coalition leadership had worked for, insurgent holdouts remained. In light of these developments, Marine leadership questioned whether aviation ordnance would do more harm than good, as collateral damage could undo the coalition's gains. During this period, Harrier pilots grew increasingly frustrated as they returned from missions without employing ordnance. Despite this, Harrier pilots still made a difference. Utilising the LITENING pods that were by this time ubiquitous, these pilots helped ground commanders build sustained situational awareness of their battlespace. As Hermley observed, *'Just because you're not releasing weapons doesn't mean you're not providing a very valuable service. When you go and do that for four hours every other day as a pilot, you don't see what happens when you're there for 24 hours and see what aviation is doing for the regimental commander and the subordinate battalions, which is building that picture and providing that sense of overwatch, that there's someone up in the sky watching out for you. I think both from the kinetic nature and non-kinetic intelligence-gathering, the Harrier made a significant difference while we were there.'*

During this same period, both aircraft in a two-ship section carried a LITENING pod. Though this normally would have required sacrificing another weapons station within the section to accommodate the pod, at this point in the conflict, tanker support from Marine KC-130s was abundant enough to allow Harriers flying from Al Asad to replace external fuel tanks with additional weapons.

The typical per-section loadout in summer of 2007 comprised two LITENING pods, one GBU-38 500lb (227kg) JDAM, one GBU-12 500lb LGB, one AGM-65 'LMAV', one four-shot pod of Zuni rockets and two GAU-12s.

As the availability of LITENING pods expanded, so too did the number of ROVER systems on the ground. Given the target-confirmation and fratricide-mitigation capabilities ROVER provided, the system quickly shifted from 'good to have' to being seen as necessary for approving release of aviation ordnance. Further enhancement of LITENING imagery came with the upgrade from an analogue datalink to a digital datalink in summer 2007. This upgrade also extended the datalink's signal range, allowing the pod's feed to be accessed from further away.

As the insurgency withered in the face of the 2008 troop 'surge' and the Anbar Awakening, Harriers took on new roles. With oil smuggling on the rise, Marines shifted their attention to interdicting tanker trucks carrying stolen oil into Syria and Turkey. The primary means of stopping smugglers was an approach known as 'aeroscout'. Aeroscout missions involved UH-1N and AH-1W helicopter crews finding suspicious activity and directing CH-53s carrying infantry Marines in to investigate. For smuggling interdiction, Harriers used LITENING to locate suspected smuggler tanker to stop and inspect. By spring 2008, the insurgency effectively ceased to exist, with Harriers flying for weeks at a time without dropping a single bomb or observing a single hostile act through the LITENING pod. With no more work, the last Harriers in Iraq – from VMA-311 'Tomcats' – left Al Asad in October 2008, formally bringing the AV-8B's role in OIF to a close.

Fighting pirates

Combatting piracy is in the Corps' DNA. The second line of the Marines Corps Hymn – 'To the shores of Tripoli' – commemorates the service's first victory on foreign soil against Tripolitan pirates during the Battle of Derna in 1805. In late July 2009, a detachment from VMA-214 spent seven months at sea aboard the USS *Boxer* attached to the 13th MEU. During this cruise, the 'Blacksheep' flew in support of counter-piracy operations near the coast of Somalia. Recalling how Harriers were used in counter-piracy operations, Captain Andrew Cano, a Harrier pilot with VMA 214 told a 13th MEU public affairs officer, '*Most of our time was spent doing non-traditional intelligence, surveillance and reconnaissance. We would fly out and locate any suspicious vessels and send back visual reconnaissance to identify whether they might be pirate vessels.*' The 'Blacksheep' also participated in the rescue of Captain Richard Phillips, who Somali pirates kidnapped while seizing the container ship Maersk *Alabama*. During the operation, Harriers flew reconnaissance missions, sharing the LITENING's feed in near real-time. Harriers again supported counter-piracy operations in autumn 2010 with a six-ship AV-8B detachment aboard the USS *Kearsarge* (LHD 3) in support of the 26th MEU. Little information about Harrier counter-piracy support on this deployment is public, aside from involvement in 'maritime interdiction' operations.

Back to Afghanistan

As the Iraqi insurgency faded in 2009, things were once again heating up in Afghanistan. Similar to USMC responsibility for al-Anbar province in Iraq, Marines in Afghanistan were accountable for Helmand Province in southern Afghanistan. The re-establishment of a consistent and consecutive cycle of Afghan deployments brought Marine Harriers back into the fight against the Taliban, with a host of new or expanded capabilities like JDAM integration and a new digital datalink. Further, the proliferation of ROVER terminals among FACs and ground commanders reduced the need for lengthy talk-ons. Throughout 2008, the LITENING/ROVER combination proved critical to getting precision strikes on insurgents emplacing IEDs approved before they had a chance to detonate the bombs – the FACs, AirOs and commanders at various levels could see the Harrier's feed in near-real time and observe unambiguously hostile acts in progress that warranted interruption with aviation ordnance. The footprint of Marine Harrier units in Afghanistan at this time expanded from a six-ship MEU detachment either operating at sea or coming ashore for a few months to a series of regular 10-ship deployments to Kandahar Air Base.

Centreline LITENING and low-collateral-damage weapons

In gaining a targeting pod, Marine Harriers lost a weapons station, as the LITENING occupied one of the inboard underwing pylons. On top of losing a weapons station, the pod's placement also limited the sensor's field of view, restricting pilot manoeuvres while keeping the sensor on a target or area of interest. For shipboard operations,

In addition to allowing the type to operate from short-deck carriers, the Harrier's short-takeoff capability allows it to operate from short or damaged runways while still carrying a potent warload. (Joe Copalman)

underwing LITENING carriage created asymmetric loading issues that complicated landings at sea. In 2008, the 'Dust Devils' of Navy Air Test and Evaluation Squadron 31 (VX-31) began testing the LITENING on the Harrier's centreline pylon. The resultant modification, known as Airframe Change 479, hit the fleet in 2009, with an accelerated conversion process allowing VMA-231 'Ace of Spades' to deploy to Afghanistan that November with a full complement of ten AV-8B+ radar birds capable of carrying the LITENING on the centreline.

Having yielded disappointing results in Iraq (partially due to incorrect collateral damage estimate tools governing its employment), low collateral-damage bombs were used again in Afghanistan. One of the common loadouts in Afghanistan included a GBU-51 low-collateral damage, or 'lo-co' laser-guided 500lb (227kg) bomb and a full-strength GBU-38 JDAM. Recounting one successful GBU-51 employment, Hermley told the author, *'I remember the first time someone employed the GBU-51. There was a machine gun that was right next to this wall. All the compounds in Afghanistan, it's a mud hut, but the wall or the fence that goes around the compound is usually part of the same wall that's part of the structure. We didn't want to damage any compounds. There was some debate in how people read that, it wasn't extremely clear, but this machine gun was up against this wall. We were watching the video of the pilot who employed the GBU-51, and he's not aiming at the wall and you go 'Wow, was it bad marksmanship there? What's happening?' In reality, the FAC told him, 'Get as close to that wall as you can, but I don't want you to target that wall. It hit a couple meters away from the wall and doesn't put a scratch in it, and that happened to be exactly where that machine gun position was.'* 'Lo-co' weapons were best utilised in cases where precision effects on a target were needed, but the 'frag' effects of a high-explosive weapon or the dispersion of cannon fire were perhaps too risky. From a pilot workload and threat-exposure standpoint, employing 'lo-co' weapons was much less challenging than diving towards a target and firing a burst from 3,000ft (914m) away with a pipper that almost completely eclipses the target.

Though not a precision weapon, the GAU-12 benefited from LITENING integration. Explaining how the pod enhances gun employment, Colonel Hermley said, *'As we're coming down the ramp in a dive, we're trying to keep that T-pod on the target that allows us then to make that visual transition to put the pipper on the actual target itself. A man-sized target, we're not going to see that in the heads-up display, but we'll see him on the T-pod, and then we'll use the T-pod to get our pipper onto the target area like that. Then at night, the T-pod has a marker capability, so with the NVGs, we can see that sparkle – it's really a laser marker, but we can see it through the NVGs, and that's what we're shooting at, because once again, we can't see that man-sized target, which was the typical target. So we're shooting the laser, either from our own aircraft or from our wingman who's holding overhead and tracking that person that's walking down the road or whatever it might be.'*

Modern Harrier at war – VMA-231 over Marjah

By the time VMA-231 arrived in Afghanistan in December 2009, the Harrier had a reputation as an effective precision-weapons CAS and strike platform. Operations throughout Helmand Province kept VMA-231 busy providing ISR coverage and CAS for Marines and other International Security Assistance Force (ISAF) troops. These efforts culminated with Operation Moshtarak, a 15,000-troop operation aimed at ridding the town of Marjah of the Taliban. Harriers helped mitigate the two greatest threats in Marjah – snipers and IEDs.

Explaining VMA-231's role during Moshtarak, Major Alex Ramthun, who served as Battalion AirO for 1st Battalion/6th Marines said, '*During the firefight phase, the Harrier carried laser-guided Maverick missiles, they had the 25mm gun, and they had their low-collateral damage laser-guided and GPS-guided weapons. The ROE (Rules of Engagement) there required us not to strike homes unless we met certain conditions, and also required us to reduce collateral damage at all costs. So, the Harrier's precision targeting, and the fact that I could show my battalion commander on the ground what the pilot was seeing and doing with his weapons system, we were able to approve fires much more quickly than other platforms.*' He continued, '*For example, the UH-1s and AH-1s – very effective CAS platforms, love them to death, but it was very challenging for our battalion to get fires approval for them because we needed to see what they were shooting at. So, the type 2 [strikes approved through an aircraft's sensor feed] didn't work that often. When we brought them in for Type 1 [approval when the FAC has visual contact with both the target and the attacking aircraft], the bad guys could usually hear their rotor noise and they'd go running away. The Harrier brought us an element of surprise because they're way up high at 16 to 17,000 feet, they're dropping weapons that take 30 to 40 seconds time-of-fall that are very accurate and have targeting so that we could see the ground. So the majority of airstrikes during that period came from Harriers.*'

The Harriers also employed the GAU-12 multiple times during Moshtarak, primarily against IED emplacers at night. Utilising the pod to catch IED emplacers in the act, a pilot could share his feed for strike approval, then use the pod to target the insurgents for attack with the gun. Because roads were the most common site for IEDs, a 500lb (227kg) bomb cratering a road used every day by the locals was not the wisest course of action to maintain their support. To this end, Ramthun praised the gun/LITENING combination as '*quintessentially the perfect weapon for that*'. Another new development for Harriers operating over Helmand province was the amount of Marine unmanned aerial systems (UAS) flying ISR missions. Though Harriers continued to fly ISR using the LITENING pod, UAS reduced that burden significantly with FACs relying on unmanned systems like the AAI RQ-7B Shadow or Boeing ScanEagle to locate insurgents and generate the essential information needed to direct attacks onto those targets.

FARP operations – validating flexible forward basing

Throughout the squadron's Afghan deployment, VMA-231 frequently used the expeditionary airfield at Camp Dwyer, a forward operating base (FOB) in Helmand province with a 4,250ft (1,295m) runway (extended to 6,000ft/1,829m in early 2010). Harrier operations out of Dwyer aligned with the expeditionary employment tactics developed in the 1970s by the initial cadre of Marine Harrier pilots, with aircraft based at a distant air base operating out of an expeditionary airfield much closer to the battlespace in support of the infantry. Marjah was only a ten-minute flight from Camp Dwyer, with most of that time spent climbing to altitude, while VMA-231 operated out of Kandahar over 80 miles (129km) to the east. With the FARP at Dwyer, a section of Harriers could respond to a CAS request in Marjah, expend its ordnance, refuel and rearm at Dwyer, and be back over Marjah within 40 minutes, as opposed to well over an hour had the section returned to Kandahar. With Marine KC-130s tied up making logistics runs, Dwyer presented a valid alternative to aerial refuelling to extend mission times. Even when KC-130s were available, hot-pitting at Dwyer still made more sense. As Hermley explained, '*We lost time on station if we go to the tanker. They're 40 miles away, so you have to have gas to get to them, keep some gas to try to get in, and then if you can't get gas, to have enough gas to get back to Dwyer as our divert. So actually, instead of having 4,000lb of gas to go to the tanker and try to make all that happen, we could be right overhead at 1,500lb of gas and go right into Dwyer. It really equated to more time on station for us to provide to the battalions, which was important because the approval for fires could take a long time. The longer you could stay overhead, the higher probably you had of getting to employ a weapon.*'

Digitally aided CAS

During Operation Moshtarak, VMA-231 took an early step into the realm of digital interoperability (DI). For the assault support community, DI has largely taken the form of situational awareness tools used for en route updates and mid-mission re-tasking. For the TacAir community, DI goes one step further into the realm digitally aided close air support, or DaCAS. One of the biggest challenges in providing effective CAS is ensuring the pilots employing ordnance near friendly troops are looking at the correct target. This ensures both the desired effects on the enemy and prevention of friendly casualties or collateral damage. Since World War II, the Marines have relied on FACs on the ground and in the air to locate targets, talk pilots onto the target area and mark targets for attack. While the means of marking targets has evolved from smoke grenades and rockets to laser designators and infrared pointers, the fundamentals of directing CAS have remained constant – getting a pilot's eyes onto a target and providing a mark to make it more conspicuous or to give corrective adjustment for follow-on attacks. Depending on the situation, terrain, weather and other factors, talk-ons could take anywhere from two minutes to upwards of 20. Laser designators and targeting pods have sped that process up, but the target's location is only one of nine pieces of information a FAC generally passes to CAS aircraft as part of what is known as a nine-line CAS brief. This brief consists of the basic relevant information needed for a successful strike – initial point (IP), heading from IP to target, distance from IP to target, target elevation, target description, target location, type of mark, location and disposition of friendly forces and egress direction after weapons release. Conversely, the FAC requires several points of critical data from the aircraft overhead – number and type of aircraft, station time, types of weapons carried (including warheads and fuses), type of targeting pod and anything else that might help the FAC maximise the capabilities those aircraft bring to the fight. With the advent of GPS-guided weapons like the JDAM, lengthy grid coordinates help ensure weapon accuracy, but also introduce more potential for transcription errors. Put simply, CAS requires the exchange of significant amounts of information, and for the sake of the troops whose survival may depend on CAS arriving quickly, the faster FACs and CAS pilot can accurately exchange that information, the better.

By 2009, the Marines had been testing a system known as StrikeLink for three years. Developed by Stauder Technologies, StikeLink held the promise of shortening the talk-on process, allowing the FAC to present a strike to his commander for approval more quickly, ultimately getting the Marines on the ground the help they need more quickly. Major Ramthun, as Battalion AirO for 1/6, was a strong advocate of StrikeLink, working closely with his FACs and JTACs on using the system prior to deploying. In his role as AirO, Ramthun was effectively the senior aviation advisor to the battalion commander, letting him know what aviation assets could and could not do, as well as reviewing strikes requested for approval from his FACs and JTACs in the field. While Ramthun and his FACs had numerous CAS coordination tools at their disposal, as AirO, he used Strikelink as often as he could, primarily for hastening approval of fires.

Describing StrikeLink, Ramthun said, '*It's like a very ruggedised iPad. It's designed for the battlefield where your JTAC can just carry this system around and be able to pick out targets, to put the target information in StrikeLink and send it directly to an aircraft via digital means. The whole point of this is to speed up the targeting process. Strikelink pushes the exact data that you put in up to the aircraft, and all the pilot has to do is read it back to verify you didn't mess up the data entry. It's very expeditious.*' He continued, '*I can also use the system to speak to my other JTACs solely through text messaging means, so if they wanted to get a strike approved, instead of reading a bunch of coordinates over the radio and taking a grease pencil to a map and using a protractor and taking an awful long time to figure out where the friendlies are at, where the enemy's at, marking all this on a map and then showing my battalion commander, they would simply do up a mission in StrikeLink, click 'send', it would go to me, and I could show it on a big screen overlaid on a moving map, and show where all the boundaries are, all the known locations of enemies, friendlies, no-fire targets, etc, and my CO could say 'Okay, I see exactly what you're saying, that's approved.' I found I could approve fires more quickly that way.*'

While Ramthun's FACs and JTACs sometimes struggled to use StrikeLink effectively, primarily due to short battery life, the system worked well for him as Battalion AirO. As he explained, '*I used it primarily in the Combat Operations Center, set up in a static position, hooked up next to my LITENING pod live feed. I was able to, on multiple occasions, shoot targeting packages up to the Harrier and watch them verify the data in their cockpits. I'd watch them snap their LITENING pods to the targets I gave them, and really alleviate the need to do long talk-ons via the radio with the aircraft to get their sensors on target.*' While the CAS publications governing employment of live weapons in proximity to friendly troops require an audible, unambiguous 'cleared hot' call authorising weapons release, StrikeLink could pass this information digitally to reinforce the call. As Ramthun explained, '*With the digital system, we are still required per our publications to get a verbal 'cleared hot'. However, I can push messages into the heads-up display of the Harrier. So he's flying around, I say 'cleared hot' in the radio, and as a backup, I can tell him or her 'cleared hot', or I can tell them to abort in their HUD. It's kind of a dual-feedback feature in which if they didn't hear my radio call, or it was garbled, they could confirm it through their HUD.*'

Prior to Moshtarak, StrikeLink had not been used to pass a digital nine-line brief to an attack aircraft in combat. During a firefight on 19 February 2010, Marines from Alpha Company, 1/6 took effective machine gun and sniper fire from a Taliban bunker compound in Marjah. While then-Major Hermley and his wingman were in their Harriers at Dwyer rearming and refuelling, the Regimental AirO briefed Hermley on the situation and asked him and his wingman to check in with an Alpha Company JTAC once they were re-established over Marjah. As Hermley and his wingman were en route from Dwyer, the JTAC used Strikelink to generate a digital nine-line with all the pertinent information, including rules of engagement and weapon fuse settings, a process that only took five minutes from the forward observer generating the grid coordinates for the target. Once Hermley checked in, the digital nine-line the JTAC 'pushed' to him resulted in positive target correlation in less than four minutes – with some of that time used to talk through an obvious elevation error. Though the Harrier had possessed the capability to receive digital nine-lines through its Automatic Target Hand-off System (ATHS) since the late 1990s, this strike represented the first time that capability had been employed in combat, as StrikeLink was the first deployed system capable of pushing that data through the ATHS. The time saved through the digital nine-line (with mandatory verbal readback) and target correlation left more time for the lengthy approval of fires, which in this case took 14 minutes. Once the battalion commander authorised the strike, the JTAC authorised weapons release via digital means, with the 'cleared hot' message appearing in Hermley's HUD, accompanied by a verbal 'cleared hot' over the radio. Hermley's GBU-51 found its mark, followed by another GBU-51 dropped three minutes later by his wingman, another direct hit on the Taliban bunker, silencing the threat.

Despite the success of this particular strike, DaCAS advocates stress that the process is digitally aided, not digital-only. Like Ramthun, Major Eric Grunke was a Harrier pilot who had served a ground tour as a FAC and was also a proponent of StrikeLink and DaCAS. Along with the battery life issue, StrikeLink could be unwieldy for use in the field, as it was an additional piece of gear along with an already robust set of tools FACs and JTACs carried on top of all the other gear required to serve alongside infantrymen. Further – as the target elevation error encountered during Hermley's DaCAS strike over Marjah demonstrated – StrikeLink was not entirely reliable. As Grunke mentioned, '*For me, sometimes it just doesn't quite work out for whatever reason. Whether it's aircrew error or JTAC error, I don't know. But eight times out of ten I'd say it doesn't really go as planned. As an air officer instructor, we say 'Try it', and if it doesn't work, then you've immediately got to shut it and go onto your normal TTPs. There's just too many kinks, and the time on station is just too precious to try and mess around with it.*' In the decade since Moshtarak, the Marines have made significant strides in both the standardisation and proliferation of DaCAS and digital interoperability. StrikeLink has been superseded by newer systems like the KILSWITCH (Kinetic Integrated Low-cost Software Integrated Tactical Combat Handheld) and APASS (Android Precision Assault Strike Suite) apps accessed primarily through ruggedised tablet computers known as MAGTABs (Marine Air-Ground TABlets).

Odyssey Dawn – Harriers over Libya

The 26th MEU's August 2010 – April 2011 cruise proved to be remarkably eventful. Having deployed a month early to provide humanitarian assistance and disaster relief in flood-ravaged Pakistan, the MEU then sent its ground combat element ashore for a planned Afghanistan deployment. With the ground forces and much of the ACE in Afghanistan, the USS *Kearsarge* (LHD 3) continued on towards the Horn of Africa to

The ability to conduct effective night operations served the Harrier community well in the skies over Libya during Operation Odyssey Dawn in the spring of 2011. Unlike Afghanistan and Iraq, Libyan dictator Muammar Gaddafi retained a potentially deadly air defence capability, making daylight operations significantly more dangerous. (USMC/Cpl Garry Welch)

support counter-piracy operations with its Harrier detachment from VMA-542 'Tigers'. With the Arab Spring uprisings raising tensions throughout the Middle East and North Africa, *Kearsarge* steamed north into the Red Sea, ready to cover the evacuation of Americans from Egypt if needed. While the Egyptian evacuation never materialised, Libyan dictator Muammar Gaddafi's use of military force against civilians elicited a US and European military response that would involve *Kearsarge* and its remaining aircraft, which along with the six Harriers included four MV-22s, three UH-1s and four CH-53Es. Known as Odyssey Dawn, the operation focused on degrading or destroying Gaddafi's ability to use his military against civilians. As detachment Officer-in-Charge for the MEU's Harrier det, then-Major Hermley said his biggest concern was '*How do we stop the regime forces advancing on Benghazi and using their weapons against civilians?*' He continued, '*That was our immediate focus. We had been watching these forces truck up and advance toward Benghazi, and we feared that they were going to get so engrained in the city that there was going to be a point where we'd have a hard time targeting and just separating them from anyone else, and then we just worried about civilian casualties as we attempted to target the pro-regime forces.*'

Odyssey Dawn represented the first time Marine Harriers faced off against a modern integrated air defence system since day one of OIF. While Air Force and Navy assets decimated most of Gaddafi's SAM sites, air defence systems around Benghazi remained untouched. Though constantly monitored for any sign of hostile action, these SAM and AAA sites never opened fire on US or NATO aircraft, but their mere presence kept the Harrier pilots on alert. Flying from the *Kearsarge* less than 100 miles (161km) from the Libyan coast, VMA-542's Harriers were ten times closer to Benghazi than most of the Air Force assets supporting Odyssey Dawn from Aviano Air Base in northern Italy, and four times closer than the Navy and NATO assets operating out of NAS Sigonella in Sicily. The proximity of *Kearsarge* to Benghazi meant that VMA-542's Harriers were among the least tanker-dependent strike aircraft during Odyssey Dawn.

During the opening pre-dawn strikes on 19 March 2011, VMA-542 launched two sections of Harriers as a 'mop-up' force to search for additional targets after Air Force F-15E Strike Eagles and F-16 Vipers dropped their bombs and egressed over the Mediterranean to rendezvous with their tankers before returning to their bases in Italy. As the Air Force strikes commenced later than planned, the Harriers faced the prospect of flying during daylight and presenting visual targets for AAA to, but all four pilots managed to drop their bombs on some of the military vehicles surrounding the town of Ajdabiya before sunrise.

On the second night of Odyssey Dawn, the Harriers were effectively the only US tactical aircraft flying over Libya. As Hermley explained, '*That first night, the US packages of F-15s and F-16s lost their tankers on the way home, so they all diverted to Sigonella. Because of the crew day and whatnot, they didn't get those aircraft back until the following day, so that first night, the only US full-motion video attack footage they had come from Harriers. That second night, we were the only US attack assets that deployed because the entire strike package was still trying to make it back to Aviano.*' As night fell, the 'Tigers' launched two sections to finish the job started the previous night over Ajdabiya. Hermley, who led that strike, recalls, '*We were thankful to the pro-regime forces for not moving their tanks for several hours. The ten-digit grids that we had that we entered into the pod, there's that tank that we'd seen in*

Major Eric Grunke at the controls of a VMA-542 aircraft while he served as an instructor pilot with MAWTS-1 at MCAS Yuma in 2014.
(Joe Copalman)

that same spot. It was hard on the conscience, like we were cheating a bit. We knew exactly where they were and they weren't moving, so it's not like they were trying either.'

Without having to accommodate for fuel-critical aircraft coming from Italy, the 'Tigers' had time to verify the positions of targets identified the night prior, then search for higher-priority targets. Hermley recounted, '*We wanted to make sure there wasn't something hiding out there that was missed that's a higher priority. So, we don't want to go after an armoured personnel carrier while there's a multi-rocket launcher sitting down the road a bit. We'd search around some more, then hit our timeframe where we said we need to start attacking now. As the lead, I'd pass coordinates to dash-2 what I wanted him to hit, he would un-stow his pod, he'd find them, we'd talk about it to make sure we're correlated on the correct targets, and then we would start employing.*' Despite the use of GPS grid locations to pass target locations along, VMA-542's Harriers carried only laser-guided weapons during Odyssey Dawn. Explaining this, Hermley said, '*We stayed all GBU-12s, primarily because of the accuracy. The -12, because it follows that laser spot, is extremely accurate. The JDAM is accurate as well, but we were attacking targets that had the potential of moving.*'

FAC(A) saves the day – the rescue of BOLAR 34

On night three of Odyssey Dawn, an F-15E from the 492nd Fighter Squadron, call-sign BOLAR 34, suffered a fuel feed issue on the right side of the aircraft, creating a weight imbalance significant enough to cause an unrecoverable spin. Short on options and running out of altitude, pilot Major Kenneth Harney and weapons systems officer (WSO) Captain Tyler Stark ejected over territory that was at best contested and at worst hostile. While Stark was quickly picked up by anti-Gaddafi rebels, Harney was on the ground, on the run and in need of rescue.

Prior to deploying, every MEU undergoes a certification exercise, in which a series of short-notice scenarios test the MEU's ability to perform certain vital tasks every MEU must be capable of. One of those tasks is TRAP – tactical recovery of aircraft and personnel. TRAP differs from combat search and rescue in that the location of an isolated service member has been determined before the TRAP package launches. In the case of BOLAR 34, the locations of the survivors were recorded and shared by Harney and Stark's wingman.

As Harrier det OIC and the most experienced AV-8B pilot on the *Kearsarge*, Major Hermley could have led the first section of Harriers that night. Instead, he chose the detachment's Weapons and Tactics Instructor, Major Grunke, to lead the first Harrier section supporting the rescue. In addition to being the det's WTI, Grunke also completed a ground tour as a FAC and recently earned his qualification as a FAC(A). Describing how his FAC(A) qualification related to TRAP missions, Grunke said, '*FAC(A), doing it airborne, what that allowed me to do was think about 'How do I handle all of these assets,' because (BOLAR 34's) wingman was overhead, some F-15s were overhead, and I was bringing in the rescue vehicles, the Ospreys were coming inbound. How do I think about this time and space problem? I was also thinking about geometries of fire, going 'Okay, how do I make sure that when I release a bomb, it's not going to affect (the survivors). For that mindset, the FAC training both on the ground and in the air was certainly helpful.*'

With Harney's location established and identity authenticated, the MEU commander gave the command to launch the TRAP package. Shortly after departure, Grunke received the codeword authorising weapons release if the mission called for it. Arriving overhead, Grunke established contact with Harney, who described seeing a vehicle heading towards his position. Finding the vehicle in his LITENING pod, Grunke stopped it with a GBU-12. Shortly thereafter, he received word the WSO had been picked up by friendly rebels and was in the back of a truck. Unable to determine the alignment or intent of a second truck approaching Harney, Grunke dropped a second GBU-12 between the truck and Harney's position to deter the driver from proceeding further. It worked.

With the threat of Harney being captured by pro-Gaddafi forces mitigated for the moment, Grunke's attention turned to finding a suitable landing zone for pickup. With a suitable LZ not far from Harney's position, Grunke guided him to the zone just before conducting a rescue on-scene command handover with an F-15E crew that guided the Ospreys to the landing zone shortly after Grunke and his wingman left the area. Regarding the role his FAC training played in the rescue, Grunke said, '*It gave me the geometries of fires consideration and asset management – thinking about the guy on the ground, picking LZs, etc. Some of that is practiced in the TRAP training, but it really was the FAC training that I relied heavily on that night.*' For his role in

While the Harrier is first and foremost an expeditionary ground attack aircraft, the addition of the AIM-120 Advanced Medium-Range Air-to-Air Missile (AMRAAM) to its arsenal in late 2011 gave Marine Expeditionary Units a true beyond-visual-range air defense capability.
(USMC/LCpl Cody Rowe)

the BOLAR 34 rescue, the Marine Corps Aviation Association named Grunke the 2012 Marine Corps Aviator of the Year.

AMRAAM

The operational demand signal for expanded Harrier air-to-air capabilities came in March 2011, when *Kearsarge* arrived off the coast of Libya to support Odyssey Dawn. The coalition arrayed against Libyan dictator Muammar Gaddafi imposed a no-fly zone, and though ideally located to enforce it, *Kearsarge*'s Harriers lacked a long-range radar-guided missile like the AIM-120 Advanced Medium-Range Air-to-Air Missile (AMRAAM). Describing the lack of an AMRAAM capability during Odyssey Dawn, Hermley recalled, '*There was an initial question about whether or not we could support the enforcement of the no-fly zone. At the time, we did not have the equipment we needed to carry the AIM-120, so we were AIM-9s only. That was all we had from an air-to-air standpoint. There were pieces of equipment that we needed that were manufactured at a slow rate. Since then, we definitely have that capability.*'

The components issue was sorted shortly after *Kearsarge*'s spring 2011 patrol. When the USS *Makin Island* (LHD 8) departed San Diego on its maiden patrol in November 2011, its Harrier det, from VMA-214 was the first to deploy with the AMRAAM. Subsequent Harrier MEU detachments have carried the AIM-120, and its use is now something all AV-8B pilots train to. While the AMRAAM does not magically transform the Harrier into a supersonic super-fighter, it provides MEUs with a much-needed long-range defensive counter-air punch. As Hermley explained, '*If the Harriers are defending you, and that's all you've got, then that's really an emergency. If they're out there with an AIM-9 against an active missile threat, or a semi-active missile, then we just don't have the 'stick' to go out there and get it. So (with the AIM-9) it really was an emergency defence. But now with the AIM-120, that's a significant capability to defend in that MEU role or that amphibious task force role to defend our friendly forces air-to-air from aviation engagement.*'

More Afghan action

When the 'Flying Nightmares' of VMA-513 arrived at Kandahar in May 2011, the squadron was the first Harrier unit to deploy with a new paint scheme. The Marines introduced a new overall dark grey scheme that supposedly made the jet harder to see, while also making it slightly lighter. In 2020, this scheme remains in limited use, as it was never applied fleet-wide. The 'Nightmares' also brought a new weapon that further increased the Harrier's flexibility. The 500lb (227kg) GBU-54 Laser JDAM carried a GPS receiver and INS kit in the tail cone like a standard JDAM, but also included a laser seeker in the nose. This meant that rather than carrying a laser-guided bomb under one wing to attack moving targets and a JDAM under the other for static targets Harriers could carry a Laser JDAM under each wing and engage either type of target with both bombs. Additionally, Laser JDAM kits could be fitted to the BLU-126 low-collateral damage bomb, giving additional flexibility against targets in urban areas or other places where collateral damage is a concern. Because of its flexibility, Laser JDAM became the weapon of choice for VMAs in Afghanistan. Major Art 'Bug' Bruggeman deployed to Camp Bastion with VMA-231 from October 2012 to April 2013. Regarding the ordnance loadouts the squadron carried then, Bruggeman recalled, '*It was almost exclusively GBU-54s on that deployment. And a lot of gun. My first deployment (VMA-542 March 2008) it was GBU-38s and GBU-12s, and we did a little bit of LMAV – carried, but never really employed them. We employed the gun more than we did the -54s on that last deployment though.*'

For years following the Camp Bastion attack, most Marine Harrier squadrons honored the memories of Lt Col Christopher 'Otis' Raible and Sgt Bradley Atwell, who were both killed in the attack, by stencilling their names on the canopy rails of at least one aircraft in the squadron. This AV-8B from VMA-211 wears Raible's name back in 2014 (Joe Copalman)

Disaster at Bastion

On 14 September 2012, 15 Taliban militants wearing US Army uniforms infiltrated Camp Bastion. Broken into three teams, they conducted coordinated attacks on three separate areas of the base, using automatic weapons, rocket-propelled grenades and explosive charges to destroy aircraft and equipment. Living up to the motto 'Every Marine a rifleman', maintainers from VMA-211 killed one insurgent and wounded another who was subsequently taken prisoner. Sadly, the Marines lost two of their own – Sgt Bradley Atwell, an aviation electrician with Marine Aviation Logistics Squadron 13 (MALS-13) and Lt Col Christopher Raible, VMA-211 Commanding Officer when both were hit by shrapnel from a rocket-propelled grenade while Raible was coordinating a counterattack against the insurgents.

At the time of the attack, the 'Avengers' had recently sent two Harriers home in accordance with an order to reduce the overall Marine footprint in Afghanistan. Those two aircraft made the first leg of the trip back to the US and were in Qatar, leaving eight aircraft at Bastion. All eight aircraft – representing 100 per cent of Marine Harriers in Afghanistan at the time – were rendered inoperable by the attack, with six destroyed and two severely damaged. In response to the attack, VMA-231, which was set to relieve VMA-211 at Bastion, sent six Harriers to replace the destroyed aircraft, while the two jets in Qatar returned to Afghanistan. Within seven days of the attack, the 'Avengers' – under the command of former VMA-214 Commanding Officer Lt Col Troy Pehrson – were flying more missions per day than before the attack.

While the two aircraft damaged in the attack were eventually returned to service at considerable expense, the loss of a full MEU detachment worth of Harriers on a single day left a hole in the Harrier fleet that could not be filled with attrition replacements, as the AV-8B was long out of production. The Harrier community continues to memorialise the Bastion attack. Several Harrier units sustain a tradition of honouring the sacrifices of Sgt Atwell and Lt Col Raible by stencilling their names on the canopy rails of at least one AV-8B per squadron.

Jump-jet jammers

For as effective as the AV-8B was at detecting and engaging IED emplacers in Iraq and Afghanistan, roadside bombs continued to maim and kill American troops. Eager to further degrade the enemy's capability to employ IEDs against American and coalition forces, the Marines initiated an in-house programme to develop an electronic warfare (EW) pod capable of eavesdropping on insurgent communications and jamming remote IED detonation signals. Known as the AN/ALQ-231 Intrepid Tiger II or IT-II, the pod was developed and tested by the Naval Air Warfare Center Weapons Division (NAWCWD) over an 18-month period. Though the Marines already had an aircraft capable of this in the Grumman EA-6B Prowler, the Prowler community was extremely small, and primarily operated as a joint force asset rather than directly in support of Marines.

Given the lack of an organic EW capability within the MEUs, the Harrier – which at the time comprised the only fixed-wing aircraft deploying with MEUs – became the priority platform for IT-II integration. The first flight of a Harrier with an IT-II pod occurred on 27 March 2012 at MCAS Yuma, with VMA-214 'Blacksheep' helping test the pod while MAWTS-1 assisted in the development of tactics for employing it. Two months later, VMA-231 deployed to Camp Bastion with several IT-II pods.

A pair of 'Ace of Spades' AV-8Bs fly over Helmand Province in December 2012 carrying AGM-65 Maverick missiles, GBU-54 'Laser JDAMs' and GAU-12 cannon, giving the pilots remarkable flexibility to engage both static and moving targets.
USMC/Cpl Gregory Moore)

Despite initial reluctance to take on the EW mission in Afghanistan, once VMA-231's pilots began receiving feedback regarding the pod's effectiveness, that reluctance turned to enthusiasm. While USMC public affairs published multiple releases about IT-II and its capabilities during development and testing, virtually all public messaging about the pod ceased once VMA-231 deployed with it. To this day, Marines familiar with the pod remain understandably tight-lipped about its capabilities. What Harrier pilots will say about the IT-II pod is that it works well and that it remains in high demand, to the point where ground troops prefer the pod to an additional bomb or missile on the wing pylon it takes up. Development of additional IT-II variants continues, with NAWCWD working on the Intrepid Tiger II Block X, which will give the pod a radar-jamming capability in addition to the communications intelligence and jamming functions of the Block 1 pods.

Out of Afghanistan

The Bastion attack occurred at the tail end of the Afghan 'surge', as the Harrier mission in Afghanistan was drawing to the close. When VMA-231 relieved the 'Avengers' in November 2012, they supported mostly non-US forces as part of ISAF, though those forces had Marine FACs and JTACs attached from an Air-Naval Gunfire Liaison Company (ANGLICO), meaning Harrier pilots still spoke to Marines on the ground. In addition to this being the Harrier's first combat deployment for the Intrepid Tiger II pod, VMA-231's Harriers also carried new ALE-47 chaff and flare dispensers. The high point of the deployment came on 7 February 2013, when a mass strike that had been on-again, off-again for several months finally received approval. Whereas the Harriers typically employed 500lb (227kg) weapons to minimise collateral damage, the loadout for this mission was four 1,000lb (454kg) GBU-32 JDAMs per aircraft, with seven Harriers total launching for the mission. Though Lt Col Hermley – who served as commanding officer of VMA-231 on that deployment – could not divulge any details of the target or ground forces supported, he did tell the author that all 28 GBU-32s were employed against multiple targets within a three-minute window. That strike was followed by another strike the following day involving six aircraft each carrying a four-bomb mix of GBU-32s and GBU-38s, releasing all 24 bombs on targets within two minutes. In Hermley's words, the attack had '*a significant and far reaching impact on the enemy.*'

When the 'Tomcats' of VMA-311 relieved VMA-231 in April 2013, the squadron flew a few larger missions against wide-ranging target sets like the ones VMA-231 flew that February, further crippling the Taliban's ability to exert military influence in Afghanistan. Aside from these pre-planned strikes, the 'Tomcats' flew convoy escort, overwatch and electronic warfare missions as Operation Enduring Freedom wound down. The squadron flew its last OEF mission on 11 September 2013, 12 years to the day after the terror attacks that brought the Marines to Afghanistan in the first place.

Last of the Nightmares

In 2010, the USMC convened a Force Structure Review Group to assess the best options for structuring the post-OEF/OIF Marine Corps. Among the group's recommendations was a reduction in the number of flying squadrons from 70 to 61 as part of an overall manpower reduction from 202,000 Marines to 186,800. Additional force-shaping discussions in January 2012 led to further personnel reduction recommendations to 182,000 Marines by 2017. Amid this reduction, the Marines selected VMA-513 for decommissioning. In a ceremony at MCAS Yuma on 13 July 2013, 'Nightmares' commanding officer Lt Col Samuel Smith and Sergeant Major Raquel Painter cased VMA-513's colours, bringing an end to 69 years of USMC service.

Though losing a squadron placed additional strain on the VMA community to provide aircraft, pilots and maintainers for the deployment and detachment commitments Harriers fulfil, there were some benefits to decommissioning a squadron. First, it helped improve the overall 'health' of the Harrier community, as the squadron's aircraft and parts were distributed to the other units. Second, with the F-35B having recently been introduced into the fleet, and with the Marines cherry-picking experienced maintainers with multiple critical qualifications from the Harrier and Hornet communities, Harrier maintenance shops lost a significant amount of experience to F-35 squadrons.

The stand-down of VMA-513 injected several high-qualification maintainers into other squadrons that sorely needed them, again, improving the overall 'health' of the AV-8B fleet.

An AV-8B from VMA-223 'Bulldogs' assigned to VMM-162 (Reinforced), the aviation combat element for the 26th MEU aboard the USS *Kearsarge* receives fuel from a US Air Force tanker aircraft. (USAF/TSgt Nathan Lipscomb)

Inherent Resolve – the fight against ISIS

The withdrawal of American troops from Iraq – and the increasing lawlessness in civil war-ravaged Syria – emboldened the re-emergence of Islamist militants who coalesced under the banner of the so-called Islamic State in Iraq and Syria, or ISIS. While the group had existed in one form or another since establishment as an al-Qaeda offshoot in 2004, it began to assert itself in earnest in 2013. With the stated goal of establishing a caliphate in the Middle East, ISIS conducted terror attacks on civilian, government and military targets throughout 2013 and 2014, causing enough death and destruction to warrant the resumption of American airstrikes over Iraq in cooperation with Iraqi security forces. Dubbed Operation Inherent Resolve, the US air campaign against ISIS began on 7 August 2014.

Marine Harriers joined the fight in January 2015, when a pair of AV-8B+s from VMA-231 attached to VMM-265(REIN) aboard the USS *Bonhomme Richard* dropped eight JDAMs on ISIS positions. This strike was unique in that one of the Harriers involved carried the new Exelis BRU-70/A Digital Improved Triple Ejector Rack, or DITER, with two JDAMs per rack. The DITER contains the necessary wiring to allow the Harrier's mission computer to 'talk' to up to three 500lb (227kg) JDAMs per rack, increasing the number the AV-8B can carry. The initial strike using DITER racks came just one year after Exelis received a contract to produce 161 BRU-70/As for the USMC. Marine AV-8Bs returned to the Arabian Gulf in August 2015, when Harriers from VMA-311 assigned to VMM-161(REIN) launched from the USS *Essex* (LHD 2) in support of OIF. *Essex* remained on station supporting OIR with its Harrier detachment until 17 October. Harriers returned to the fight on 19 November 2015 when *Kearsarge* arrived in the Arabian Gulf with a Harrier detachment from VMA-223 'Bulldogs'. Images from this cruise depict VMA-223 Harriers carrying centreline LITENING, one GBU-38, one GBU-54 and no gun. During this deployment, the 'Bulldogs' occasionally carried a seven-shot pod of Advanced Precision Kill Weapons System 2.75in (70mm) laser-guided rockets in place of one of the JDAMs. APKWS provides a first-hit low-collateral damage precision munitions capability for use on the same types of targets Harrier pilots would typically employ the gun against.

Combat employment of the DITER racks appears to have resumed in winter 2016 when VMA-231 deployed to Sheik Isa Air Base in Bahrain in support of Special Purpose MAGTF – Crisis Response – Central Command. VMA-231 also employed APKWS rockets against ISIS, the weapon being especially useful in urban areas to minimise collateral damage. The most recent Harrier deployment in support of OIR concluded in October 2019, when the 'Tomcats' of VMA-311 returned to Yuma after deploying as part of SMPAGTF-CR-CC for several months. In addition to multiple JDAM and Laser JDAM carried on DITER racks and pods of APKWS rockets, VMA-311 loaded its Harriers with AIM-9M Sidewinders, as Syrian and Russian tactical aircraft in the region posed a potential aerial threat.

Continuing upgrades

Though fighting relatively low-tech insurgents consumed the majority of the Harrier community's attention since the turn of the century, AV-8B pilots are committed to adapting their platform for the high-end fight against prospective near-peer competitors. As then-Major Brett McGregor explained while head of MAWTS-1's TACAIR department in 2014, '*We have focused more on 'let's get back to our roots, let's work on not just OEF/OIF.' As challenging as they were, they were very one-dimensional for TacAir. It was just one thing, it was the same thing every day. We got very good at that one thing, which was medium-altitude PGM CAS from the overhead with no threat. That was challenging for different reasons, but we're trying to go back into a full-spectrum mindset, looking at more threats, higher-intensity situation, higher tempo, getting a little bit more of an even focus.*'

With only three squadrons currently operating the F-35B as of this writing, Harriers remain critical assets for ensuring the Marines retain STOVL capability and capacity for maritime and expeditionary operations throughout the F-35 transition. Recent upgrades such as Link 16, DITER racks, APKWS, Intrepid Tiger II capability, and the AIM-120 have all made the AV-8B a far more lethal and versatile multi-role platform than most Harrier pilots at the turn of the century could have dreamed. Yet the Marines are far from finished improving the Harrier.

Ongoing integration of the Advanced Tactical Data Link (ATDL) is expanding the scope of aircraft and systems AV-8Bs can exchange information with, both in air-to-ground and air-to-air operations. The first eight examples of the ATDL were purchased for the AV-8B community in FY2019, with a total of 120 systems planned for acquisition by FY2024. With the release of H7.0 Operational Flight Plan software in 2020 and the H7.1 upgrade scheduled for implementation in 2021, the AV-8B fleet is set to gain significant weapons capabilities. With H7.0 OFP, ground attack capabilities will include the AGM-154C Joint Stand-Off Weapon (JSOW). The AGM-154C is an upgraded variant of the JSOW GPS/INS-guided glide bomb equipped with an imaging infrared seeker for improved terminal guidance and two-stage warhead for hardened target attack capability. The H7.1 upgrade will bring improved air-to-air capabilities in the form of the AIM-9X Block II high-off-boresight dogfighting missile with a lock-on-after-launch capability and the AIM-120C-7 with a better radar and further range than the AIM-120B. The H7.1 OFP upgrade will also unlock the full capabilities of Link 16 for the Harrier, including fighter-to-fighter messaging, further increasing the type's lethality in counter-air operations. Additional upgrades scheduled for implementation include a helmet-mounted cueing system, high-definition video capability in the cockpit, upgraded survivability equipment, and the inclusion of Variable Message Format (a messaging language used by F/A-18s, F-35s, and C2 systems) and satellite communications (SATCOM) capabilities, most of which are scheduled for implementation in 2023.

The Marines will continue operating the Harrier until FY2028, when VMA-223 is scheduled to begin its transition to the F-35B Lightning II. Until then, the Marines remain committed to keeping the Harrier as lethal, survivable, and relevant through continued upgrades and tactics revisions. Summarising this approach to Harrier sustainment, Lt Col McGregor observed, '*We are going to the transition to the F-35. The Harrier is going to go away, we know that. We want to make sure it's effective until that day, so we're trying to maximise its potential and make it as good as we can.*'

The Advanced Precision Kill Weapons System (APKWS) mates laser-guidance kits to 2.75in (70mm) rockets. Laser guidance ensures first-hit accuracy, while the small warhead limits the blast radius of the weapon. (USMC/LCpl Stormy Mendez)

VMAQ | MARINE TACTICAL ELECTRONIC WARFARE

Electronic Warfare has long been one of the six primary functions of Marine Corps aviation. With the USMC operating as an expeditionary force-in-readiness, often being the first branch of the military to have boots on the ground or aircraft overhead trouble spots throughout the world, this function is critical for enabling Marines to disrupt, delay and deny the enemy's access to the electromagnetic spectrum. Historically, Marine Corps EW aircraft focused on the suppression of enemy air defences (SEAD) mission, temporarily disabling surface-to-air missile (SAM) and anti-aircraft artillery (AAA) with radar and communications jamming, or permanently destroying them with anti-radiation missiles. For over 40 years, the Marines relied on the Grumman EA-6B Prowler as their dedicated EW workhorse. With the final Marine EA-6Bs retired in Spring 2019, the service is transitioning to a new EW construct that spreads capabilities far more broadly than the previous Prowler-centric model.

Electronic legacy – the EA-6B Prowler

The Prowler has its roots in the Vietnam War, where the Marines needed a replacement for the long-serving Douglas EF-10B Skyknight that could keep pace with the Air Force and Navy strike aircraft in need of tactical jamming support over North Vietnam. The answer for the USMC was the Grumman EA-6A, an EW variant of the A-6 Intruder which entered service in December 1965. At the same time the Marines were flying the EA-6A in Vietnam, the US Navy was developing an even more robust EW variant of the A-6, the EA-6B Prowler. The Prowler entered Navy service in 1970, with the Marine Corps adopting the type in 1977.

Only one USMC squadron – Marine Tactical Electronic Warfare Squadron Two (VMAQ-2) 'Playboys' based at MCAS Cherry Point – operated the Prowler between 1977 and 1990 when reserve squadron VMAQ-4 'Seahawks' transitioned from the EA-6A to the EA-6B. Two years later, the Marine Corps restructured its Prowler fleet, breaking VMAQ-2 into three squadrons – VMAQ-1 'Banshees', VMAQ-2 and VMAQ-3 'Moondogs'. Additionally, VMAQ-4 transitioned from the reserve component to active duty and relocated from Naval Air Station Whidbey Island in Washington State to join the other three squadrons at Cherry Point under Marine Aircraft Group 14.

Marine Prowlers served in every major conflict from the bombing of Libya in 1986 through the continuing fight against the so-called Islamic State in Iraq and Syria (ISIS). While the foundational principle of Marine Corps aviation is that it exists to support the Marine on the ground, the EA-6B primarily supported joint force and coalition air operations far beyond the reach of Marine infantry. In the cases of Bosnia, Kosovo and Libya, Marine ground units were not even committed to land operations. While Marine ground forces in Afghanistan and Iraq routinely received Prowler support, Marine ground combat element commanders never 'owned' the aircraft, which were instead controlled by joint force combatant commanders.

This joint force tasking kept the VMAQ community cycling through a near-continuous deployment rotation after Desert Storm, with combat deployments to Southern Europe in support of NATO's Operation Deliberate Force over Bosnia in 1995 and Operation Allied Force in 1999. The VMAQs also supported Operation Northern Watch and Operation Southern Watch supporting no-fly zone enforcement over Iraq through the beginning of Operation Iraqi Freedom in March 2003, which demanded extensive support from Marine EA-6Bs. The VMAQ squadrons saw action over Afghanistan, participated in Operation Unified Protector over Libya and provided crucial capability in the fight against ISIS in what proved to be the final conflict for the Prowler. Being such a small community and in such high demand, at various points over the past two decades, Prowler squadrons experience dwell times between deployments as little as six months.

Prowler crews

The Prowler was manned by a crew of four, with a pilot and three Electronic Countermeasures Officers, or ECMOs, seated sedan-style with two seats up front and two seats close behind. The pilot sat in the left front seat, with mostly analogue displays and gauges betraying the Prowler's age. Accompanying the pilot up front was ECMO 1, who handled communications, navigation, defensive electronic countermeasures (ECM) and dispensing chaff and flares. Additionally, EMCO 1 operated the communications receivers and jammers and could serve as overall mission commander in the EA-6B. The two ECMOs in the rear cockpit – ECMO 2 on the right and ECMO 3 on the left – sat at identical panels, primarily conducting electronic surveillance and operating the Prowler's ALQ-99 jamming pods. Side-by-side seating allowed the ECMOs in back to coordinate their efforts, targeting individual antennas in the ALQ-99 pods at numerous threat emitters simultaneously. All three positions enabled ECMOs to select and prioritise targets for the AGM-88 High-Speed Anti-Radiation Missile (HARM), the Prowler's sole kinetic weapon.

A point of pride among many Marine EA-6B pilots was that they were the last 'stick and rudder' TACAIR pilots in Marine Corps aviation. In an age when digital fly-by-wire flight control systems are ubiquitous among tactical jets, the Prowler retained its analogue flight controls, complete with cables and pulleys, giving pilots direct control of aircraft manoeuvring. As one former EA-6B pilot explained, '*If I move the stick, the control surfaces move, because the stick moved the cables and it moves. It's not fly-by-wire where I make a control input and the jet decides how it wants to move the control surfaces and decide what to do for me. You have a lot of feedback, you feel like you're actually flying a flying machine.*'

Improved Capability

Beginning in April 2010, the USMC upgraded its EA-6Bs to ICAP III (improved capability) standard, with the modification work being performed at the Fleet Readiness Center in Jacksonville, Florida. Along with greatly improved computer processing

The EA-6B Prowler proved highly effective in the low-threat skies of Iraq and Afghanistan, intercepting insurgent communications for intelligence exploitation, jamming those communications when necessary, and jamming remote detonation signals for improvised explosive devices. (Joe Copalman)

speed and capacity over the previous ICAP II Prowlers, ICAP III saw the introduction of a tactical networking capability with the Multi-Function Information Distribution System (MIDS) with Link 16 datalink compatibility. The incorporation of Link 16 gave crews aboard other aircraft in the network an accurate picture of the battlespace, including the location of threat emitters. Another change introduced with the ICAP III upgrade was the standardisation of the three ECMO displays with the Multi-Mission Advanced Tactical Terminal, allowing ECMO 1 to see the same things EMCOs 2 and 3 could see on a modern colour display. The ICAP III upgrade increased the effectiveness of the Prowler's jammers by 30 per cent, while also introducing a selective reaction jamming capability that automatically identifies, prioritises and jams threat signals, while also enabling the ALQ-99 jamming pods to match a threat emitter's frequency hopping. The 1970s-vintage ALQ-99 receiver was replaced with the far more capable ALQ-218 receiver system. More reliable radios, a night-vision optimised cockpit, a Joint Mission Planning System and an improved interface for the LITENING targeting pod rounded out the ICAP III upgrades. Though further upgrades had been discussed, the ICAP III proved to be the ultimate variant, with capabilities Prowler crews

In autumn 2007, the USMC added the LITENING targeting pod to the Prowler's arsenal, enabling EA-6B crews to be even more effective in protecting ground convoys and foot patrols from ambushes and IEDs, able to tie the picture on the ground to insurgent communications being intercepted. (USMC/Cpl Neysa Huertas Quinones)

could honestly say enabled them to operate the EA-6B at the top of its game in its final years of military service.

Tools of the trade

Referred to as the 'heart' of the EA-6B by later-era Prowler pilots, the Northrop-Grumman ALQ-218 digital receiver suite, which provides Radar Warning Receiver, Electronic Support Measures and Electronic Intelligence functionality, replaced the ALQ-99 receiver in the iconic 'football' fairing atop the Prowler's tail as part of the ICAP III upgrade. The ALQ-218 brought a faster and more accurate capability to identify, locate and prioritise threat emitters for targeting. Whereas the ALQ-99 receiver could determine the general direction a threat signal was being emitted from, the ALQ-218 could pinpoint the emitter's location. One unique feature of the ALQ-218 is that it permitted 'look through' capability, allowing ECMOs to continue receiving and processing signals from emitters in the battlespace while simultaneously employing its jamming pods. Once an emitter is detected, located and classified, the three ECMOs have numerous options at their disposal to monitor, mitigate, or eliminate the threat.

For the Prowler's traditional EW/SEAD mission, the ALQ-99 Tactical Jamming System was the primary tool employed, having been used since the EA-6B was introduced into US Navy service. Continual upgrades kept the ALQ-99 relevant and able to deal with current and emerging threats, but even the US Navy, which employs the ALQ-99 on the EA-18Gs it replaced the Prowlers with, is seeking a replacement. Known as the Next-Generation Jammer, the future pod will be more reliable, powerful and capable than the ALQ-99, as well as more adaptable to emerging threats.

Along with jamming, Marine Prowlers employed kinetic effects against hostile radar systems. As one EA-6B pilot explained, '*We've got the High-speed Anti-Radiation Missile, or HARM, that we can fire. It's our only kinetic weapon, if we need to use that.*' The Raytheon AGM-88 HARM has been the Prowler's go-to weapon for destroying enemy radars.

The EA-6B could also create electromagnetic 'smokescreens' to obscure strike aircraft from enemy radars. In this role, Prowlers carried the AN/ALE-43(V) bulk chaff pod, which dispenses chaff strips to create radar-reflective clouds that degrade the ability of radar systems to pick individual aircraft out for tracking or targeting. The use of chaff corridors dates back to World War II and was still something the VMAQ com-

In addition to jamming enemy radars with ALQ-99 jamming pods, marine EA-6Bs could create chaff clouds with the ALE-43 chaff dispenser (seen on the port-side outboard pylon) to further confound enemy air defense radar operators. (Joe Copalman)

munity trained to through the end of the Prowler's service life, especially during large force training events.

For communications surveillance and jamming, the Prowler utilised the powerful BAE Systems USQ-113 communications jamming suite. In the SEAD role, the USQ-113 prevented or degraded communication between air defence forces, making coordinated responses to air attacks difficult. Combined with the ALQ-99's radar jamming capabilities and the lethality of the AGM-88 HARM, the USQ-113 made the EA-6B a potent triple threat to modern air defence networks. Though the EA-6B's receiving and jamming capabilities were developed for and tailored towards the high-end SEAD mission, the Prowler's EW systems could be used effectively across the broad spectrum of conflict, as the Marines demonstrated in the skies above Afghanistan, Iraq, Libya and Syria over the first two decades of the 21st century.

Marine Prowlers at war in the 21st century

At the turn of the century, the four VMAQ squadrons regularly rotated in and out of Saudi Arabia and Turkey providing EW and SEAD support for no-fly zone enforcement over Iraq as part of Operations Northern Watch and Southern Watch (OSW). Both VMAQ-1 and VMAQ-2 were flying OSW missions out of Prince Sultan Air Base in Saudi Arabia on the eve of Operation Iraqi Freedom (OIF). Crews from VMAQ-1 supported one of the opening OIF strikes on 20 March 2003, an Air Force F-117 Nighthawk attack on a mansion outside of Baghdad where intelligence indicated Saddam Hussein was that evening. The Prowlers had already been airborne supporting another tasking and were re-tasked mid-mission, coordinating with an E-3 AEW&C and the F-117s carrying out the strike.

With much of Iraq's integrated air defence network decimated during Operation Desert Storm, and post-war sanctions restricting Saddam Hussein's ability to rebuild it, Marine Prowlers escorted numerous strikes throughout Iraq, but had little in the way of radars to jam or SAM sites to destroy.

Counterinsurgency EW – jamming the Jihadis

The Global War on Terror saw a dramatic shift in the role of the Prowler, with the VMAQ community reorienting from defeating robust air defence networks to supporting infantry units during prolonged ground operations. One of the earliest instances of Marine EA-6Bs directly supporting ground troops occurred on 7 April 2003, when Regimental Combat Team One (RCT-1) took fire from an Iraqi artillery battery while attempting to cross a bridge over the Diyala River just outside of Baghdad. With RCT-1's Regimental Air Officer (AirO) being a Prowler ECMO serving on a ground tour and familiar with the type's communications jamming capabilities, he requested EA-6B support from VMAQ-2. Once on station, the ECMOs aboard the Prowler successfully jammed the communications between the Iraqi artillery battery and the forward observers adjusting fire for them, effectively suppressing the threat. Though the Prowler's utility in support of the infantry was becoming more apparent, no playbook for integrating EA-6Bs into ground operations existed at that point.

In mid-2003, Marine Aviation Weapons and Tactics Squadron One (MAWTS-1) began developing tactics, techniques and procedures (TTPs) for EA-6B EW support for the ground combat element (GCE). The conduit for Prowler support to the infantry was the Marine radio battalions, the GCE's organic EW specialists. In December 2003,

VMAQ-3 supported the first integrated radio battalion exercise. Over the next several months, VMAQ and radio battalion Marines refined the integrated air and ground EW TTPs during multiple training exercises. Additionally, the VMAQ community adopted the radio battalions' Technical Control Analysis Center (TCAC) signals analysis system, aligning the analysis capabilities of the Marine Corps' air and ground EW communities. Marines from VMAQ-2 employed the new tactics operationally beginning in July 2004 when the squadron deployed to Talil, Iraq.

The first major test of those tactics came in November and December 2004 during Operation Phantom Fury, the effort to retake Fallujah. Prowlers from VMAQ-2 maintained almost constant orbits over the city, jamming insurgent communications, complicating enemy attempts to coordinate ambushes or any effective response to coalition progress on the ground. The success of EA-6Bs in Fallujah was followed by a dramatic increase in Joint Tactical Air Requests (JTARs) specifically asking for Prowler support. During VMAQ-2's July 2004 through January 2005 deployment, the 'Death Jesters' logged over 2,000 combat hours in support of Marine and coalition ground units. When the squadron returned to Iraq in January 2006 for another six-month deployment, VMAQ-2 logged 3,286.7 combat hours. Demand for Prowler support in Iraq continued to grow, with the 'Jesters' peaking at 4,423 combat flight hours over the course of a deployment from July 2007 to January 2008 – setting a utilisation rate record not just within the Marine EA-6B community, but among every type of aircraft in the USMC. This growth in EA-6B utilisation was not unique to VMAQ-2, as it impacted all four VMAQs deploying to Iraq.

The distinctive 'football' fairing atop the EA-6B's vertical tail housed the ALQ-218 digital receiver suite, capable of receiving signals from across the electromagnetic spectrum for analysis, classification and geolocation, enabling the crew to take appropriate action against threat emitters. (Joe Copalman)

Countering the IED threat

Beginning in November 2005, Marine EA-6B crews assisted in preventing the detonation of radio-controlled improvised explosive devices (IEDs), which had become the preferred weapon of insurgents in Afghanistan and Iraq. Cell phones, walkie-talkies and even garage door openers were cheap and efficient means of remote detonation and eliminated the need for a wire or cable and could lead back to the triggerman's location if discovered. As US forces got better at early detection of command-wire detonated IEDs, insurgents began employing radio-controlled IEDs – which by 2006, comprised 70 per cent of the IEDs used in insurgent attacks in Iraq. While these decreased the risk of detection and allowed insurgent triggermen to be as far from the device as signal strength allowed, radio-controlled IEDs relied on access to the electromagnetic spectrum, meaning the Prowler could jam the detonation signals.

The 'Banshees' of VMAQ-1 took on the counter-IED mission in late 2005 while deployed to Al Asad, utilising the EA-6B's USQ-113(V)2 communications jammer to block signals from cell phones and two-way radios, saving the lives of countless American and allied troops on the ground. With IEDs presenting the greatest ground threat, the VMAQs were hardly alone in their counter-IED efforts. The joint-force air response to the IED threat eventually became so overwhelming that aerial EW assets tasked with counter-IED missions began to interfere with one another's efforts, as well as those of EW troops on the ground. This resulted in the formation of a joint EW cell in the Combined Air Operations Center at Al Udeid Air Base in Qatar, which processed all EW-related JTARs and managed frequency deconfliction between EW aircraft.

The ALQ-99 Tactical Jamming System consisted of jamming pods powered by ram air turbines. Based on the mission, the number and placement of the pods could vary. (Joe Copalman)

The Prowler community's counter-IED capabilities evolved further in autumn 2007 with the pairing of the Northrop-Grumman AN/AAQ-28(V) LITENING AT target-

An EA-6B from VMAQ-1 'Banshees' banks away from a tanker after receiving the fuel needed to continue its mission over eastern Afghanistan in November 2009. (USAF/SSgt Michael Keller)

ing pod with the EA-6B. First fitted to a VMAQ-4 EA-6B during a tactical demonstration (TACDEMO) with MAWTS-1 in August 2007, LITENING allowed the ECMOs to observe possible IED emplacement sites ahead of ground convoys or foot patrols, identify potential danger areas and report on the positions of suspected IED emplacers or trigger men, all while using the USQ-113 to monitor insurgent communications and provide jamming to neutralise the IED threat. The 'Banshees' of VMAQ-1 were the first to take the LITENING to war, deploying to Al Asad in July 2008, carrying the targeting pod operationally and evaluating the TTPs that MAWTS-1 established. The Prowler's endurance allowed crews to fly non-traditional intelligence, surveillance and reconnaissance (NTISR) missions with the LITENING pod as well. Marine Prowlers retained the LITENING capability through the type's retirement in 2019.

Prowlers over Afghanistan

Given the low-tech nature of the enemy in Afghanistan and the lack of anything resembling an integrated air defence system, Marine Prowlers remained largely absent from Operation Enduring Freedom in the wake of the 9/11 terror attacks. The 'Moondogs' of VMAQ-3 became the first Marine EA-6B unit to deploy to Afghanistan in January 2005, relieving a US Navy expeditionary Prowler squadron at Bagram. Prowler crews in Afghanistan worked closely with US Air Force EC-130H 'Compass Call' SIGINT (signals intelligence) aircraft. Linguists aboard EC-130Hs intercepted and interpreted Taliban tactical communications, the pushed relevant information to Marine EA-6Bs, allowing the crews to prioritise targets for communications jamming.

With the US drawdown in Iraq, US President Barack Obama turned his attention to Afghanistan, where after nearly a decade of fighting, the Taliban remained a significant threat to that nation's stability. Seeking to hasten an end to the US role in Afghanistan, Obama authorised a 30,000-troop 'surge' in late 2009, aimed at breaking the Taliban's grip on various area of the country, and accelerating completion of hundreds of civil reconstruction projects.

Marine Prowlers played a significant role in supporting the Afghan surge, providing communications jamming and counter-IED support for ground forces. Regarding the diverse missions flown by Prowlers in Afghanistan, one EA-6B pilot remarked, '*If an adversary's mission involves use of the electromagnetic spectrum, we can find a means to influence it.*' During a late 2009 deployment to Bagram, VMAQ-1 conducted psychological operations broadcasts in support of coalition information operations, a capability the Prowler possessed, but used infrequently. As the surge wound down in 2011, Marine EA-6B operations in Afghanistan slowed considerably. The final USMC Prowler Afghan deployment ended early, with VMAQ-2 redeploying to Qatar in mid-2012.

Unified Protector – NATO support over Libya

At the same time operations in Afghanistan were winding down, long-simmering political tensions in Libya began boiling over. Among the various anti-government uprisings during the 'Arab Spring' in early 2011, the clashes between forces loyal to Libyan dictator Muamar Gaddafi and anti-Gaddafi militias stood out as the most violent. With Gaddafi employing his armed forces against civilians in Libya, NATO initiated Operation Unified Protector to impose a no-fly zone and provide kinetic aerial support to Libyan rebel groups fighting Gaddafi's troops on the ground. Unlike Afghanistan and post-'Mission Accomplished' Iraq, Libya possessed modern SAM and AAA systems, demanding SEAD workhorses like the Prowler to protect NATO strike aircraft.

Having initially prepared for a deployment to Afghanistan in mid-2011, VMAQ-1 instead deployed to Aviano Air Base in Italy to support NATO strikes over Libya as part of Unified Protector. On 10 September 2011, VMAQ-1 Prowlers supported strikes against air defence targets near Sirte, where Gaddafi and his remaining loyalists were making their last stand. After Libyan rebels captured and executed Gaddafi on 20 October, VMAQ-1 left Aviano, continuing on to Afghanistan to relieve VMAQ-4 as originally planned.

Training changes

Since the EA-6B entered Marine Corps service in 1977, Marine Prowler pilots and ECMOs received their conversion training at VAQ-129, the joint Navy/Marine Fleet Replacement Squadron (FRS) at NAS Whidbey Island in Washington State. With the Navy committed to the EA-18G Growler as its EA-6B replacement, and with the type facing its impending retirement from Navy service in 2015, VAQ-129 ceased training Prowler aircrews in March 2014. The USMC, which planned to fly the EA-6B for another five years, needed to maintain a training pipeline for pilots and ECMOs. As such, VMAQ-1 'Banshees' re-designated as Marine Electronic Warfare Training Squad-

ron One, or VMAQT-1 on 14 June 2013. Along with the re-designation came a change in mission, from being an operational squadron to being an FRS. While this took one of only four VMAQs out of the deployment rotation, the Navy's Prowler retirement freed up enough additional airframes and spare parts to increase the VMAQ table of organisation from five to six jets, enabling the last three deployable squadrons to fly more sorties.

Keeping the SEAD skills sharp

Despite being heavily tasked in Afghanistan and Iraq, Marine Prowler crews retained the skills needed for the high-end SEAD mission the EA-6B was designed for. The two most common venues in which VMAQ aircrews honed and refined these skills were the Marine Corps' Weapons and Tactics Instructor (WTI) course held twice a year at MCAS Yuma and the US Air Force's 'Red Flag' large-force exercises held multiple times per year at Nellis Air Force Base in Nevada. In addition to sending pilots and ECMOs through WTI as students, one of the four Prowler squadrons would deploy to Yuma during each course to support numerous large force events, often using the course as a pre-deployment work-up. These events involved EA-6Bs escorting large strike packages on the Yuma ranges as well as one long-range strike over the Nevada Test and Training Range. On most of these missions, threat emitters on the ground – designed to replicate the same frequencies expected from air defence systems in a peer-level fight – are used to detect, track and target inbound strike aircraft, and it fell to the Prowler crews to neutralise those emitters. Red Flag exercises put these skills to the test in an even larger venue, with the Prowlers acting as joint force and coalition EW assets in support of large strikes against simulated peer state adversaries. Maintaining the SEAD skills at the core of the VMAQ mission statement served the Prowler community – and the American and allied aircrews who relied on them to render the enemy's air defences blind, deaf and mute – considerably well in the skies over Libya and Syria.

Back to Iraq – Operation Inherent Resolve

Operation Inherent Resolve (OIR) – the US-led military effort aimed at defeating ISIS signalled the type of changing tactical environment the Marines have been preparing for through sustained focus on peer-threat SEAD. While OIR is in many ways a continuation of the counter-insurgency fights against radical Islamist militants that characterised the last two decades of conflict, the presence of a modern air-defence capability in Syria and the military support the Syrian government has been receiving from Russia added threats to locate, classify, monitor and defend against should they be used with hostile intent. Beginning in late 2014 with a VMAQ-4 deployment to Al Udeid Air Base in Qatar, Marine EA-6Bs supporting OIF employed nearly the full range of the Prowler's capabilities, doing everything from jamming walkie-talkies used by insurgents to monitoring Russian SAM sites, to providing escort jamming for Air Force B-1 bombers.

Over the final three years of Marine EA-6B operations, OIR remained the primary focus for the three remaining VMAQ squadrons, with the 'Jesters', 'Moondogs', and 'Seahawks' rotating through either Al Udeid or Incirlik Air Base in Turkey. In addition to supporting OIR joint force EW requests, the Marine Prowler crews flew over Afghanistan in support of Operation Resolute Support (the NATO-led successor mission to Operation Enduring Freedom) and Operation Freedom's Sentinel (the smaller US-only force protection and counter-terrorism mission in Afghanistan). Regardless of

Marine EA-6Bs stayed relevant through the type's final deployments in support of Operation Inherent Resolve over Iraq and Syria both aiding US and allied forces in the fight against ISIS while protecting friendly aircraft from potential engagement by Syrian air defences. (USAF/SSgt Trevor McBride)

where Prowlers operated, missions lasted six to eight hours, with crews using the electromagnetic spectrum to track and monitor high-value individuals in Iraq and Syria, as well as to intercept and jam insurgent communications, denying them the ability to coordinate attacks or tactical movements.

Prowler sundown

As the scheduled 2019 EA-6B sundown drew closer, the Marines began deactivating VMAQ squadrons, starting with training unit VMAQT-1 'Banshees' on 29 April 2016. The next squadron stood down was VMAQ-4 'Seahawks', which cased its colours at MCAS Cherry Point on 2 June 2017. Having returned from deployment in October 2017, VMAQ-3 'Moondogs' deactivated on 11 May 2018, leaving VMAQ-2 – which had already deployed by then – as the sole remaining EA-6B squadron in the US military.

During the final Prowler deployment from April through November 2018, VMAQ-2 integrated into the USAF's 379th Air Expeditionary Wing at Al Udeid. One of the more interesting missions the squadron flew occurred on 14 April 2018, when a single Prowler provided escort jamming for two B-1B Lancer bombers on a strike into Syria to destroy the Barzah Scientific Research Centre, believed to be a key facility in Syria's chemical weapons programme. Though occurring early in the deployment, this mission demonstrated that, despite its age, the EA-6B was going out at the top of its game.

Prowler crews took exceptional pride successfully performing their mission, protecting aviators and ground troops alike from enemy action. Describing what he enjoyed most about flying the Prowler, one EA-6B pilot told the author, '*We're the only Marine Corps platform that's dedicated to EW. We have our receiver system, comms system, comms jamming, and radar jamming systems that can go out there and protect strike aircraft, protect ground forces, and degrade the enemy's ability to communicate and coordinate attacks. A lot of what we do can't be seen visibly, like if how somebody drops a bomb, you see an explosion. What we do is visible in the fact that nobody died. There's an inherent satisfaction that goes along with protecting forces on the ground.*'

After completing the final EA-6B deployment in November 2018, VMAQ-2 returned to Cherry Point to begin the deactivation process. While the 'Jesters' continued to fly for several months, pilots, ECMOs, maintainers and other support personnel left the squadron to begin transitioning to their next assignments. The squadron formally stood down on during a combined VMAQ-2 deactivation/EA-6B retirement ceremony at Cherry Point on 8 March 2019. The last ever flight of an EA-6B occurred on 14 March, then VMAQ-2's colour bird – bureau number 162230 – was flown from Cherry Point to Dulles International Airport near Washington DC, where it was inducted into the collection of the Smithsonian Air and Space Museum's Steven F. Udvar-Hazy Center, where it is now on public display.

Limits of the Prowler

For all the capabilities the Prowler brought to Marine, joint force and coalition SEAD and EW air and ground operations, for the Marine Corps' unique amphibious, expeditionary mission, the type lacked a critical capability – the ability to launch and recover from an amphibious carrier as part of a Marine Expeditionary Unit's Aviation Combat Element. As America's seaborne force in readiness, MEUs need to be able to respond to crises virtually anywhere in the world. With the EA-6B unable to operate from the short-deck carriers at the centre of a MEU's Amphibious Readiness Group (ARG), MEUs historically have lacked an organic, dedicated aerial electronic attack capability.

Further, with only four squadrons of five aircraft each at the height of USMC EA-6B operations, the Prowler fleet was simply too small to meet the Corps' growing need for aerial EW. At any given time, the Corps has at least two MEUs on seagoing patrols, plus the 31st MEU in Japan, two WTI courses per year requiring EW support, and at various points throughout the first decade of the 21th Century, ongoing combat operations in Iraq and Afghanistan. With inter-deployment dwell times needed for rest, recovery and training, only half of the Corps' EA-6B capacity was typically available to support operations worldwide. On a good day, when all aircraft are available, this meant that – at best – the Marines had ten Prowlers total to rely on for EW support.

Lastly, though assigned to Marine squadrons and flown and crewed by Marines, USMC Prowlers primarily served joint force commanders, rather than being attached to Marine Air-Ground Task Forces (MAGTFs). As Lt Col Greg Sand, EW Requirements Officer at Headquarters Marine Corps Department of Aviation explains, '*Following (Operation) Desert Storm and the subsequent deactivation of the USAF EF-111A Raven, Marine Corps EA-6B squadrons served in a joint capacity as a Department of Defense tactical Airborne Electronic Attack (AEA) platform, not as a MAGTF asset.'* This is an important point in any discussion of the Prowler's retirement. While Marine Prowlers undeniably supported Marine ground units, MAGTF commanders typically did not have EA-6Bs at their immediate disposal, as the type typically covered the EW needs of all joint and coalition forces within a given area of operations. With the renewed regional ambitions of peer-level competitors like China and Russia, both of which are investing heavily in advanced EW systems, the Marines needed a credible, organic EW capability spread across the entirety of Marine aviation worldwide.

MAGTF-EW

Long before the twin Pratt & Whitney J52-P-408A engines of the final EA-6B ever to fly spooled down for the last time, Marine Corps leadership laid the foundation that the future of USMC EW would be built on. Combat experience in Iraq and Afghanistan revealed that demand for aerial EW support far exceeded the Corps' capacity to fulfil those requests, highlighting a need to move away from a Prowler-centric EW model that relied almost solely on a low-density/high-demand asset nearing the end of its service life. Explaining the genesis of the new construct, Lt Col Sand said, *'Marine Air Ground Task Force – Electronic Warfare, or MAGTF-EW, is a Marine Corps Combat Development Command concept from 2007 that provided focus for future combat development efforts in the area of electronic warfare. The concept was intentionally broad in scope and designed to allow the MAGTF to continue to mitigate the EW threats of today, as well as dominate the electromagnetic spectrum of the future.'* Rather than relying on a single aircraft type to manage Marine EW, MAGTF-EW is a platform agnostic, system-of-systems spread across fixed-wing, rotor-wing, tiltrotor and unmanned aircraft throughout the Marine Corps.

Enter the Tiger

The most mature component of MAGTF EW is Intrepid Tiger II (IT II), a precision communications jamming pod developed by the US Naval Air Warfare Center Weapons Division's Joint Electronic Attack and Compatibility Office. Most of the IT-II pod was constructed using commercial off-the-shelf components to limit the development timeline and keep costs to a minimum. Designed to utilise an open-architecture design, the IT-II's software is rapidly reprogrammable. Importantly, the pod could be carried and used aboard the AV-8B Harrier II without the need for new software. Though the Harrier was the first intended platform for Intrepid Tiger, VX-9 'The Vampires' conducted initial integration testing and assessment of the pod on an F/A-18C, with assistance from the Jammer Techniques Optimisation Group at Point Mugu.

Introducing IT-II into the Harrier community brought an organic aerial electronic attack capability to MEUs that hadn't existed previously. The first flight made by an operational Harrier squadron with the IT-II pod occurred on 27 March 2012 by VMA-214 'Blacksheep' at MCAS Yuma. Two days later, the 'Blacksheep' partnered with the 1st Radio Battalion to participate in the first integrated air/ground IT-II training event at an expeditionary airfield just outside Yuma. During this training, radio battalion Marines controlled the IT-II pod from the ground, taking the initial steps in establishing Harrier-Radio Battalion interoperability TTPs to maximise the effects of the IT-II pod.

Initially developed for communications intelligence and jamming for fixed-wing aircraft like the Harrier and Hornet, Intrepid Tiger capabilities are being expanded to include a counter-radar capability. This AV-8B assigned to the 13th MEU flies above Djibouti carrying an IT-II pod under its starboard wing in 2013. (USMC/SSgt Matt Orr)

IT-II at war

Making its operational debut in Afghanistan with VMA-211 'Avengers' in May 2012, IT-II was employed on missions similar to those in which Prowler crews utilised the USQ-113 for communications intelligence and jamming. This had the dual effects of providing communications AEA for more units on the ground while providing much-needed relief for the long-overworked Prowler fleet. While the Marines are understandably reluctant to discuss specifics when it comes to IT-II, the pod has no shortage of fans in both the air and on the ground.

Lt Col Shawn 'Junk' Hermley served as commanding officer of VMA-231 on a 2012–2013 deployment to Afghanistan, during which the squadron employed the IT-II pod in support of US and coalition ground operations. Reflecting on this, Hermley said, '*Once I got my guys over the fact that they didn't want to be electronic attack guys and showed the ground forces how capable this thing was and what we could do with it and how we could fit it into the fight, it came to the point where they were asking for it constantly. We always had to have a backup aircraft when we flew these missions, and we'd ask them 'Alright, for our backup aircraft, do you want Intrepid Tiger or do you want more weapons?' And they'd say 'No, we want the Intrepid Tiger,' so we'd make sure that that aircraft had IT-II because that was so important to the scheme of manoeuvre.*'

Hermley also noted that incorporating a single IT II pod into a two-ship section of Harriers gave his Marines the capability to conduct electronic attack in support of assault support aircraft during the most vulnerable point of inserting or extracting troops, then being able to switch to an overwatch or close air support role. That is something the Prowler simply could not do, nor could it do it from the deck of an amphibious assault ship like the Harrier can. Current plans call for adding IT-II – which is also being flown on Marine F/A-18 Hornets and UH-1Y Venoms as of this writing – to the quivers of Marine KC-130 'BattleHerks', AH-1Z Vipers, CH-53 Super Stallions and MV-22 Osprey.

With an internal payload bay, the RQ-21A Blackjack UAV was seen as a potential platform for a repackaged Intrepid Tiger II system to provide communications intelligence and jamming in an unmanned system. While the Blackjack proved too small and underpowered to carry the IT-II systems, it has been tested with the AN/DSY-4 'Spectral Bat' Signals Intelligence and electronic warfare support payload. (Joe Copalman)

Intrepid Tiger II variants

In addition to the proven IT-II(v)1 pod utilised by the Harrier and the Hornet, the Marines have three other IT-II variants at different stages of development. In service aboard the Bell UH-1Y Venom since 2016, the IT-II(v)3 pod offers expanded frequency range and enhanced direction-finding capability over the (v)1 pod. Like the (v)1, the (v)3 primarily provides a communications EW capability and can be operated from either aboard the aircraft or controlled by radio battalion Marines on the ground. Marine AH-1Z Vipers will gain IT-II(v)3 capability in 2021.

The concept of providing Marine unmanned aerial systems (UAS) with an electronic warfare capability dates back to the mid-1980s, when young officers within the Corps' nascent remotely piloted vehicle community sought expanded roles beyond reconnaissance and artillery adjustment. The Boeing-Insitu RQ-21 Blackjack is the Corps' first step towards an unmanned EW capability, with a utility bay that can carry payloads weighing up to 39lb (18kg). Intrepid Tiger II(v)4 is the unofficial designation for the as-yet-unfunded IT-II variant intended for integration into the Blackjack's payload bay. Though eager to gain an EW capability, some in the RQ-21 community remain sceptical that the IT-II payload can be scaled down enough for the Blackjack, as two variants of IT-II pods currently in service both weigh in around 300lb (136kg).

With the delay and eventual cancellation of the Marine Corps' proposed all-in-one MUX (MAGTF Unmanned Expeditionary) UAV, the service began operating a pair of General Atomics MQ-9A Reaper UAVs over Afghanistan in September 2018. (USMC/LCpl Colton Brownlee)

While the 2018 Marine Aviation Plan (AvPlan) projected a functional IT-II payload for the RQ-21 within the 2021-23 timeframe and cited the RQ-21/IT-II pairing as 'the foundation for further EW expansion within the VMUs', the 2019 AvPlan gives the impression this is no longer being pursued. The 2019 Aviation Electronic Warfare plan makes no mention of the RQ-21, and the Unmanned Aircraft Systems (VMU) plan makes no mention of the IT-II. Despite this, the Marines appear to be finalising development of the AN/DSY-4 'Spectral Bat' Signals Intelligence (SIGINT) and electronic warfare support (ES) payload for the RQ-21, which will give the Blackjack a signals detection and geo-location capability. Developed specifically for the RQ-21 payload bay, Spectral Bat requires no scaling-down of a much larger system, easing integration. In anticipation of the (now-cancelled) Marine Air-Ground Task Force Unmanned Aerial System – Expeditionary (MUX) group 5 UAV, the Marine Corps recently began flying the General Atomics MQ-9 Reaper over Afghanistan on a contractor-owned, contractor-operated basis. While not explicitly stated as a justification for acquiring MQ-9s, the Reaper's ability to carry underwing stores heavier than existing IT-II pods is something the Marines may very well exploit moving forward to help bridge the EW gap.

The fourth IT-II variant under development is the Intrepid Tiger II Block X. While the IT-II pod has mitigated the impact of losing the EA-6B and its robust communications EW capabilities, existing variants of the pod cannot jam radar signals like the Prowler's ALQ-99 pods could. The Marines plan to rectify this with the introduction of the Block X, which will add a significant radar-jamming capability while retaining the comms-jamming functionality of earlier variants. The lead platform for integration of IT-II Block X is the MV-22B Osprey, which will operate the system as an internal payload rather than in a pod mounted externally. A podded version will be developed for Harriers and Hornets as well, giving both aircraft – especially the HARM-equipped Hornet – significant SEAD capabilities.

F-35 – Stealthy SEAD

Once fully developed, the IT-II system will be integrated into every manned aircraft community within a MEU's ACE, with one exception – the Lockheed Martin F-35 Lightning II. Along with replacing the Harrier and Hornet in Marine Corps service, the F-35 has picked up the peer-threat SEAD torch from the EA-6B. As Maj Brian Hansell, an F-35 instructor pilot with MAWTS-1 explained, '*As the Prowler has sunset, the F-35 has become the Marine Corps' SEAD platform. We understand the importance of the SEAD mission, and we actively train to it.*' As a low-observable, fifth-generation aircraft with different sensors and EW systems than the EA-6B, the F-35 approach to SEAD is inherently different from how Prowler crews performed the mission.

At the heart of the Lightning II's EW capability is the BAE Systems AN/ASQ-239 electronic warfare suite. Designed to provide offensive and defensive electronic warfare capabilities, the ASQ-239 can locate, identify and target threat emitters while using the Link 16 datalink to share that data with other aircraft. Additionally, the F-35's Northrop-Grumman AN/APG-81 active electronically-scanned array radar is both impressively jam-resistant and can be employed as a jammer for airborne electronic attack. Though seemingly novel, the Northrop AN/APG-77 AESA utilised by the Air Force's Lockheed F-22 Raptor has long possessed an electronic attack capability. For electronic attack,

Despite the concerns of many that retiring the EA-6B from service and disestablishing dedicated electronic warfare squadrons would rob the Marine Corps of the potent EW capabilities it needs to defeat peer-level air defence threats, pilots in the Marine F-35 community are enthusiastic about the type's prowess as a suppression of enemy air defences platform. (Joe Copalman)

the APG-81's precision emitter geo-location capabilities work in the other direction as well, enabling the pilot to jam a specific emitter with the radar's energy.

Currently absent from the arsenal of munitions the F-35 employs is any kind of dedicated anti-radiation missile like the AGM-88 HARM typically associated with the SEAD mission. As of this writing, Northrop-Grumman is working with the US Navy on the development of an upgraded and redesigned variant of the HARM specifically for the F-35. Known as the AGM-88G Advanced Anti-Radiation Guided Missile – Extended Range (AARGM-ER), the new missile features smaller control surfaces and ventral strakes, eliminating the tall fins that prevented the HARM from internal carriage in the F-35's weapons bay. Due to the missile's length, the AARGM-ER will likely fit inside the F-35C carrier-based F-35 variant, but not in the weapons bay of the STOVL F-35B, which traded a full-length bay for a lift fan enabling expeditionary and amphibious operations. The AARGM-ER is currently scheduled to enter flight testing in 2021.

Though many have expressed scepticism over the F-35's efficacy as a SEAD platform, those within the F-35 community have been impressed with its effectiveness. Describing the Lightning II's aptitude in its three primary mission sets, Maj Hansell at MAWTS-1 observed, '*It is extremely capable. It does very good air-to-surface, where it is comparable to that fourth-generation type platform. That's really where it needs to be. But it absolutely excels at SEAD and in kind of an escort air-to-air role.*'

Criticism of MAGTF-EW

Despite holding the promise of giving MAGTF commanders control of aerial EW capabilities they had not had previously, MAGTF-EW is not without its critics. One of the most common concerns expressed by MAGTF-EW sceptics is the timing of the Prowler retirement. With the IT-II Block X still under development and with only three active, deployable F-35 squadrons at the time VMAQ-2 disestablished, neither of MAGTF-EW's strongest pillars were fully developed. Critics also cite a potential Marine EW 'brain drain', as the number of former EA-6B pilots and ECMOs on active duty continues to decline. The corporate EW knowledge amassed by veteran ECMOs over the past 10-15 years is of immeasurable value towards the development of future EW systems and TTPs, yet with MAGTF-EW and many of its component systems still very much works in progress, many of these EW experts will have retired, separated from service, or been promoted out of positions in which they could have a direct impact on the future of Marine EW.

Lastly, MAGTF-EW sceptics remain concerned that eliminating a community focused solely on EW and making it just another trade for multi-mission aircrews to be jacks of will dull the Corps' cutting edge when it comes to EW. To this end, MAWTS-1 established a Spectrum Warfare Department in 2013 to ensure that the Marines retain an enduring EW centre of excellence for the development of TTPs as new systems and capabilities are introduced into the fleet.

The value of MAGTF-EW is most apparent when looking at the entirety of Marine Corps operations worldwide. During the final four years of EA-6B operations, the three remaining VMAQs rotated through deployments almost exclusively in support of OIR. With threats in Iraq and Syria ranging from low-tech insurgents with small arms to frontline Russian surface to air missiles, OIR rightfully demanded the attention the VMAQ community paid it. But with only six aircraft deployed at any given time as the other two squadrons worked through their training and readiness cycles in preparation for another deployment, other deployed units that could have benefitted from the Prowler's EW capabilities went without them.

As AFRICOM's casualty evacuation and embassy support force, Special Purpose MAGTF – Crisis Response – Africa could find itself flying into situations where the ability to intercept insurgent communications or jam them to prevent coordinated attacks on Americans would be considerably useful. Yet with the Prowler being the high-demand, low-density, joint-force asset it was, SPMAGTF-CR-AF would likely never have rated a dedicated EA-6B detachment had the Prowler continued to serve. Plans to equip Marine KC-130Js and MV-22Bs – the two aircraft that comprise the SPMAGTF-CR-AF aviation combat element – with Intrepid Tiger II systems will give the aircrews and the Marines they support a credible organic aerial electronic attack capability they never previously enjoyed.

Chapter 9

VMFA | MARINE FIGHTER ATTACK

The F/A-18 Hornet entered the 21st century as the most capable tactical aircraft the Marines flew at the time. As of September 2020, the F/A-18 equips seven Marine Fighter Attack Squadrons (VMFAs), plus a fleet replacement squadron (FRS) for training.

Hornet variants

As of this writing, the Marines operate four deployable variants of the F/A-18: the F/A-18C, F/A-18D, F/A-18A++ and F/A-18C+. For a brief period in the 2017 to 2018 time-frame, several fleet squadrons operated a fifth variant, the F/A-18B, but that appears to have been withdrawn from service. Though all Hornet variants flown by the Marines are similar enough to require only minimal training for pilots transitioning from one to the other, each has its own unique history of upgrades that warrants examination.

The single-seat F/A-18C comprises the backbone of the USMC Hornet community. A late-1980s development of the F/A-18A, the 'C' introduced the capability to employ the AIM-120 Advanced Medium-Range Air-to-Air Missile (AMRAAM), the AGM-65 Maverick air-to-ground missile and the AGM-84 Harpoon anti-ship missile. The F/A-18C gained credible night attack and precision ordnance capabilities with the Raytheon AAR-50 NAVFLIR (Navigational Forward Looking InfraRed) navigation pod and the AAS-38A NITE Hawk targeting pod. Though the NITE Hawk initially lacked the ability to laser-designate for on-board weaponry, a 1993 upgrade enabled pilots to designate targets for laser-guided munitions. A 1988 upgrade added night-vision-goggle-compatible cockpit displays that include a colour moving map and two-colour multi-function displays (MFDs). Rounding out the early C-model upgrades were self-protection jammers and NACES ejection seats.

Concurrent with the development of the F/A-18C, McDonnell-Douglas introduced an update of the two-seat F/A-18B, which had primarily been utilised for training. Known as the F/A-18D, the new two-seater came in two sub-variants – one with dual controls for training F/A-18 pilots, and another specifically for the Marines with a 'missionised' rear cockpit for a weapons systems officer (WSO). Having relied on the Grumman A-6 Intruder for all-weather and night attack for decades, the Marines sought a replacement as the Intruder neared the end of its service life. While the USMC lost a pure 'bomb truck' in the A-6E with its impressive 18,000lb (8,165kg) bombload, it gained a credible supersonic strike aircraft that could self-escort and conduct Forward Air Controller (Airborne), or FAC(A) missions.

The F/A-18 Hornet has been the Marine Corps' primary fighter/attack platform since the mid-1980s and remains a potent air-to-air and air-to-surface platform.
(Joe Copalman)

Some upgraded F/A-18A variants continue to serve, though these are being phased out. While most VMFAs upgraded to the F/A-18C or D by the turn of the century, the four Marine Reserve Hornet squadrons (and two active-duty squadrons) had not. Concerned with a capabilities gap limiting the reserve's ability to support and integrate with the total force, anticipating F/A-18C inventory shortfalls, and seeking operational and logistical commonality with the C and D-model Hornets, the Marines pressed for the conversion of 76 F/A-18As to F/A-18A+ standard. The A+ incorporated improved displays and faster processors, GPS navigation, new SJU-17 ejection seats, AMRAAM and AIM-9X Sidewinder capability and APX-111 combined interrogator-transponder IFF system. With the number of reserve VMFA squadrons cut from four to one between 2004 and 2008, most of the Marine F/A-18A+s became active-component aircraft.

To keep pace with F/A-18C upgrades, the Marines initiated another upgrade known as the F/A-18A++, adding compatibility with the Joint Helmet-Mounted Cueing System (JHMCS), better displays, the multi-function information distribution system (MIDS) with Link 16 datalink and 'four-bucket' ALE-47 chaff and flare dispensers. Regarding the advantages of the A++, one Marine F/A-18 pilot said, '*The A++ really stepped up the avionics of the jet way beyond what it was designed to do. It has increased display capability – all three of our MFDs are colour. We have Link 16, we have our LIT-*

The Marine Corps upgraded its older F/A-18A Hornets to retain commonality with the more advanced F/A-18C. The resultant F/A-18A++ remains in service as of this writing, primarily with reserve squadron VMFA-112, but is being rapidly replaced by F/A-18Cs pulled from former US Navy stocks, as the navy has retired its 'legacy' Hornets from active-duty service. (Joe Copalman)

ENING G4 pods, we have JHMCS, we have APG-73 radars instead of the -65s they were originally installed with, we have ALE-47. We basically have all of the combat systems that a legacy Hornet can have in a very old airframe.'

The final variant still in service is the F/A-18C+. Though US Navy divestment of its 'legacy' Hornets freed up F/A-18Cs for the Marines, most of these aircraft are just as old and worn-out as the A-models. Planning to fly the F/A-18 through FY2030, and with the F/A-18 being the primary bridging platform to the F-35, the Corps initiated another upgrade programme, bringing 23 F/A-18Cs out of war-reserve storage storage (and another seven from former US Navy stocks) and putting them through a programme similar to the A++.

Under a 2014 contract, the Marines contracted Boeing to convert these aircraft to F/A-18C+ standard. The upgrade includes ALE-47 dispensers, JHMCS compatibility, MIDS/Link 16, the multi-purpose display update including embedded tactical aircraft moving map capability (TAMMAC), the APX-111 CIT IFF, and all the weapons capabilities of F/A-18Cs. Boeing began modification work in 2014, with the first C+ completed (BuNo 163755) being delivered to VMFA-115 'Silver Eagles' at MCAS Beaufort in mid-2016. As of mid-2020, reserve squadron VMFA-112 'Cowboys' continues to accept deliveries of F/A-18Cs to replace its F/A-18A++ Hornets.

Tactical Reconnaissance

In addition to performing the FAC(A) mission, the F/A-18D conducts tactical aerial reconnaissance (TACRECCE), utilising the Advanced Tactical Aerial Reconnaissance System (ATARS).

ATARS consists of two electro-optical cameras and an infrared line scanner mounted in a modified nose. Aircraft equipped with ATARS are easily identifiable by the lack of a gun port and the flat-bottomed nose section with glassed-over camera ports. In addition to the EO and IR cameras, ATARS utilises the APG-73 synthetic aperture radar to generate mapping imagery. The system initially recorded imagery from all three sensors (EO/IR/Radar) onto a digital tape system designed in the 1980s. This system was notoriously unreliable, with a tape failure rate around 50 per cent. When it worked, the system allowed WSOs to review imagery shortly after each pass to ensure success. Compared to traditional 'wet' film, digital tape also shortened the time it took to get imagery to analysts for exploitation. ATARS was designed to employ a datalink that could share imagery while the aircraft was still airborne, but this system never quite worked as intended.

ATARS Hornets retain all the offensive weapons capabilities of the F/A-18D with the exception of the M61 20mm cannon, and can participate in standard strike, CAS and FAC(A) missions when not fulfilling photoreconnaissance requests. Capable of employing the AIM-9 and AIM-120, the ATARS Hornets can self-escort as well.

ATARS at war

By the time Operation Iraqi Freedom (OIF) began in March 2003, each of the three all-weather VMFA squadrons in theatre had ATARS aircraft. ATARS-equipped 'Deltas' helped First Marine Expeditionary Force (I MEF) planners know what awaited their Marines on the other side of Kuwait's border with Iraq and on the roads up to Baghdad,

With the retirement of the RF-4B Phantom and the USMC lacking a photo-reconnaissance platform, several F/A-18Ds were modified with the Advanced Tactical Aerial Reconnaissance System.
(Joe Copalman)

identifying choke points, locating enemy armour and artillery, and assessing the suitability of planned FARP (forward arming and refuelling point) sites. Once US forces crossed into Iraq, ATARS imagery remained crucial for target development along I MEF's route of advance.

Hornet weapons

Tasked with both air-to-air and air-to-ground missions, Marine Hornets are capable of employing a diverse variety of weapons to meet every challenge the type could encounter in combat.

For air-to-ground missions, the F/A-18 carries a vast array of free-fall ordnance, primarily from the Mk 80-series of general-purpose bombs. In addition to carrying the 500lb (227kg) Mk 82, 1,000lb (454kg) Mk 83 and 2,000lb (907kg) Mk 84, Marine Hornets employ laser-guided (GBU-12, -16 and -10, respectively) and GPS-guided (GBU-38, -32 and -31) variants of all three, including hardened penetrator variants like the 2,000lb BLU-109 and 'low-collateral damage' weapons like the 500lb BLU-126. During OIF and Operation Enduring Freedom (OEF), Marine Hornets typically carried a mix of GPS-guided Joint Direct Attack Munitions (JDAMs) and laser-guided bombs to provide maximum flexibility.

In recent years, the dual-mode GBU-54 500lb Laser JDAM has provided this flexibility in a single weapon, which has been employed extensively in Afghanistan and against the Islamic State in Iraq and Syria (ISIS).

Forward-firing ordnance still plays a critical role in the Hornet's arsenal. The AGM-65E 'Maverick' anti-tank missile was chosen by the Marines for its reliance on laser designation. This has proven an effective means of fratricide mitigation over the electro-optical and infrared-guided variants of the AGM-65. A personal favourite of many Hornet veterans who employed it in Iraq and Afghanistan, the 'LMAV' offered a

The Hornet's ability to carry a wide range of guided and unguided ordnance make it a remarkably flexible ground attack aircraft. This F/A-18A++ from VMFA-115 'Silver Eagles' carries two four-shot pods of 'Zuni' rockets under the left wing and a pair of GBU-12 laser-guided bombs on the other.
(Joe Copalman)

fast, responsive and highly accurate alternative to 500lb (227kg) laser-guided bombs while also mitigating collateral damage with its smaller 300lb (136kg) warhead.

Suppression of Enemy Air Defences (SEAD) is a core VMFA mission, and one Marine Hornets perform with the AGM-88 High-Speed Anti-Radiation Mission (HARM). In use since the 1980s, the HARM's seeker targets radar energy emitted by surface-to-air radar systems, with the ability to 'remember' a targeted system's location even after it stops emitting.

A weapon that has become more relevant for VMFA units operating in the western Pacific region is the AGM-84D Harpoon anti-ship missile, with a range of 120nm (220km) and a 487lb (221kg) penetrating high-explosive warhead. A variant of the Harpoon, the AGM-84H/K Standoff Land Attack Missile – Extended Range (SLAM-ER) gives Marine Hornets the ability to strike land and sea targets from ranges as far as 155nm (270km). Another standoff weapon employed by Marine Hornets is the AGM-154 Joint Standoff Weapons (JSOW). A glide bomb with a maximum range of 70nm (130km), JSOW delivers a payload of 145 BLU-97/B Combined Effects submunitions, which provide anti-armour, fragmentary and incendiary effects.

In USMC use since the Vietnam War, 'Zuni' 5in (127mm) rockets remain a viable weapon in the Marine Hornet community. Zuni rockets with white phosphorous warheads, which create a persistent cloud of dense, white smoke, are still occasionally employed by F/A-18D FAC(A) crews to mark targets. Zunis are used more frequently with high-explosive warheads, and though not precision-guided, have a reputation for accuracy, able to be employed against point targets like trucks or bunkers. Though the F/A-18 can carry pods of 2.75in (70mm) Hydra unguided rockets, the VMFAs typically do not employ these outside of training. That said, Hydra rockets have been used recently as part of the Advanced Precision Kill Weapons System (APKWS), which utilises a guidance system with laser-seekers in pop-out wings, transforming the Hydra from an area weapon into a highly accurate low-collateral damage weapon.

With the exception of ATARS-equipped F/A-18Ds, all Marine Hornets are equipped with the proven M61 'Vulcan' 20mm Gatling-type cannon, capable of a 6,000-rounds per minute rate of fire. Used against both air and ground targets, the Vulcan is even capable of destroying armoured vehicles. Though not a precision weapon, the M61 offers pilots and ground commanders a relatively accurate low-collateral damage weapon with minimal concussive and fragmentation effects.

While cluster munitions have fallen out of favour with many air arms around the world, the CBU-99 cluster bomb remains in the Marine F/A-18's arsenal for anti-tank and area target usage. Despite its proven effectiveness when the bomb functions correctly, CBU-99s employed during OIF were plagued by a high dud rate, with the 'clamshell' halves failing to open in flight, causing the cannister to impact the ground with the bomblets having not been armed.

Though Marine Hornet pilots still train to use the Mk 77 firebomb, its last operational employment was in 2003 during OIF, when Marines needed to secure a bridge held by Iraqi troops. With no concussive or fragmentation effects, the Mk 77 was chosen to neutralise the defenders without damaging the bridge, while having a secondary psychological effect to keep reinforcements away.

In addition to engaging ground targets, Marine F/A-18s are responsible for keeping the battlespace free of enemy air threats. For counterair missions, the Hornet employs the active-radar homing AIM-120 Advanced Medium-Range Air-to-Air Missile for

An F/A-18D wearing the colours of VMFA(AW)-225 'Vikings' returns to MCAS Yuma carrying an inert AGM-88 High-Speed Anti-Radiation Missile (HARM) under its wing at the conclusion of a Suppression of Enemy Air Defences mission during a Weapons and Tactics Instructor course. (Joe Copalman)

longer-ranged engagements and the infrared-seeking AIM-9M and AIM-9X Sidewinder for shorter-ranged engagements. The AIM-9X is a high-off-boresight missile capable of engaging targets nearly 90° off the aircraft's axis of movement in conjunction with the JHMCS helmet system.

War in the 21st century

The F/A-18 was the first Marine aircraft to respond to the terror attacks of 11 September 2001. After sorting out some coordination issues with North American Aerospace Defence Command, reserve squadron VMFA-321 'Hell's Angels' at Andrews AFB flew combat air patrols (CAP) over Washington DC on 12 September. With the immediate threat gone and the Air National Guard firmly established as the lead service for what became known as Operation Noble Eagle, VMFA-321 stood down on the evening of 12 September, having only flown the DC CAP mission for one day. This was not the end of Marine participation in Noble Eagle, as VMFA(AW)-332 'Moonlighters' took on the air defence mission over Guam, a US territory in the western Pacific, in January 2002.

Marine Hornet pilots were also first in their service to bring the fight to the enemy after 9/11, when on 18 October 2001, the 'Thunderbolts' of VMFA-251 flew strikes against Taliban targets in Afghanistan from the deck of the USS *Theodore Roosevelt* (CVN 71). The 'Thunderbolts' continued to support special forces teams through February 2002 before the 'TR' returned to the US. Marine Hornet support for OEF remained limited, with no VMFA squadrons deploying directly to Afghanistan until 2010. In April 2002, VMFA(AW)-121 'Green Knights' deployed to Manas, Kyrgyzstan, flying 900 OEF sorties before returning to Miramar that October. Additionally, single-seat VMFAs attached to carrier air wings (CVWs) flew off of Navy carriers at numerous points throughout the Afghan conflict.

An F/A-18A from VMFA-115 carrying a GBU-12 laser-guided bomb under the right wing and a GBU-32 Joint Direct Attack Munition en route to a target in northern Iraq in April 2003. (USAF/TSgt Robert Horstman)

Marine Hornets over Iraq

In the weeks preceding OIF, Marine Aircraft Groups 11 (Miramar) and 31 (Beaufort) sent five squadrons to Kuwait. In order of arrival, these were VMFA(AW)-225 'Bengals', VMFA-232 'Red Devils', VMFA(AW)-121 'Green Knights', VMFA(AW)-533 'Hawks', and VMFA-251 'Thunderbolts', giving commanders a total of 60 land-based Hornets to rely on. Additionally, two squadrons were assigned to CVWs supporting OIF. The 'Death Rattlers' of VMFA-323 flew from the USS *Constellation* (CV 64) as part of CVW-2 in the Northern Arabian Gulf (NAG), while VMFA-115 'Silver Eagles' flew as part of CVW-3 aboard the USS *Harry S Truman* (CVN 75) in the eastern Mediterranean. Whereas the Kuwait-based squadrons supported the USMC drive on Baghdad, VMFA-115 flew in support of special operations forces working alongside Kurdish Peshmerga guerrillas and the US Army's 172nd Airborne Brigade in northern Iraq. While the 'Silver Eagles' participated in deep strike missions like the 'shock and awe' raids on the opening night of the war and a large force strike employing GBU-31 2,000lb (907kg) JDAMs on Al Taqaddum Air Base, the squadron's primary focus remained CAS for special operators using tactics refined by Navy Hornet squadrons flying similar missions in Afghanistan.

The 'Death Rattlers' aboard the *Constellation* spent the first ten days of OIF flying night strikes against regime targets in the Baghdad area with the rest of CVW-2, focused on crippling Ba'ath Party leadership, degrading air defences and disabling communications. With the majority of targets struck by CVW-2 being buildings, VMFA-323 primarily employed GPS-guided weapons, including 30 GBU-31 2,000lb (907kg) JDAMs, 11 BLU-109 2,000lb penetrating JDAMs, 42 GBU-32/35 1,000lb (454kg) JDAMs and 25 AGM-154 JSOWs. During this period, one VMFA-323 pilot also fired a weapon rarely employed by Marine Hornets – the AGM-84H SLAM-ER – one of only two fired during the initial phase of OIF.

While the carrier-based Hornets dealt with regime targets in Baghdad and northern Iraq, the Kuwait-based Hornets assisted the three Regimental Combat Teams and Task Force Tarawa, all racing northwest towards Baghdad. The F/A-18Ds played a major role in clearing the RCTs' routes of advance. Flying with FAC(A)-qualified crews, the 'Delta' squadrons flew strike control and reconnaissance (SCAR) missions, seeking out targets and directing other aircraft to attack them. Refining an approach successfully employed during Operation Desert Storm, planners divided Iraq into a series of 'kill boxes', which two-ship sections of F/A-18Ds would be assigned to search for targets in. Each 30nm (56km) square kill box was further divided into nine 10nm (18.5km) square 'keypads', set up like the buttons on a telephone – '1' in the upper left, '2' upper middle, etc. Operating in sections allowed one aircraft to leave the area to aerial refuel while the other continued to search for targets or prosecute an attack. When not directing airstrikes, F/A-18D crews flew battlefield aerial interdiction (BAI) missions, close air support (CAS) and ATARS missions.

While their 'Delta' brethren focused on locating targets for attack, the single-seat Hornet pilots engaged almost solely in battlefield shaping through kill box BAI, hitting targets – especially artillery – designated by F/A-18Ds ahead of the ground forces' advance. In addition to precision-guided munitions like GBU-12s and laser Mavericks used extensively during this period, Marine Hornets also employed unguided ordnance like Mk 83 1,000lb (454kg) general purpose bombs and CBU-99 cluster bombs on targets far from friendly troops or civilian populations. While the CBU-99 could be highly effective against area targets and armoured vehicles, a high dud rate plagued employment of the weapon throughout OIF. In addition to battlefield interdiction, the shore-based VMFAs also participated in occasional 'decapitation' strikes aimed at destroying Iraqi military and Ba'ath Party leadership. One such mission validated the JDAM as an all-weather precision weapon for Marine Hornets, with successful engagement of targets under thick cloud cover using coordinates provided by special operations JTACs near Baghdad.

After the fall of Baghdad and the transition to stability operations, the Kuwait-based VMFAs returned to the US and the *Constellation* and *Truman* continued their scheduled cruises. With the emergence and growth of the insurgency in Iraq, the country once again demanded the Marine Corps' attention. The first VMFA to participate in post-'mission accomplished' OIF was VMFA-312 'Checkerboards', deployed as part of CVW-1 aboard the USS *Enterprise* (CVN 65) in October 2003.

From NITE Hawk to LITENING

By the start of OIF in March 2003, the AAS-38A NITE Hawk targeting pods used by Marine Hornets were eclipsed by newer, more capable pods. The NITE Hawk's poor resolution made finding artillery – the highest-priority target in the opening weeks of OIF – difficult. The pod's laser also suffered from poor reliability, often requiring the use of buddy-lasing. Flying from the *Truman* during OIF 1, VMFA-115 relied on Navy F-14 Tomcats utilising the Lockheed Martin AN/AAQ-25 LANTIRN pods, which would find and identify targets the Hornet's NITE Hawk could not. Lastly, the NITE Hawk lacked a downlink capability, meaning FACs and JTACs could not access the pod's feed to confirm targets – a capability that became critical as the wars in Iraq and Afghanistan progressed.

Over a year prior to OIF, Marine F/A-18D pilots specifically requested the Northrop-Grumman AN/AAQ-28(V) LITENING II pod for the 'Delta' community, as its higher resolution and reliable laser designator were both critical for the FAC(A) mission. At the same time, single-seat Hornet pilots assigned to 'boat' squadrons advocated for the Raytheon AN/ASQ-228 ATFLIR, the Navy's intended replacement for the NITE Hawk, as it could fit on the Hornet's 'cheek' stations along the sides of the lower fuselage, allowing carrier-based Hornets to carry a much-needed centreline fuel tank. For F/A-18D pilots, a centreline-mounted pod made sense, since cheek-mounted pods were subject to 'masking' by the fuselage or underwing drop tanks at longer ranges or certain aspects relative to the target. In the end, both groups got what they wanted, with the carrier-based squadrons getting the ATFLIR and the VMFA(AW) squadrons getting the LITENING II.

Highlighting the advantages of the LITENING II, retired WSO Major Doug Glover said, '*What it gave us was an amazing sensor. The resolution was so much better than our displays, it gave us a high-res sensor that was TV and infrared in the same pod, so I could look at it through pure electro-optical or infrared.*' An additional advantage of the LITENING was the provision for a super-wide field of view to help F/A-18D WSOs observe the broader tactical situation on the ground. As Glover explained, '*You could scroll all the way out in E/O mode. It was great for situational awareness. A lot of times when you get sucked into the pod, you lose the big picture. It will be like 'I am on a road somewhere in the desert and I see a vehicle.' You could go out to the super-wide field of view, not lose your designation, and see something like a 28° field of view. That was amazing, and huge for talking people onto the target.*' The LITENING II's downlink capability allowed its feed to be shared with FACs and others on the ground.

OIF 2

The 'Bats' of VMFA(AW)-242 were the first 'D' squadron to deploy to Iraq, as well as the first to deploy with the LITENING, arriving at Al Asad Air Base in August 2004. During this deployment, two of the squadron's LITENINGs were datalink-capable, enabling

Marine F/A-18s were a near-constant fixture in the skies over Anbar between 2004 and 2008, flying from Al Asad Air Base like this F/A-18D from VMFA(AW)-242 'Bats' in January 2007. This example carries a 500lb (227kg) JDAM under the right wing and an AGM-65E Laser Maverick under the left wing. (USMC/LCpl James Cline III)

FACs and JTACs on the ground to view the pod's feed on screens connected to ROVER devices. This resulted in Hornets taking on the new, non-traditional role of intelligence, surveillance and reconnaissance (ISR), giving ground commanders an overhead view of the battlespace in near-real time. The dramatic increase in image resolution enabled the 'Bats' to see insurgents emplacing improvised explosive devices (IEDs) at night and to employ laser-guided weapons close to friendly troops, sometimes dropping 500lb (227kg) GBU-12s as close as 200 yards (183m) from them. In addition to ISR and CAS, VMFA(AW)-242 also flew convoy escort and counterbattery missions against insurgent mortar crews.

Operation Phantom Fury, the battle to retake Fallujah starting on 8 November 2004 gave the 'Bats' the opportunity to prove the F/A-18D's worth as an urban CAS platform. In addition to relying heavily on the LITENING pod for 'danger-close' CAS during troops-in-contact firefights on the streets of Fallujah, the 'Bats' were the first Marine squadron to employ the 500lb (227kg) GBU-58 JDAM in combat, putting it to good use during Phantom Fury. Despite supporting a dynamic and often confusing close-quarters fight in urban terrain, VMFA(AW)-242 supported the Marines on the ground with no fratricide incidents, a result many credit to the LITENING pod.

As the insurgency dragged on for the next five years, VMFA squadrons regularly deployed to Al Asad at six-month intervals. Through this period, the use of unguided free-fall ordnance effectively stopped, replaced almost entirely by laser-guided and GPS-guided munitions. The introduction of low-collateral damage versions of 500lb (227kg) LGBs and JDAMs offered considerable promise for urban CAS, but a faulty collateral damage estimate tool resulted in disappointing effects. One notable deployment during this period was VMFA-115's February through September 2008 'dirt det' to Al Asad, as the 'Silver Eagles' were the first FAC(A)-capable single-seat Hornet squadron to deploy in combat. The final Hornet unit deployed to Iraq was VMFA-112 'Cowboys', a reserve squadron from Texas that supported the US withdrawal, working closely with US Army special forces teams advising the Iraqi military, returning to the US in Spring 2010.

Refocus on Afghanistan

Following the drawdown of US forces in Iraq and in keeping with US President Barack Obama's focus on 'surge' operations in Afghanistan, Marine Hornets joined the OEF fight in earnest. In May 2010, VMFA-232 deployed to Kandahar with a mix of F/A-18Cs and F/A-18Ds, making the 'Red Devils' the first USMC Hornet squadron to land-base in Afghanistan. Three months later, the 'Werewolves' of VMFA-122 joined VMFA-232 at Kandahar to support the surge. During this deployment, VMFA-122 amassed 4,900 combat hours over 1,700 sorties, releasing 71,000lb (32,205kg) of ordnance and firing over 20,000 rounds of 20mm ammunition in support of ISAF (International Security and Assistance Force) ground troops.

Upgrades

With the Marines planning on flying the F/A-18 through 2030, the USMC has leveraged numerous avionics, armament, interoperability, survivability and readiness upgrades for its Hornet fleet. The introduction of the Raytheon AIM-9X Sidewinder advanced short-range air-to-air missile in 2004 provided Marine F/A-18s with enhanced lethality that allowed for successful engagements at high off-boresight angles. Utilising a

The Joint Helmet-Mounted Cueing System (JHMCS) introduced numerous capabilities to Marine Corps Hornets, including off-boresite engagement with the AIM-9X Sidewinder, the ability to 'slave' the targeting pod or radar to wherever a pilot is looking, and spending more time 'eyeballs out' with a heads-up display projecting basic flight data onto the inside of the visor. (Joe Copalman)

wide-angle imaging infra-red focal-plane array seeker and a thrust vectoring propulsion system, the AIM-9X provides Hornet pilots the ability to engage targets at roughly 80° off-boresight – a significant tactical advantage in a within-visual range dogfight. Further, with a streamlined design reducing drag, the AIM-9X yields a significant range increase over the AIM-9M it is largely replacing.

Tied closely to the introduction of the AIM-9X, the Joint Helmet-Mounted Cueing System (JHMCS) enables Hornet pilots to target the new missile off-boresight, and can also be used for air-to-ground employment. JHMCS enables an aircraft's LITENING pod to 'snap' to wherever a pilot or WSO is looking, and can be used to direct the APG-73 radar in the same manner. Introduced in the 2008-2009 timeframe, JHMCS utilises a magnetic system to track a pilot's or WSO's head position to determine where on the ground or in the air he or she is looking. JHMCS gives Hornet aircrew a heads-up display inside their visors, providing flight data like airspeed, heading, altitude and other information regardless of where they are looking. Using datalinks like Link 16, Hornet crews can share information that can be input into the JHMCS system, which is particularly useful for FAC(A) crews needing to get the sensors of strike aircraft arriving on station onto the intended target or area of interest. As former WSO Major Glover explained, '*The ability to quickly push coordinates between airplanes via datalink, whether it was MIDS/Link 16 or VMF messaging was huge. You could then take that coordinate and put it into your helmet. You'd put it into your system, look outside the aircraft, and the aircraft puts the target designation diamond in your helmet. Is it perfectly on the mark? No. Is it close? Yes. That systems fusion was a game-changer.*'

Another significant upgrade is the replacement of the Raytheon AN/APG-73 multimode radar with Raytheon's AN/APG-79(V)4 active electronically scanned array (AESA) radar. Whereas the AN/APG-73 relied on a mechanically actuated antenna, the AN/APG-79's antenna is an array of stationary antennas that can electronically 'steer' the radar's beam in different directions. AESA radars offer numerous advantages over the pulse-Doppler radars that equipped most fourth-generation fighters when they first entered service. Among these advantages are reliability, with no mechanical parts that wear out from fatigue, the ability to utilise multiple frequencies and perform several functions at once, a lower probability of intercept by enemy radar warning receivers and a higher resistance to jamming.

One upgrade requested by Marine Hornet pilots is the installation of an F-35-style fifth-generation cockpit display. As Hornet pilot Captain Thomas Frey explained, '*If you look at a fifth-generation cockpit, it generally has a large iPad-like display, whereas an older aircraft has multiple displays that all show different information, and now my brain has to process what's going on in all three of these to create a three-dimensional picture in my mind, whereas theirs, the software is ultimately much better.*' While such an upgrade has not been approved for Marine F/A-18s yet, it could very well be a game-changer if approved and implemented.

EW Hornets

When the Marines retired the last EA-6B Prowler electronic warfare (EW) aircraft in March 2019, they did so with no dedicated EW platform to take its place. Rather, the Marines are moving forward with a distributed system of air and ground EW systems known as Marine Air-Ground Task Force – Electronic Warfare, or MAGTF-EW. Though many decried this move as an abandonment of a longstanding EW capability, in practice, the Prowlers were effectively theatre-level assets, tasked to support joint force and coalition EW requests far more than the type directly supported Marines.

In 2011, seeking to provide Marine ground commanders with aerial EW support they could control, the Marine Corps – in conjunction with the US Naval Air Warfare Center Weapons Division (NAWCWD)'s Joint Electronic Attack and Compatibility Office (JEACO) at China Lake – developed the AN/ALQ-231 Intrepid Tiger II electronic warfare pod. As a precision communications intelligence and jamming pod, IT-II can intercept hostile communications to determine enemy intent, jam those communications to prevent enemy coordination via radio and jam radio-frequency signals used to set off command-detonated IEDs. In addition to being controlled by the pilot aboard the F/A-18 carrying it, the IT-II pod can be controlled from the ground by Radio Battalion Marines tasked with conducting electronic warfare.

After testing, IT-II was cleared for use on the Hornet, being used by Marine F/A-18s on a 2014 Middle Eastern deployment. In addition to the IT-II Block 1 pod for communications EW tasks, a new variant is being developed to expand the Hornet's EW capabilities significantly. Known as the IT-II Block X, the new pod will provide a counter-radar capability that will drastically increase survivability in higher-threat air defence environments.

Hornet Standard Game Plan

The F-35 is changing the way Marine aviation trains and fights, as evidenced by the 2015 introduction of an air-to-air combat tactics revision in the VMFA community. Known as the Hornet Standard Game Plan (HSGP), this revision has two major components. First, it leverages the fifth-generation low-observability, sensor-integration and data-sharing capabilities of the F-35 with the existing capabilities of the Hornet. Second, HSGP aligns the Corps' air-to-air combat tactics, techniques and procedures (TTPs) with that of the United States Air Force – a significant break from the Corps' traditional alignment with naval aviation air-to-air tactics as taught by the Naval Fighter Weapons School.

Marine Aviation Weapons and Tactics Squadrons One (MAWTS-1) at MCAS Yuma manages all tactics revisions in Marine aviation, and the squadron's F/A-18 division was tasked with developing the HSGP. Then-Captain Tom Frey, an F/A-18 instructor with MAWTS-1, took on the responsibility of writing new TTPs for the F/A-18 to integrate with the F-35. Regarding the genesis of the HSGP, Frey explained, '*Now that we are flying the F-35 operationally, we need to find a way to integrate that with our F-18s. It was very quickly realised that the F-35 is a joint platform, it's going to do the same thing regardless of the service that's utilising it. That's the goal here, to get us all on the same page. They're obviously not going to change the way they do business for the old F-18 A through D, so in order to integrate seamlessly, we're going to have to update how we conduct business.*'

Though the Marines stood up the first operational F-35 squadron and were first to achieve initial operating capability with the Lightning II, by 2015 the Air Force had a solid decade of experience operating the fifth-generation F-22 Raptor alongside its fourth-generation fighters like the F-15 Eagle and F-16 Fighting Falcon. With the USAF being the only service with fourth-gen/fifth-gen integration experience, and with the Marines' F/A-18 being similar in performance and capabilities to the F-16, MAWTS-1 turned to the 16th Weapons Squadron 'Tomahawks' at Nellis Air Force Base in Nevada for assistance in developing the HSGP tactics. The 16th WPS is effectively the MAWTS-1 Hornet division's equivalent in the USAF F-16 community, responsible for developing or revising the tactics employed by F-16 pilots. Initially, Frey gave the F/A-18 air-to-air combat tactics manual to instructors at the 16th WPS for review, to 'poke holes' in the tactics and advise on what they would do differently. After the 16th WPS reviewed the F/A-18 TTPs and made its recommendations, the Hornet division staff at MAWTS-1 made their own revisions where applicable or necessary. Based on these recommendations, the Marines aligned their air-to-air tactical doctrine with Air Force Doctrine Document 3-01: *Counterair Operations*, which is the joint and coalition standard for intercept control.

The fundamentals of the HSGP apply whether the F/A-18 pilots are integrating with F-35s or operating independently. Having instructed several courses worth of Marine Hornet pilots on the HSGP, Frey said the conversion to the new tactics has been fairly seamless. '*What I tell everyone when I teach new tactics is: I didn't just give you a new airplane. We're flying the same airplane. A lot of your manoeuvres, how you actually stick-and-throttle to control the airplane, work your sensors, work your weapons are all going to be pretty similar to our previous tactics that we would execute in the Marine Corps air-to-air wise. But how we interact as four or greater F-18s is going to be much different. It's going to utilise a lot more manoeuvre warfare fundamentals in order to take into account what the enemy is actually doing, and then based upon what they're doing, let me now manoeuvre my forces in order to counter what they're doing.*'

Readiness and recovery

Heavy combat use in multiple conflicts led to airframe fatigue and depletion of spare parts inventories long before programmed, resulting in a post-OIF/OEF Hornet fleet struggling to meet the minimum readiness rates needed to maintain pilot proficiency. The 2013 budget sequester further exacerbated this problem, limiting funds available for maintenance and flight hours. While the US Navy began transitioning to the F/A-18E/F Super Hornet in 2001, several Navy 'legacy' Hornet squadrons remained in service, competing with Marine VMFAs for serviceable airframes and spare parts. In 2014, aircraft availability was so low that the Marine Corps lowered the primary mission aircraft inventory for active-duty VMFAs from 12 F/A-18s to 10.

All this occurred among existing efforts to prolong the life of USMC Hornets through the F-35 transition. The first major attempt to extend the life of the Hornet fleet was the Center Barrel Replacement Program, which began in 2000 and replaced the centre fuselage assembly on fatigued F/A-18s. By 2015, 200 of these replacements had been completed. More recently, the Navy and Marine Corps initiated a service life extension programme (SLEP) in 2008, aimed at extending F/A-18 service life from 6,000 hours to 10,000, and from 8,300 landings (2,000 arrested) to 17,000 total. Despite these life-extending programmes, they simply could not keep pace with the high utilisation rates during OIF and OEF.

On 10 April 2016, Deputy Commandant for Aviation, Lt Gen Jon Davis, testified to the US Senate that out of 276 Hornets in the USMC inventory at the time, only 87 were mission-capable. The majority of those were split between VMFAT-101 with 30 'up' jets for training, and 40 combat-ready Hornets distributed among the four squadrons deployed overseas, leaving only 17 mission-capable aircraft for the remaining squadrons at various points in their own pre-deployment training and readiness cycles. This critical shortage of aircraft limited flight hours, impacted pilot proficiency and stunted career progression as the focus turned to simply maintaining currency. Compounding this shortage, the Hornet community at that time struggled with a 55 per cent 'break rate', meaning that out of all aircraft a squadron launched for a first sortie, less than half would be available to fly a second.

With the F/A-18 designated as the primary bridging platform to the F-35B/C throughout the transition period, the Hornet has received high priority for funding and action taken on readiness recovery. Building off the success of the Center Barrel Replacement and SLEP programmes of the previous decade, the USMC and Naval Air Systems Command embarked on a recovery programme aimed at drastically improving the Hornet fleet's mission capable rate. Following an F/A-18 Independent Readiness Review (IRR), the VMFA community began implementing more efficient maintenance practices, a depot readiness initiative aimed at speeding up depot-level maintenance and a consumable parts management system that reduced wait times for parts. Further, a new maintenance capacity model balancing the needs of operations and maintenance has so far resulted in 20-30 per cent gains in productivity in squadrons that have implemented it. In FY2017, the Marines invested over USD1.6 billion in spare parts, specifically flight surface spares.

While all of these initiatives have helped increase and sustain readiness levels in the F/A-18 community, one of the strongest factors in the recovery process has been Navy divestment of its 'legacy' Hornet fleet, freeing up dozens of airframes and tens of thousands of spare parts. A programme known as the Stricken Aircraft Reduction and Disposal Program introduced over 96,000 repairable parts into the USMC Hornet supply system. As a result, supply issues do not factor into non mission-capable rates anywhere near as much as they used to.

The result of all these efforts is a Marine Hornet fleet far better prepared for what the Corps calls 'the fight tonight'. In October 2018, then-Secretary of Defense James Mattis mandated that all Marine TACAIR communities reach an 80 per cent mission-capable rate by the end of 2019. While the Hornet community has fallen short of this goal, the mission-capable rate among all VMFAs increased from 48 per cent in 2017 to 64 per cent in 2019, with a two-month period in which the mission-capable rate reached 76 per cent. As more squadrons transition from the F/A-18 to the F-35B/C,

Marine Corps Hornets played a significant role in the war against the so-called Islamic State in Iraq and Syria, such as this colourful example from VMFA-232 'Red Devils', armed with both standard and laser JDAMs, as well as a live AIM-9X. (USMC/1stLt Matthew Gregory)

more Hornet airframes will become available for spares and for culling 'best of remaining breed' fleets. Additionally, with most foreign F/A-18 operators currently seeking Hornet replacements, the USMC is considering purchasing these aircraft to ensure it has the parts and airframes necessary to sustain the Hornet through the planned 2030 completion of the F-35 transition.

Operation Inherent Resolve

Marine F/A-18 squadrons remain extremely busy, supporting Special Purpose Marine Air-Ground Task Forces (SPMAGTFs), Marine Rotational Forces, Theater Security Packages, Unit Deployment Program commitments, TACAIR Integration deployments aboard navy aircraft carriers, and dozens of exercises and courses annually. Additionally, the type remains a critical component of joint force combat operations in the Middle East.

Since 2015, VMFAs have deployed to 'undisclosed locations' along the Arabian Gulf in support of Operation Inherent Resolve, the US combat effort aimed at destroying the so-called Islamic State in Iraq and Syria (ISIS). Deployed as the aviation combat element for SPMAGTF – Crisis Response – Central Command, these squadrons provide the full range of Hornet combat capabilities in support of special operations forces, Iraqi military and Syrian rebel groups engaged in the fight against ISIS. Ordnance employed during OIR has predominantly been 500lb (227kg) JDAMs, both the standard GPS-only GBU-38 and the dual-mode GBU-54 Laser JDAM, with occasional employment of Laser Mavericks and the new APKWS laser-guided 2.75in (70mm) rockets.

In addition to land-based deployments in support of OIR, Marine Hornets aboard Navy carriers have also contributed to the fight against ISIS. As the Navy has completed its transition from the legacy F/A-18C to the F/A-18E/F Super Hornet, Marine Hornet deployments aboard carriers have tapered off, with only one squadron – VMFA-323 'Death Rattlers' – remaining committed to the Corps' TACAIR Integration (TAI) agreement with the Navy as of early 2020. The 'Death Rattlers' embarked on the final Marine Hornet carrier deployment in summer 2020 aboard the USS *Nimitz* (CVN 68). Moving forward, Marine F-35Cs will pick up the TAI torch, with VMFA-314 'Black Knights' at Miramar being the first C-model F-35 squadron in the Marine Corps.

Transforming VMFA – the F-35 Lightning II

The Lockheed Martin F-35 Lightning II is the Marine Corps' first fifth-generation fighter. While some disagreement exists over precisely what constitutes fifth-generation features, the term generally applies to aircraft designed for low-observability (including low radar cross-section, reduced infrared signature and low-probability-of-intercept sensors), multirole capability, high manoeuvrability and the ability to network with other aircraft and ground systems to share tactically-relevant data quickly. The appearance of the F-35 echoes that of Lockheed's F-22 Raptor – the world's first fifth-generation fighter – complete with low-observable design and a radar-absorbent coating to reduce its 'visibility' to radar. What separates the F-35 from any previous tactical aircraft – including the F-22 – is the number of advanced sensors it employs and the aircraft's ability to fuse data from those sensors onto a unified display. Using a variety of datalinks, the F-35 can share data collected by its sensors with other aircraft, enhancing the lethality and survivability of those aircraft. The current acquisition plan includes a total of 420 F-35s for the Marine Corps, with 353 being short take-off/vertical landing F-35Bs and 67 being F-35Cs for operation aboard US Navy aircraft carriers.

The F-35's sensor system consists of the Northrop-Grumman AN/APG-81 AESA radar, the AN/AAQ-37 Distributed Aperture System (DAS), the AN/AAQ-40 Electro-Optical Targeting System (EOTS) and the BAE AN/ASQ-239 Electronic Warfare/Countermeasure (EW/CM) system. Individually, each of these sensors represents a potent combat system equal to or better than similar systems equipping current fourth-generation fighters. But unlike those aircraft, the F-35 fuses data from these sensors into a single cockpit display (L3's Large Area Avionics Display), with much of that information also being projected onto the inside of the pilot's visor through the Rockwell-Collins Helmet-Mounted Display System (HMDS).

The HMDS is a more advanced development of the concept utilised by the JHMCS used by Marine F/A-18 pilots. Instead of a heads-up display providing basic flight data like heading, airspeed and altitude directly in the pilot's forward line of sight, that data is projected on the inside of the pilot's visor, meaning anywhere he or she looks, that data is visible. Like the JHMCS, the HMDS displays target symbology as well, able to provide directional cues for the pilot to look to find a target or other item of interest. Targets displayed in the HMDS could come from the EOTS, radar, EW system, or DAS – often a combination of one or more sensors working together.

The transition from the F/A-18 to the F-35 is well underway. As of mid-2020, three Hornet squadrons have transitioned to the F-35B, while VMFA-314 'Black Knights' at MCAS Miramar began transitioning to the F-35C in March, the first USMC squadron to accept the conventional naval variant of the Lightning II. (US Navy/LCDR Darin Russell)

The HDMS is coupled to the DAS, which consists of six IR sensors positioned to give overlapping coverage all around the aircraft, resulting in a system that provides pilots with spherical 360° situational awareness during day or night. Of note, DAS gives pilots the ability to 'see' through the aircraft by projecting a fused image from its sensors onto the visor. The DAS provides missile warning through plume detection and tracking of a missile's heat signature as well as identification and tracking of other aircraft, providing pilots with unprecedented awareness of potential ground and air threats. The sensors used by the DAS provide extremely high resolution, advertised as being 'near 20/20 acuity'. The system can also track moving targets on the ground and detect the wakes of watercraft long after they are no longer perceptible to the human eye.

In lieu of an external targeting pod, the F-35 employs the on-board EOTS. Housed in a stealthy, faceted sapphire enclosure under the nose, the EOTS consists of an infrared sensor capable of detecting and tracking surface and air targets and functioning as an infrared search and track (IRST) device, a laser rangefinder, laser spot tracker and a laser designator to 'lase' targets for attack with laser-guided weapons or generate target grid coordinates for engagement with GPS-guided weapons. The EOTS utilises many components from Lockheed's proven Sniper XR pod, which remains one of the most capable targeting pods available for fourth-generation aircraft. In 2015, Lockheed Martin announced development of the Advanced EOTS, which will add a high-definition electro-optical sensor, a short-wave IR sensor and a laser pointer to direct JTACs and other pilots to targets without having to use a targeting laser. Advanced EOTS will be introduced with the Block 4 software package.

The electronic warfare system provides defensive and offensive EW capabilities, able to detect, classify and accurately locate threat emitters, with relevant threat information fed to the pilot's fused cockpit display and into the HMDS. The F-35 can share threat data with other aircraft via Link 16 or – if sharing with other F-35s – the Multifunction Advanced Datalink (MADL). When active countermeasures are required to defeat a threat, the EW/CM system automatically deploys chaff or flares. In addition to the EW/CM system, the F-35 employs another BAE product – the ALE-70 towed decoy – as an additional defence against radar-guided missiles. Some defence experts have speculated the decoy has an offensive function as well, with the ability to 'bait' an enemy into switching his radar on long enough for the F-35's sensors to locate it for precision attack.

The Northrop-Grumman AN/ASQ-242 Communications, Navigation and Identification (CNI) system is an integrated avionics package performing 27 functions that typically require over a dozen separate systems in other aircraft. In addition to the numerous datalinks utilised by the F-35, the CNI manages voice and data communications across multiple waveforms, multiple navigation aids, identification friend or foe, a radar altimeter, and numerous landing systems, with the ability to perform multiple functions simultaneously.

F-35 weapons

For surface attack, the F-35B employs precision-guided bombs and an optional 25mm cannon carried in a centreline pod. Derived from the Harrier's five-barrelled GAU-12,

The F-35 was designed from the outset to carry external ordnance and stores for 'day 2' operations once an enemy's air defence infrastructure has been crippled. Here ordnance Marines aboard the USS *Wasp* load live GBU-12 laser-guided bombs onto an F-35B from VMFA-121. (US Navy/PO 3rd Class Sean Gal)

Cannons have long been effective close air support weapons. Marine F-35Bs and F-35Cs can carry the GAU-22 cannon in a low-observable external pod. With a rate of fire of 3,300 rounds per minute, the GAU-22 is a four-barrelled variant of the combat-proven GAU-12 cannon carried by Marine AV-8B Harrier IIs. (US Navy/Cmdr Victor Chen)

the General Dynamics GAU-22/A four-barrelled Gatling-type 25mm fires up to 3,300 rounds per minute and is ideal for attacking everything from dismounted infantry to heavy armour. Though highly accurate, the pod only carries 220 rounds of ammunition, limiting its use to a handful of passes.

The F-35B is cleared to carry a broad range of precision-guided munitions, but primarily carries 500lb (227kg) laser-guided bombs and 1,000lb (454kg) JDAMs. As Major Brian Hansell, F-35 division head at MAWTS-1 explained, '*We're carrying GBU-12s and GBU-32s like we always have, and now we are carrying (dual mode) GBU-49s as well, so a moving-target weapon.*' The F-35B has the ability to carry two 500lb or 1,000lb bombs internally for missions in which low observability is required. Additionally, the B-model can carry four additional bombs externally on four underwing pylons. Emphasising the flexibility this offers, Major Hansell said, '*That's the beauty of the F-35. It can be a fifth-gen, low-observable aircraft on day one (of a conflict), but on day 30, I can configure my aircraft to be just like any fourth-gen aircraft. I can load my bombs externally, I can strap on a gun pack, and I can provide everything that a legacy fourth-generation aircraft could provide. It gives you that flexibility.*'

The F-35C, which the Marines are acquiring for service aboard Navy aircraft carriers under the TACAIR Integration agreement, can employ the same air-to-surface weapons as the B, but with its larger weapons bays can also carry 2,000lb (907kg) weapons like the GBU-31 JDAM internally. For counterair operations, both variants can carry up to four AIM-120C AMRAAMs internally (two if carrying internal bombs) and two AIM-9X Sidewinders on launch rails mounted under the wingtips.

The Navy's new Advanced Anti-Radiation Guided Missile — Extended Range, or AARGM-ER – is being designed by Orbital ATK for carriage inside the weapons bay of the F-35C. Based on the AGM-88E AARGM (itself a development of the AGM-88 High-Speed Anti-Radiation Missile), Orbital's design takes the guidance system and warhead of the current missile and places them in an entirely new design. With strakes running along either side of the missile's fuselage and no mid-body control surfaces, the AARGM-ER's design is optimised for internal carriage in the weapons bays of the F-35C (and conceivably, the F-35A) and enhanced resistance to countermeasures.

F-35 tactics

Historically, the USMC and US Air Force have clashed over how best to employ aircraft in combat, particularly regarding Marine aviation's *raison d'etre*, CAS. Investment by both services in the F-35 has closed that gap, with the Marines, US Air Force and US Navy all working together to develop a common set of tactics, techniques and procedures (TTPs) for F-35 employment. As the source of training and readiness manuals for all Marine aircraft, MAWTS-1 is the lead Marine unit in helping develop the joint tactics manual for the F-35. As Major Hansell explained, '*We integrate with TOPGUN and the 6th Weapons Squadron, which are the Navy and Air Force weapons schools. As a tri-service effort we continually refine our TTPs, so we work on the next version of our tactics manual. That is a non-stop, never-ending process, where we're always refining our tactics.*' He continued, '*We all take advantage of each other's test resources, each other's tactical test and evaluation efforts, and we work to come up with the right answer together, so that when we publish a tactics manual, we feel confident as to our answer. Certainly, there will always be different interests. The Navy will be focused on carrier air wing integration more than the Air Force, but ideally, we're all coming to that right answer on how to optimise F-35 tactics and then publish that as a tri-service effort.*'

Marines take delivery – pilot perspectives

Lockheed Martin delivered the Marine Corps' first two production F-35Bs to Marine Fighter-Attack Training Squadron 501 (VMFAT-501) 'Warlords' at Eglin Air Force Base, Florida on 11 January 2012. Though under operational control of the Air Force's 33rd Fighter Wing at Eglin, VMFAT-501 reported to Marine Aircraft Group 31 (MAG-31) at MCAS Beaufort in South Carolina, where the squadron has since relocated. The Warlords' mission at Eglin was to train the initial batch of Marine F-35 pilots, who were hand-selected from the Harrier and Hornet communities. Pilots chosen for the F-35 were second or third-tour aviators with multiple instructor qualifications, with many having experience running various departments within a squadron such as maintenance, operations and logistics. As the initial group of pilots would be tasked with building the Marine F-35 community from the ground up, the Marine Corps deemed these qualifications and this administrative experience critical to the programme.

33rd Fighter Wing

After graduating from the F-35 course at Eglin, pilots either stayed at VMFAT-501 to help build the instructor cadre and further develop the training syllabus, or they went to Yuma to help establish VMFA-121 'Green Knights' – which had been an F/A-18D squadron – as the Corps' first operational F-35 squadron. The 'Green Knights' received their first two F-35Bs on 20 November 2012.

These first deliveries occurred while Lockheed Martin was still doing developmental testing on the F-35. Known as 'concurrency', this arrangement allowed the services to accept early production aircraft with full knowledge they were not representative of the final F-35 configuration. This approach presented numerous advantages, such as allowing the services to establish TTPs for the new type, test maintenance forecasts and scheduling in a far more realistic environment than a test unit, and simply build pilot and maintainer experience in the type before it was cleared for deployment. Concurrency had several disadvantages as well, the most significant being that as more aircraft were delivered, any major deficiencies identified through ongoing testing would have to be corrected in more fleet aircraft. Concurrency also ran the risk of bad publicity, with early software blocks not having anywhere near the capability of the Block 2B update the Marines set as a benchmark for VMFA-121 to declare initial operational capability (IOC) in July 2015 with ten aircraft in that configuration. Defence media reporting on the F-35 during this time trended negative, focusing on what these early-build aircraft could not do, which was both a function of software maturity and flight envelope restrictions based on airspeed, G-limit and manoeuvring conditions the test team simply had not cleared yet.

These flight envelope restrictions frustrated the experienced pilots who transitioned from Harriers or Hornets to the F-35. Major Hansell at MAWTS-1 recalled those early days: '*The frustrations were in the earlier days of the F-35 with concurrency. We were flying a very early-build aircraft that wasn't fully mature. The Block 1 aircraft didn't have the maturity or the capability that the jets we're currently flying have.*' Addressing the flight envelope restrictions, Hansel said, '*I can't recall the exact specifics, but it was something like no faster than .85 Mach. The G-limit was really low. You really couldn't take the jet through its full envelope or to its full tactical capability in those days. With concurrency, that's a natural thing you would expect, but you're interacting with fleet pilots flying F-18s, so they're getting a false impression of the F-35 early on, which is different from the impression you'd get now flying a fully-capable F-35. (Concurrency) created a lot of bad publicity, because the message didn't get out that we were flying a pre-IOC, early-lot aircraft. It was just viewed as 'Why isn't this thing as capable as it should be?' Now, if we started from today, people would be like 'Oh my God, that's an amazing aircraft!' But we have five years of baggage that is frustrating sometimes.*'

In 2013, then-Captain Rob Guyette was an F-35B pilot who recently transitioned from the F/A-18D and was serving as VMFA-121's flight officer. Though he experienced the same frustrations as Major Hansell at the time, he also had high praise for the Lightning II's flight control systems. '*As a pilot, I love it. It's extremely easy to fly. In terms of stick and rudder skills, compared to a Cessna 172 or something like that, I would say a Cessna 172 is much more challenging to stick-and-rudder fly than the F-35. The test pilots have done a really nice job of refining the flight control laws, so that if you want to put the jet in a place, it just goes there. I make the comparison where the F-18 was kind of like a hatchet, you know, where it's like 'I wanna go that way,' and the F-18 would just use power and aerodynamics to get there – and I love the F-18 – but the F-35 is more like a scalpel. I mean, it is right there. Very, very precise to a level that almost kind of lulls you to sleep a little bit, because everything is so automated, whereas an F-18 is a digital fly-by-wire flight control system aircraft. The F-35 is the next level of that, I mean the landing checklist for an F-35 is 'landing gear handle down, taxi light on,' that's it. It puts the flaps down, reconfigures its angle of attack, trims itself out.'*

While the early-block F-35s were easy to fly, the sensor-fused display – one of the key components making the F-35 a fifth-generation fighter – took some getting used to. Describing his experiences with sensor fusion in the Block 2A in 2013, Guyette said, '*What we're running into now that we're starting to develop the tactics for fighting the aircraft, because there's so much information being presented to you in such*

The F-35B relies on a downward-vectoring exhaust nozzle and a lift fan for short and vertical takeoffs and landings.
(Lockheed Martin/Andy Wolfe)

a digestible way, that it's almost like you have to increase the bandwidth of your brain, literally, to be able to assimilate all of that tactical information, and then make decisions.' Fine-tuning sensor fusion and filtering what should get displayed out of the all the information being gathered by the radar, the EOTS, the DAS and the EW system has been a major focus of the test community. In an interview six years later while flying Block 30P02 aircraft, Major Hansell observed, '*It's better. The fusion itself has gotten much better in the later software builds. It is a fused picture that we're being presented with, but you still need to process that on your own.*' The end result of all that information being presented to pilots is greater situational awareness – unprecedented in Marine Corps aviation history – not just for the F-35 pilot, but for any aircraft or ground systems connected to the aircraft via datalink.

When asked what the F-35 brings to the fight, Hansell replied, '*Lethality and survivability, and I would go so far as to say relevance. It is a different fight in the year 2019 than it was in 2000-2001. It is fundamentally a more advanced threat, and to be survivable and lethal in that battle, you need a more advanced, more capable aircraft. If you reference the Commandant's planning guidance, the most recent version of that, we are expected to live inside the WEZ (Weapons Engagement Zone) and go up against the peer threat, and to do that, you need a capable aircraft. I feel like with the F-35, we can operate in that environment successfully, be lethal and survivable, and I couldn't do that in a previous platform.*' Describing the enhanced situational awareness, the sensor-fused display gives, Hansell told the author, '*As an F-35 pilot – not because I'm a good pilot, but because it's a very good aircraft – I have a lot of situational awareness. The jet sees a lot, and it provides me with a fused picture that tells me what's going on in the battlefield. I'm able to communicate that verbally or via datalinks and provide that information to anyone that's in the battlespace with me. That's probably one of the biggest benefits.*'

The road to IOC

Between taking delivery of its first F-35Bs and declaring initial operational capability with the type in July 2015, VMFA-121 worked diligently to develop the initial training and readiness (T&R) manual for the F-35 community, as well as all the in-house departments critical to the functioning of a deployable fighter squadron. Though MAWTS-1 is typically responsible for developing and revising T&R manuals, the squadron lacked an F-35 division at the time, leaving VMFA-121 to lay the foundation future F-35 squadrons would be built upon. Speaking in May 2013, then-Captain Jack Cronan, an F-35 pilot with VMFA-121 said of the process, '*Whatever standard we come up with here, that's going to be the building blocks that the other squadrons are going to branch off of. We have a couple of F-35 subject matter experts (at MAWTS-1). Their MOS is not F-35 at this point, but there's a Hornet pilot and a Harrier pilot over there who are the F-35s SMEs, and they help us as far as tactics development.*'

In addition to working locally on developing the T&R manual and ensuring it aligned with all the expected tasks for IOC, VMFA-121 sent pilots to Lockheed Martin's plant in Fort Worth, Texas to fly forthcoming software blocks in a simulator. As Guyette explained, '*We travel to Fort Worth and fly that software block (2B) in a kind of developmental simulator. Then the pilot comes back to Yuma and develops a plan with 'Okay, here's what the jet will be able to do, here's how we're going to start flowing our training plan to get x number of pilots ready to go in July 2015.*'

As VMFA-121 worked towards IOC, the squadron also began flying with other Yuma and Miramar-based pilots and crews on other platforms to integrate operations with the F-35. In October 2013, the 'Green Knights' flew F-35s in the WTI course for the first time, exposing students and instructors alike to the type's capabilities. January 2014 saw the establishment of an F-35 division at MAWTS. By that October, the two MAWTS-1 F-35 instructors had established a WTI syllabus for the F-35B, and went through the fall WTI course (1-15) as students for a dry-run of the syllabus before accepting the first WTI students from the fleet in April 2015.

Out to sea – F-35B OT-1

The Marine Corps purchased the F-35B with the intent of operating it aboard L-class carriers in support of MEUs. Before any squadron could deploy aboard a ship, the Marines needed to establish the TTPs for shipboard operations. From 18 to 28 May 2015, 10 pilots from VMFA-121, VMFAT-501 and VMX-22 embarked aboard the USS *Wasp* (LHD 1) for Operational Test – One (OT-1), an intensive period of shipboard operations intended to evaluate and establish foundational TTPs for operating the F-35B aboard a carrier.

Using a mix of four Block 2B and two Block 3I aircraft, OT-1 built off data gathered during developmental testing (DT), which started in October 2011. The *Wasp* had supported the DT-1 and DT-2 embarks, as the ship had deck spots 7 and 9 reinforced with a thermal coating to withstand the down-blast from the F-35's powerful Pratt & Whitney F135 engine. Additionally, the Navy installed servers for the F-35's Autonomic Logistics Information System (ALIS), which allows F-35 squadrons to effectively manage maintenance and readiness, aboard the *Wasp* in 2014. Though the aircraft utilised for OT-1 belonged to VMFA-121 and VMFAT-501 and most of the pilots participating hailed from those squadrons, planning and oversight for the detachment fell to VMX-22. Along with

Captain Nikhil Kesireddy (left), an AV-8B Harrier pilot , and Major Nathan Corkill (right), an F-35B pilot, both with VMFA-211 'Avengers' walk back to the hangar after a mixed formation flight that represented -211's final Harrier flight as the squadron has transitioned to the F-35. (Joe Copalman)

evaluating shipboard flight operations during both day and night, the objectives of OT-1 included assessments of the suitability of F-35-specific support equipment for shipboard operations, the ability of maintainers to work on the aircraft in a shipboard environment, communications interoperability between the ship and the F-35, and the effectiveness of the launch and recovery software used by F-35 landing signal officers (LSOs).

Making the grade

Prior to declaring Initial Operational Capability (IOC) on 31 July 2015, VMFA-121 had to pass an Operational Readiness Inspection. This week-long inspection evaluated the squadron's ability to deploy and conduct the full spectrum of combat operations expected of the type at the time – CAS, armed reconnaissance, anti-air warfare, large-force strikes, assault support escort and interdiction. Addressing a media briefing at the 2016 Royal International Air Tattoo at RAF Fairford, then-Deputy Commandant for Aviation Lieutenant General Jon Davis spoke highly of VMFA-121, which passed the ORI. '*We started with a variety of scenarios, and in every one, the squadron exceeded our expectations. The CAS missions went really well, but the mission that stood out for me was the visual armed reconnaissance, where we simulated a high-end SAM threat in the target area. It was up to the pilots to find the threat using the jet's sensors, locate the ground targets, and hit them as well,*' Davis recalled. He continued, '*With an older legacy jet, you've had to take out the SAM site first and work from there – not in this case. These four F-35 pilots did it all simultaneously. In the debrief afterwards, they told us 'we found all the targets in 22 minutes and had destroyed them all within 30 minutes – with just our four aircraft.*'

Redesignation, relocation and first deployments

The Marine F-35 community reached another milestone on 30 June 2016 as Marine Attack Squadron (VMA)-211 became the first Harrier squadron to transition to the F-35B. The 'Avengers' held a re-designation and change of command ceremony at MCAS Yuma to mark the transition. The transition began in January 2016, with the transfer of personnel from Yuma-based VMFA-121 to VMA-211 to begin setting up the maintenance infrastructure for the F-35 while the squadron continued to operate the Harrier through the beginning of May. The 'Avengers' received the first two of a planned 16 F-35s on 9 May, were declared 'safe for flight' after an inspection the week prior to the re-designation ceremony and made the squadron's first official F-35B flight on 29 June. The experienced hands at VMFA-121 assisted the 'Avengers' throughout the transition process, with incoming VMFA-211 commanding officer Lt Col Chad Vaughn telling the author, '*They gave birth to the squadron. The Marine Corps made -121 very big. They added a lot of extra people and extra aircraft, and those people and aircraft detached at the beginning of the year and came over (to -211).*'

Another major milestone for the Marine F-35 community came in January 2017, with the permanent relocation of VMFA-121 from Yuma to MCAS Iwakuni in Japan. The squadron departed Yuma on 9 January with ten aircraft, with six more F-35Bs following a few months later, bringing the squadron to full strength. As of this writing, VMFA-121 remains the only US F-35 squadron from any service permanently stationed abroad, but that will change in 2021 with the basing of two USAF F-35A squadrons at RAF Lakenheath in the UK. Upon relocation to Iwakuni, VMFA-121 began working closely with the 31st MEU, the Marine Corps' permanently forward-deployed Indo-Pacific response force.

On 5 March 2018, VMFA-121 became the first Lightning II squadron to deploy at sea, embarking six F-35Bs aboard the USS *Wasp* (LHD 1) supporting the 31st MEU's spring patrol, spending two months at sea before returning to Japan. This was followed shortly by VMFA-211 making the first combat deployment with the F-35, embarking aboard the USS *Essex* (LHD 2) in July 2018 for an eight-month cruise as part of the 13th MEU's Aviation Combat Element. During this deployment, the six F-35Bs flew combat missions against the Taliban in Afghanistan in support of Operation Freedom's Sentinel and against ISIS in Iraq and Syria in support of Operation Inherent Resolve. In addition to validating the F-35B in combat and as part of a MEU, this deployment gave Marine and Navy maintainers and logisticians an opportunity to assess how to better support the F-35 during sustained at-sea operations. It also allowed both services to evaluate how the F-35 interfaces with ships, other aircraft and ground forces in an operational environment, data from which is being used to refine TTPs for future F-35 MEU deployments and improve the communications infrastructure aboard the Navy's fleet of amphibious assault ships.

An F-35B from VMFA-121 departing the *Wasp* in February 2019 on another 31st MEU deployment. The 'Green Knights' of VMFA-121 made the first F-35B shipboard deployment aboard the USS *Wasp* (LHD 1) in support of the 31st MEU in March 2018. (US Navy/MC2 Sarah Myers)

Initial accession pilots

In a sign of the program's maturity, in February 2017, VMFAT-501 graduated the Corps' first two initial accession/*ab initio* Lightning II pilots at MCAS Beaufort. Up to that point, all F-35B pilots had converted from other platforms with several years and hundreds, if not thousands of flight hours before even touching an F-35, the two recently graduated pilots entered the training pipeline with no military flight experience. After graduation, both pilots reported to VMFA-121 at Iwakuni.

The third operational squadron to transition to the F-35B was VMFA-122 'Flying Leathernecks' (previously the 'Werewolves' or 'Crusaders', depending on the dominant religion of the region the squadron deployed to), an F/A-18C squadron from MCAS Beaufort. After standing down with the Hornet, VMFA-122 relocated to MCAS Yuma, making its first flight with the F-35B on 29 March 2018.

First Marine F-35 loss

As of this writing, the Marines have only lost one F-35. On 28 September 2018, an engine fuel tube in a VMFAT-501 F-35B ruptured, forcing the pilot to eject over Little Barnwell Island near MCAS Beaufort. While the pilot survived with minor injuries, the aircraft was a total loss, resulting in a temporary grounding of Marine F-35s so that all engines could be checked for defects. These inspections – and that of the wreckage – revealed a manufacturing defect on 117 engines that was quickly rectified.

Sensor-shooter integration

In addition to sharing targeting and threat information with other aircraft, the F-35 can use its sensors and datalink to push data to land and sea-based systems. Though the multi-function advanced datalink (MADL) had initially been designed for secure data exchange between F-35s within a four-ship division, the Marines and Navy learned that equipping a ship employing the Aegis Combat System with MADL antennas gave the ship a powerful, far-reaching sensor to augment the Aegis radar and enhance the fleet's situational awareness. On 13 September 2016, a Marine F-35B from VMX-1 conducted an integration test with the Navy's unimaginatively named USS *Desert Ship* (LLS 1), a simulated warship with a functioning AEGIS Combat System installed. During the test, the F-35 detected and tracked an MQM-107 target drone, pushing targeting data to the AEGIS via MADL. This provided enough information for the 'ship' to launch a Standard SM-6 surface-to-air missile at the drone, scoring a direct hit.

Marine F-35s have also worked closely with ground-based artillery systems, specifically the M142 High Mobility Artillery Rocket System, or HIMARS. Based on the US Army's five-ton Family of Medium Tactical Vehicles truck chassis, HIMARS utilises a six-shot launcher firing the same rockets as the M270 Multiple Launch Rocket System (MLRS). While costlier to acquire and operate than the Corps' 155mm (6.1in) M777 towed howitzers, HIMARS is far more mobile and can engage targets at longer range – both important attributes with the services focusing on operating in anti-access/area denial (A2/AD) environments. In recent years, the Marines have added the GPS-guided M31 Guided MLRS (GMLRS, pronounced 'GIMM-lers') rocket to the HIMARS arsenal, giving the system the ability to deliver a 200lb (91kg) warhead over 43.5miles (70km) with the same accuracy as a JDAM.

During WTI course 1-19 in October 2018, an F-35B located a target on the Chocolate Mountain Aerial Gunnery Range, used its sensors to generate a targetable coordinate, then passed that information via datalink to a HIMARS crew for engagement. This was the first time a HIMARS had fired a live GMLRS rocket at a target passed along by an F-35, and it resulted in a successful engagement, with the target – a Conex shipping container – being destroyed.

Given the Corps' renewed focus on maritime integration with the Navy and A2/AD operations in the Pacific, the ability for a C-130-transportable long-range precision rocket system to receive targeting data from a stealthy F-35 operating within an enemy's air defence weapons engagement zone could be extremely useful. Further, the Marines recently proved the utility of HIMARS in a maritime environment, successfully engaging a target with an M142 tied down to the deck of an amphibious assault ship. Two further developments – the 2020 introduction of the GMLRS-ER extended-range GPS-guided rocket with a maximum range of 93mi (150km), and the Marine Corps' intent to acquire an anti-ship missile compatible with the MLRS launch pods will further enhance the range, versatility and lethality of F-35/HIMARS teaming in the future.

'Lightning Carrier' development

For decades, the standard complement of AV-8B Harriers assigned to MEUs at sea has been six aircraft. This has been expanded in times of war, with some L-class amphibious carriers taking on up to 24 AV-8Bs to serve as 'Harrier carriers', which the Navy and Marine Corps used to good effect in Operation Desert Storm and Operation Iraqi Freedom. With the two newest L-class carriers – the USS *America* (LHA 6) and USS *Tripoli* (LHA 7) – built without well decks for launching and recovering amphibious assault vehicles and other seaborne ship-to-shore connectors, both ships have more space below deck for aircraft, spare parts and maintenance equipment, increasing the feasibility of 'Lightning carriers'. The Navy and Marine Corps have been incrementally

In September 2020, 10 F-35Bs from VMFA-211 'Avengers' joined the Royal Air Force's No. 617 Squadron aboard the HMS *Queen Elizabeth* (R08) for the first cross-decking operation in a planned long-term relationship between the UK Armed Forces and the US Marine Corps. (Royal Navy/LPhot Mark Johnson)

increasing the number of F-35s operating aboard L-class carriers to develop TTPs for 'Lightning Carrier' operations.

In early April 2019, VMFA-121 flew at least ten F-35Bs from the deck of the USS *Wasp* in the Philippine Sea during exercise Balikatan 2019. That September, VMFA-122 'Flying Leathernecks' participated in carrier qualification aboard the *America* with a detachment of 12 F-35Bs. A month later, the squadron returned to the *America* with 13 aircraft, the largest shipboard contingent of F-35Bs to date, for 'Harrier Carrier' trials, testing sortie rates, deck cycles and the ship's ability to support sustained F-35 surge operations at sea. Additionally, the detachment gave the other ships in the *America* Amphibious Ready Group (ARG) experience working with F-35s. As the F-35's communications and data-sharing capabilities currently exceed those of the ships in the ARG, experience in overcoming this imbalance is critical until the Navy upgrades its systems to better receive and exploit the information pushed to ships by F-35s. In September 2020, VMFA-211 sent a 10-aircraft detachment to the UK to begin work-ups for cross-decking aboard the Royal Navy's new carrier, HMS *Queen Elizabeth* (R08), the first steps in a partnership expected to endure over the coming decades.

Enter the F-35C

On 21 January 2020, the first of a planned 67 Marine F-35Cs arrived at MCAS Miramar. The 'Black Knights' of VMFA-314 are the first of four Marine squadrons to receive the C-model Lightning II, as the Corps remains committed to its TACAIR Integration obligation to provide four carrier-capable squadrons to the US Navy. Given the lim-

In addition to the F-35B, the Marines Corps is also acquiring 67 F-35Cs to sustain its commitment to its TACAIR Integration obligation with the US Navy. The first Hornet squadron to transition to the F-35C is VMFA-314 'Black Knights', with the first C-model Lightning II arriving at MCAS Miramar on 21 January 2020. (Kevin Whitehead)

ited number of the variant being acquired for USMC service, there is no Marine fleet replacement squadron (FRS) for pilots transitioning to the F-35C. Rather, they train with Navy F-35C FRS units like VFA-125 'Rough Raiders' at NAS Lemoore. Naval Air Systems Command certified the 'Black Knights' safe for flight on 20 March 2020, enabling the squadron to begin flight operations at Miramar.

Block 4 upgrade and the future of the F-35

While advances in F-35 capability have mostly come with the introduction of new software blocks – 2B for IOC, 3F for full warfighting capability, etc – updates within these software blocks occur every April and October utilising a construct called Continuous Capability Development and Delivery (C2D2). The C2D2 construct enables the introduction of new capabilities or expansion of existing ones, as well as the ability to fix minor software bugs. In mid-2019, Marine F-35Bs flew with Block 30P02 software, the '02' indicating it was the second production tape for that block, which was then upgraded to 30P03 in October. At the same time, a major upgrade to Block 4 was just starting to be implemented in fall 2019, bringing a wide range of new and expanded capabilities to Marine F-35s.

The Block 4 upgrade includes 53 upgrades or enhancements, with 80 per cent of those coming from new software, and 20 per cent coming from new hardware like the Advanced EOTS mentioned previously. To configure aircraft for the Block 4 upgrades, Marine F-35s have undergone a process called Technology Refresh 3. This boosted the system memory, installed faster processors and updated the cockpit display. Block 4 capabilities will not hit the fleet all at once, but will be spiralled in via the C2D2 construct between 2020 and 2024.

Block 4 will introduce – among other capabilities not publicly divulged – the following:

- Automatic Ground Collision Avoidance System
- Unmanned teaming capabilities, allowing pilots to control UAVs and possible 'unmanned wingman' systems
- Extended range via 600-gallon (2,271-litre) external drop tanks
- 11 radar and EOTS upgrades
- 13 EW upgrades extending threat detection ranges and speeding up engagement times
- A lower-weight HMDS helmet to reduce pilot neck strain
- AIM-9X Block II compatibility, including a lock-on-after-launch mode allowing the missile to be carried internally
- Expansion of maritime strike capabilities, particularly for the F-35C, which will be able to employ the AGM-153 JSOW-C1
- Tactical nuclear weapons capability, employing the GPS-guided B61 Mod 12 with a variable .3 to 50-kiloton yield and hard-target penetration capability
- Potential inclusion of the dual-mode GBU-54 Laser JDAM
- Various classified capabilities upgrades

The F-35 relies on an unprecedented variety of powerful sensors. Visible in this image are the AN/AAQ-40 Electro-Optical Targeting System under the nose, and two apertures from the AN/AAQ-37 Distributed Aperture System (one forward of the US roundel and one in the base of the windscreen). The AN/APG-81 AESA radar is housed under the nose cone. Data from these sensors is fused on both the pilot's panoramic cockpit display and projected onto the inside visor via the Helmet-Mounted Display System. (Joe Copalman)

When General David Berger took command as the 38th Commandant of the Marine Corps in July 2019, he issued a Commandant's Planning Guidance aimed at transforming the service from a largely static counterinsurgency focus to that of an agile maritime strike force capable of meeting and defeating a peer threat like China in the vast deep-water battlespace of the western Pacific. On 23 March 2020, Marine Corps Combat Development Command released a force-shaping initiative aligned with General Berger's Planning Guidance, which includes the Commandant's intent to reduce the primary aircraft authorised for F-35 squadrons from 16 to 10.

Though seemingly drastic, the F-35 community has long been programmed for a tiered Primary Aircraft Authorization (PAA) structure, with nine of the 20 planned F-35 squadrons set up for 16 aircraft, and the remaining 11 already having a planned 10-aircraft PAA. As of this writing, the Marine Corps has not announced a reduction in the total number of F-35s it plans to acquire, but with a stated need for 54 fewer aircraft, it is likely that such an announcement is forthcoming.

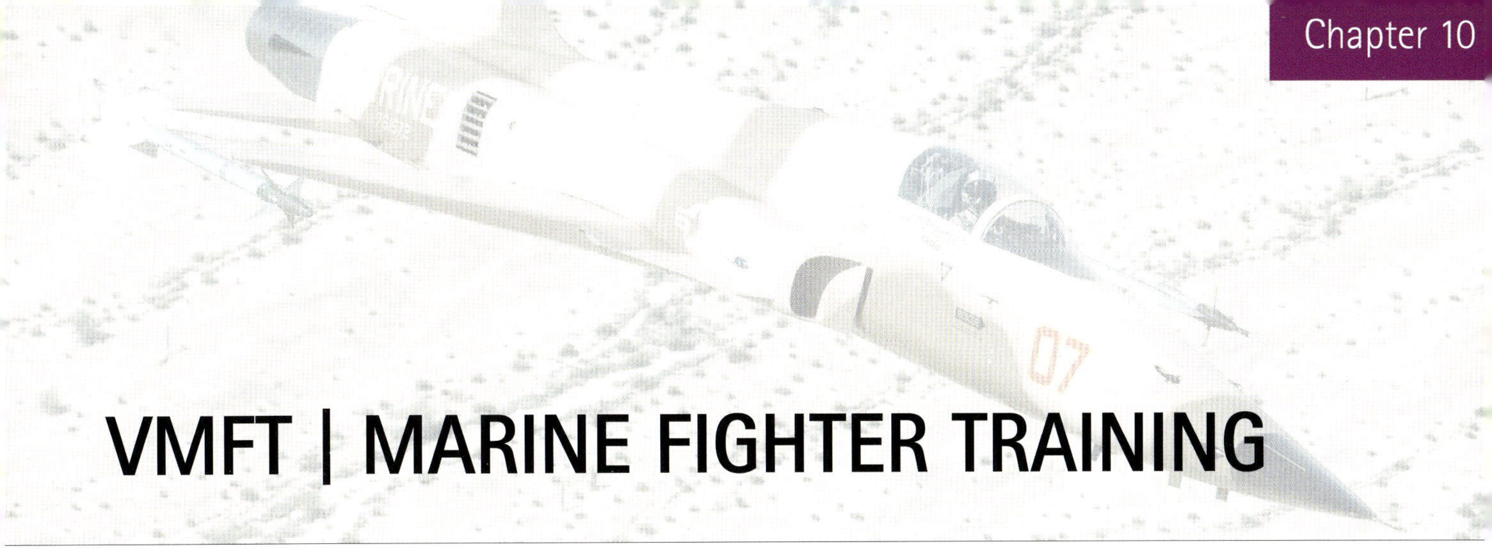

VMFT | MARINE FIGHTER TRAINING

The 'Snipers' of Marine Fighter Training Squadron 401 (VMFT-401) are the sole Marine adversary unit, tasked with providing replication and simulation of threat-nation aircraft and tactics for all deployable aviation communities within Marine aviation. Established at MCAS Yuma in 1986, the 'Snipers' have been flying the Northrop F-5 Tiger II since 1989. While the 'Snipers' support all Marine aviation communities, the squadron's primary 'customers' are the F/A-18 Hornet, F-35 Lightning II and – increasingly – the AV-8B Harrier II communities.

Since its inception, VMFT-401 has been assigned to the 4th Marine Air Wing, the aviation component of Marine Forces Reserve. While most 4th MAW squadrons are comprised mostly of Select Marine Corps Reserve (SMCR – drilling reservists) pilots with a handful of active-duty pilots running the squadron between drill weekends, high demand for adversary support requires a higher proportion of active-duty pilots. The current split in VMFT-401's ready room is about 50 per cent active and 50 per cent SMCR.

Pilots assigned to VMFT-401 typically come from the Marine F/A-18 Hornet community, with a handful coming from the AV-8B Harrier. Given the challenges of flying as

As the Marine Corps' sole adversary squadron, VMFT-401 is tasked with providing 'red air' threat replication and threat simulation for every Marine flying community. Pilots assigned to the unit study threat nation tactics extensively to provide high-fidelity threat presentations. (Joe Copalman)

an adversary, the 'Snipers' recruit only those pilots with around 1,500 or more hours in tactical aircraft, with flight lead and instructor qualifications. In addition to the active-duty and reserve pilots assigned to the squadron, the 'Snipers' rely on F/A-18, F-35 and AV-8B instructor pilots from Marine Aviation Weapons and Tactic Squadron One (MAWTS-1) to provide additional depth to the squadron's bench when needed.

Simulating the bad guys

In the adversary role, the 'Snipers' excel at simulating and replicating threat nation aircraft, tactics and weapons. While VMFT-401 pilots fly the F-5, they do not fly it as an F-5 per se, but rather as if it were any number of threat nation aircraft, aligning as much as they can with known threat nation tactics, techniques and procedures (TTPs). Explaining how the squadron does this, the squadron's Operations Officer Lieutenant Colonel Chad Fitzgerald said, '*The tactics come from a publication called the* Adversary Threat Replication Guide. *It's a classified publication that is our standard. If it's in there, most of us know it and understand it. That's part of the syllabus as you become an adversary pilot, to read that and be familiar with what's in there and how to replicate certain threats.*' The result of this is not just 'metal in the air' for Marine pilots to shoot at, but a competent, thinking adversary providing as faithful a reproduction of threat nation tactics as is possible with the F-5.

Heavily committed

The 'Snipers' support several recurring commitments throughout the year, foremost among these is the Weapons and Tactics Instructor (WTI) course run by MAWTS-1 every spring and autumn. During WTI, the 'Snipers' provide red air for every type of aircraft in the course, supporting each community's air combat manoeuvring or defensive tactics training. It is also the busiest time of year for the squadron, with eight-turn-eight-turn-eight flying schedules (three waves of eight aircraft) being common.

The 'Snipers' also support the Marine F/A-18 Hornet and F-35 Lightning II fleet replacement squadrons (VMFAT-101 'Sharpshooters' at MCAS Miramar and VMFAT501 'Warlords' and VMFAT-502 'Nightmares' at Beaufort, respectively). Presentations flown for FRS support are far more basic than the threat-specific presentations flown against fleet squadrons or during WTI. Despite the simplicity of presentations flown for FRS students, it is a job the 'Snipers' take very seriously. As former VMFT-401 Operations Officer Major Ben Apple said, '*We get to help the blue instructor make his student better. If, at the end of the day, a new student from –101 or –501 goes 'Oooh, that's what I did wrong', and then the next day he goes up and he doesn't make that mistake – that's very rewarding.*'

The squadron's third major commitment is to what was called the Marine Division Tactics Course (MDTC) until recently. This course trains experienced F/A-18 pilots in leading formations of four or more aircraft in air-to-air combat. As MDTC was a prerequisite for WTI, the course was offered twice a year. The introduction and maturation of the F-35 drove a revision of MDTC to a new course simply called 'Pre-WTI', which includes more ground classes and simulator work, with less overall flying time. Aside from these major commitments, the Snipers provide fleet support sorties throughout the year.

Marine adversary pilots typically come from the F/A-18 Hornet community, with roughly 1,000 hours and multiple instructor certifications. Increasingly, AV-8B Harrier and F-35B Lightning pilots have been flying with VMFT-401, either assigned to the squadron or as augments from Marine Aviation Weapons and Tactics Squadron One. (Joe Copalman)

Limits of the F-5

The F-5 remains popular in the adversary community due to its reliability and low operational costs. Despite the type's advantages as an adversary platform, the F-5 has several significant limitations. Thin wings and a small fuselage leave little room for fuel, giving it 40-to-50-minutes endurance. Yuma's proximity to the TCTS (Tactical Combat Training System, a system used to track aircraft during air combat manoeuvring to review during debriefs) range is a saving grace in this regard, but even then, the F-5's short legs sometimes impact the blue team's training objectives.

Another major limitation of the F-5N is its lack of a radar capable of stimulating blue-force threat receivers like fourth- and fifth-generation adversaries can. The capabilities of the Tiger II's Emerson Electric AN/APQ-159 radar are so limited that most F-5 pilots speak of the type as not having a radar at all. Though the radar falls short of providing a useful capability against modern radar warning receivers, some of the F-5Ns flown by VMFT-401 possess a limited electronic attack capability in the form of the AN/ALQ-237 adversary jamming system.

The ALQ-237 is an internal repackaging of the popular AN/ALQ-167 'Filthy Badger' jamming pod used by military adversary and aggressor units to simulate known threat-nation electronic attack capabilities, as well as postulated electronic threats aircrews could reasonably expect to encounter operationally in combat with peer-level threats. When equipped, the system is mounted in the Tiger II's empty gun bays in the nose, with two antennae protruding slightly from the two channels where the gun barrels used to be. The presence of these two black 'nubs' is a tell-tale sign that an F-5 is equipped with the system.

Kremlin controllers

Given the limitations of the F-5's radar, the 'Snipers' have long relied on ground-controlled intercept (GCI) controllers to vector them to intercepts and provide situational awareness. Historically, this aligned with the GCI-centric tactics of most threat nation air arms flying third and early-fourth-generation aircraft, helping provide threat fidelity in addition to general situational awareness.

The 'Snipers' typically have two adversary controllers assigned, on loan from a Marine Aviation Command and Control Squadron (MACCS) and using the radio callsign 'Kremlin'. Describing the role of the 'Kremlin' controllers, VMFT-401 Commanding Officer Lieutenant Colonel Eric Geyer said, '*They truly have a unique and important mission. Without having a super high-fidelity radar (in the F-5) to do presentations, they are giving us callouts on ranges and direction, not only to each other for deconfliction, but to where the threat is as well. They know the picture we're trying to set up and they can help direct that.*' During all adversary sorties over Yuma's TCTS range, a 'Kremlin' controller will sit in the TCTS control facility beside a 'Snipers' pilot (using the callsign 'Comrade') serving as the range training officer for that event.

Staying relevant in the age of fifth-generation fighters

The introduction of the fifth-generation Lockheed F-35 Lightning II has not only increased the demand for adversary support, but the complexity of that support as well. Additionally, the capabilities of threat-nation systems have evolved considerably in recent years, forcing American adversaries to up their threat-replication game. According to Lieutenant Colonel Geyer, '*The threat has progressed so much in the*

VMFT-401 routinely supports the USMC F-35 community. Despite flying a bare-bones 1970s-vintage jet, the 'Snipers' get high marks from Marine F-35 pilots for providing effective simulation of fourth-generation threats. (Joe Copalman)

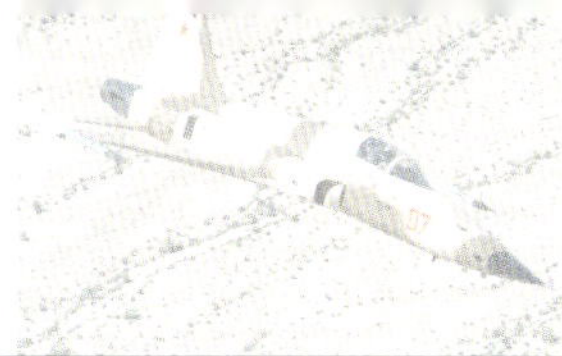

past five years. When I was a mid-level captain to young major, we were talking MiG-29s and a base Flanker threat. These days, with the proliferation and the quick build-up between China and Russia and the new (Flanker) variants, it's tough, especially for a fleet squadron to stay up to date with all that.' As it falls on VMFT-401 to provide Marine fleet pilots with exposure to threat-nation tactics and simulations of enemy technology, the GCI-centric tactics of third-generation Cold War threats fall short of the threat presentations needed to stay relevant. Reliance on GCI for situational awareness has limited the degree to which the 'Snipers' can operate autonomously, as a later fourth-generation threat would. To address the demand for more complex threat presentations, while remaining committed to the reliable, low-cost F-5, the 'Snipers' recently incorporated two major changes that are already having a noticeable impact on the quality of the training the fleet gets from them.

RedNet

For as competent and well-versed in threat-nation tactics as VMFT-401's pilots are, and for as good as the 'Kremlin' controllers are at their jobs, the squadron's reliance on GCI has limited the squadron's ability to provide presentations of late fourth-generation threats. In 2018, the 'Snipers' began using a tablet-based app known as RedNet to help provide more autonomous, higher-level threat presentations. Hailed as a 'game-changer' by Sniper pilots, RedNet effectively gives them the same view of the fight that the 'Kremlin' controller has in the TCTS facility, enabling replication of threats with high-fidelity radars and tactical datalinks.

The technology used in RedNet allows Sniper pilots to see any aircraft carrying a TCTS pod displaying the bearing, range and altitude information for each of them. The only blue air assets not visible on RedNet are F-35s, which do not currently carry TCTS pods, though Lieutenant Colonel Fitzgerald does not see this as a problem. '*With the F-35s, we don't see them. That's actually not a bad thing, because that presents a pretty accurate problem. I shouldn't be able to see them.*' Even with the inability to see F-35s with the system, RedNet gives the 'Snipers' a level of situational awareness about the blue forces unprecedented in the squadron's history. As Lieutenant Colonel Geyer explained, '*I don't have a radar, but if I'm simulating a threat that's got a radar and a link system, I have all the information I need to utilise the weapon systems that have been briefed for the day. It can make you autonomously lethal in a manner that high-end Flankers certainly could be, without having Kremlin having to tell me where everything is all the time.*'

RedNet is a valuable debriefing tool, giving Sniper pilots a record of where and when in the fight they had a valid shot on a blue fighter with the briefed threat weapons for that event. Lieutenant Colonel Geyer explained, '*I can screen-capture stuff, so if I hit a button on there, it saves it to my file so I can go back during the debrief and cycle through the screen captures. We look at 'Okay, there was a shot opportunity here', and run it through a whole system to make sure that yes, the threat missile could have done that and could have killed that person there.*'

In addition to helping the 'Snipers' detect, track and target blue air fighters and validate shots taken during the fight, RedNet has helped the squadron provide tighter and safer presentations for the blue forces. One of the biggest safety issues for adversaries flying the F-5 is kill removal during large-force engagements in which the sky is full of manoeuvring fighters. Describing how RedNet makes kill removal safer, Geyer

The cockpits of the F-5s flown by VMFT-401 are little different than when these aircraft were delivered to the Swiss Air Force in the late 1970s. Recently, the 'Snipers' began using a tablet-based system called 'RedNet' to enhance situational awareness and operate with significantly more autonomy than before when the squadron relied almost entirely on ground controlled intercept controllers. (Joe Copalman)

VMFT-401 flies F-5s in a variety of earth-tone and blue-toned camouflage schemes to make the aircraft even more difficult to track visually against either the ground or the sky. (Joe Copalman)

said, '*As soon as you die you don't just go away, you need to get out of the play of the problem. You want to turn and get out so you're not muddying the picture. Before, you didn't know where everybody was. You're not in Link 16 with them, and they're fighting all around you. I'd get a call from Kremlin, but do those other guys know I'm going to turn that way? Now, Kremlin is still watching, but I can look at my RedNet and know where everybody is, and I can see their altitude on my screen, and I can kill remove in the smartest direction away from everybody.*'

New adversary qualifications

In an effort to further professionalise VMFT-401 as an adversary squadron and ensure it is delivering the most credible and authentic presentations it can to fourth and fifth-generation blue forces, the squadron recently partnered with MAWTS-1 on new advanced qualifications for Sniper pilots. In Marine aviation, the WTI qualification is the pinnacle 'qual' a pilot can receive. Becoming a WTI certifies pilots not just to train their squadrons on the latest tactics, techniques and procedures for their assigned aircraft, but to also serve as planners and integrators with other aviation and ground units in large, combined Marine Air-Ground Task Force operations.

The 'Snipers' regularly support large force events throughout the year. While MDTC can see upwards of a dozen red players all under the command of a single red air mission commander, some of the anti-air warfare events during the WTI course can involve a mixed force of up to 40 aircraft on the red team. While leading such a large force on the blue side nearly always falls on the shoulders of a WTI, the 'Snipers' have historically relied on mission commanders to manage these larger red-force formations. That changed in 2016, when two of VMFT-401's active-duty pilots proposed the creation of an Adversary WTI qualification. As MAWTS-1 lacks an adversary department, the Adversary WTI course is administered in-house at VMFT-401 in accordance with a curriculum the squadron developed with MAWTS-1. Explaining what 'Snipers' with the Adversary WTI qualification bring to the fleet, Major David Haas – himself an Adversary WTI – said, '*It's effectively a doctorate-level adversary qualification. They have an advanced understanding of the adversary picture and are really focused on providing the customer with the best product. They're trained to manage an overwhelmingly large number of assets for presentations that could go on for six hours.*'

MATIs and SMEs

Sniper pilots on track for the Adversary WTI patch prepare for it by first earning the Marine Adversary Tactics Instructor (MATI) qualification. This path mirrors that of Marine F/A-18 pilots on track for WTI, who complete MDTC/Pre-WTI as a prerequisite for the WTI course in Yuma. Just as MDTC trained Hornet pilots to lead formations larger than four aircraft in air-to-air combat, the MATI qualification builds the skills needed for a Sniper pilot to plan, brief, execute and debrief missions involving larger red air formations. Another component of the Adversary WTI qualification training as subject matter experts (SMEs) on specific threat nation tactics or systems. Prospective SMEs spend two to three weeks at Nellis Air Force Base in Nevada working closely with the 64th Aggressor Squadron and the 547th Intelligence Squadron. After being assigned a subject to specialise in, such as Chinese Flankers, Russian radar-guided missiles or any other threat system, the prospective SME studies the subject intensely and prepares a threat brief on that subject for a board of Air Force evaluators. Afterward, the Air Force certifies him similar to an Air Force aggressor pilot going through the same process.

Once a newly certified SME returns to VMFT-401, he is the go-to pilot on his assigned subject, be it a specific Chinese fighter, Russian fighter, or a particular class of missile or other threat system. This is particularly helpful when a blue air 'customer' requests presentations of that specific threat aircraft, as the SME can help the 'Snipers' ensure the highest fidelity in flying that presentation. As Fitzgerald explained, '*We've got those guys immediately on-hand in the brief to say 'Hey, can you tighten us up on this?' And they'll give us the classified rundown on everything we need to know about the bounds that we can operate within for the replication of that threat.*' Elaborating on the depth of expertise the SMEs bring to the squadron, Fitzgerald continued, '*They know stuff that's even outside of the pub because they took that SME course with the 64th Aggressor Squadron, which is a great resource for us to have. Staying tied into a relationship with that unit has paid huge dividends here, not just for our squadron, but we're taking those lectures to the fleet as well. Those guys are giving lectures over at WTI as part of ground school academics, and it's available to fleet squadrons on request as well.*'

Marine F-5s (and their 'blue team' opponents) fly primarily over ranges equipped with the Tactical Combat Training System (TCTS), a network of transponders on the ground that track the movements of aircraft equipped a special TCTS pod. The Snipers use the AN/ASQ-T50(V)2 P5 pod to track air combat training engagements, which are recorded and reviewed during the debrief. (Joe Copalman)

Expansion

The path Marine aviation takes is charted in a document called the Aviation Plan (AvPlan), which is updated annually and reflects the service's aviation priorities as expressed by the Corps' Deputy Commandant for Aviation. For the past several years, the AvPlan has called for an expansion of VMFT-401, with the acquisition of more F-5s and establishment of permanent detachments at Beaufort, Cherry Point and Miramar. With the 2013 budget sequester limiting funds across the breadth of the US military, these dets have not yet been established.

The 2020 Department of Defense budget includes a provision for the purchase of 22 F-5Es from the Swiss Air Force to augment VMFT-401's fleet, as well as those of the two F-5-equipped Navy adversary squadrons. As of this writing, it is not known how many jets from this purchase will go to VMFT-401, nor where they will be based. The 2019 AvPlan calls for the establishment of adversary detachments at Beaufort, Cherry Point and Miramar, with Beaufort taking priority due to the 'Snipers' FRS and MDTC/Pre-WTI commitments there.

The proposed detachments are part of a larger plan called the Composite Training Squadron Concept. In addition to providing air-to-air combat training with F-5s, this concept expands the adversary charter to include the training of Joint Terminal Attack Controllers (JTACs) with light attack aircraft like the Beech AT-6 Coyote or Embraer EMB-314 (A-29) Super Tucano. Just as adversaries free fleet squadrons from burning flight hours on red air sorties that do not check any training and readiness boxes, dedicated JTAC support allows pilots in fleet squadrons to focus on their training and readiness requirements instead of helping JTACs meet theirs. The Marines currently rely on civilian contract support to meet some of their JTAC training needs, but a small fleet of turboprop aircraft capable of employing ordnance would reduce the reliance on contractors.

Whatever path the 'Snipers' commit to, additional F-5s will give the squadron more flexibility to support detachments away from Yuma throughout the year while still being able to consolidate aircraft at one location for large-force events like WTI. Recent developments like RedNet and the Adversary WTIs and SMEs will ensure that the blue pilots will receive the best threat simulation that any F-5 adversaries in the world are capable of providing.

Arguably the most credible assessment of the 'Snipers'' effectiveness is that from Marines who rely on their services, particularly those flying the fifth-generation F-35. Major Brian Hansell, head of MAWTS-1's F-35 Division, had this to say about VMFT-401, '*I will say definitively they are the best at replicating an advanced peer threat, and they do it with some of the oldest red air platforms out there. You're talking about a 1970s F-5, and I'm asking him to replicate an Su-35 or something else from the current decade. That's an incredibly challenging task, yet they're able to do it by training hard and coming up with replication TTPs that work.*'

VMGR | MARINE AERIAL REFUELER TRANSPORT

Few military aircraft can match the longevity and versatility of the Lockheed C-130 Hercules. Having flown the 'Herk' since 1962, the Marines have relied on the type's multi-mission capability perhaps more than any other C-130 operator by maximising the number of mission sets executed by a single variant. Flown by three active-duty and one reserve Marine Aerial Refueler Transport (VMGR) squadrons, the KC-130J is the current Hercules variant operated by the USMC (a second reserve squadron, VMGR-452, is transitioning to the J from the older KC-130T). Known within the VMGR community as the 'Battleherk', the KC-130 provides Marine Air-Ground Task Force (MAGTF) commanders with a long-range heavy-lift asset that is both versatile and flexible.

The Marines currently perform more missions with a single variant of the C-130 than any other Hercules operator worldwide. Per the service's KC-130J/T plan, Marine Battleherks are tasked with the following:

- Conduct aviation operations from expeditionary shore-based sites
- Conduct combat assault transport
- Conduct fixed-wing, rotor-wing and tiltrotor air-to-air refuelling (AAR)
- Conduct aviation-delivered ground refuelling (ADGR)
- Conduct air delivery (AD)
- Provide aviation delivered battlefield illumination (BI)
- Conduct close air support with the Harvest HAWK system
- Conduct multi-sensor image reconnaissance (MIR) with the Harvest HAWK system

Marine KC-130s also routinely perform airborne command and control, with ground and air mission commanders utilising the type's extensive radio suite to coordinate insertions and extractions of raid forces. Recent years have seen Marine Battleherks used in 'shoot and scoot' precision rocket artillery raids when paired with the M142 HIMARS (High-Mobility Artillery Rocket System). With the planned integration of the AN/ALQ-231 Intrepid Tiger II pod, the VMGR community will be adding electronic warfare to its list of mission sets in the near future.

Early operations in Afghanistan

When the Marines entered the fight against al-Qaeda and the Taliban following the 11 September 2001 terror attacks, the VMGR squadrons were flying some of the oldest aircraft in Marine Corps service. Operating from Jacobobad, Pakistan in support of

Tasked with a variety of missions including cargo and troop transport, aerial refuelling, airdrop operations and battlefield illumination, the KC-130J 'Battleherk' is a force multiplier and force extender for the Marine Air-Ground Task Force. (USMC/LCpl Allison Herman)

the 15th and 26th Marine Expeditionary Units (MEUs), a mixed detachment of six aircraft from VMGR-352 'Raiders' and VMGR-252 'Otis' consisted of older KC-130F and KC-130R models, including one F-model built in 1960. Only three of the six aircraft carried any kind of defensive countermeasures system, and none had cockpits compatible with night-vision goggles. Two 'Raider' KC-130s from this detachment participated in the earliest Marine missions in Afghanistan, providing aerial refuelling for AV-8B Harrier IIs from VMA-311 'Tomcats' making the first Harrier strike against al-Qaeda on 3 November. While Pakistan-based 'Herks' continued to provide aerial refuelling for Harriers operating from amphibious assault carriers on Pakistan's coast, the highest-profile mission the KC-130 detachment supported was the 25 November movement of Marines from the USS *Peleliu* (LHA 5) and USS *Bataan* (LHD 5) to a remote, deserted air base dubbed Camp Rhino. While most Marines in the initial wave into Camp Rhino arrived aboard six CH-53E Super Stallions, this movement was supported by two KC-130s providing aerial refuelling for the CH-53s en route, and four more to deliver the equipment and supplies needed to begin building infrastructure to support sustained operations from the base. With the runway having been cleared by an Air Force special tactics team for C-130 use, the first 'Herk' landed at Rhino within 90 minutes of the first CH-53s touching down, initiating a steady flow of KC-130s into the base that resulted in the delivery of 403 Marines, four tactical vehicles and several tons of supplies and equipment within the first day of operations. Additionally, one KC-130 provided aviation-delivered ground refuelling (ADGR) for two CH-53Es that had been unable to 'plug' into a tanker on the first wave – a contingency the Marines accounted for with a secondary fuel plan. Tragically, VMGR-352 lost a KC-130R and seven Marines on the night of 9 January 2002 when the crew lost situational aware-

ness while approaching an expeditionary airfield in Shamsi, Pakistan. Though not the primary cause of the mishap, the lack of night vision capability was listed as a contributing factor. This mishap led to the retrofit of night-vision compatible cockpit displays in the active component KC-130F and R models beginning in 2002. The reserve component's KC-130Ts already started receiving night-vision cockpits in the mid-1990s. With KC-130s increasingly flying logistics missions at night, this upgrade was to prove critical throughout Operation Enduring Freedom (OEF) and Operation Iraqi Freedom (OIF) as the VMGR community transitioned to the KC-130J.

Hercules Aircraft Group over Iraq

Supporting the initial push into Iraq and the drive on Baghdad were 24 KC-130s from a composite unit known as the Hercules Aircraft Group, or HAG. Comprised of VMGR-352 'Raiders' with additional aircraft, aircrews and maintainers from reserve squadrons VMGR-234 'Rangers' and VMGR-452 'Yankees', the HAG provided aerial refuelling, aviation-delivered ground refuelling at forward sites in Iraq, and resupply of fielded forces, as well as providing aircraft for the Direct Air Support Center – Airborne (DASC-A) mission. Though based at Sheikh Isa Air Base in Bahrain throughout the run-up to and execution of Operation Iraqi Freedom (OIF), the HAG began operating out of an expeditionary airfield in northern Kuwait known as Forward Operating Base (FOB) Joe Foss, named in honour of the of World War II Marine fighter ace. Built in just three weeks by Marine Wing Support Group 37, FOB Joe Foss featured two 6,000ft (1,829m) hard-packed dirt runways and parking areas covered with AM-2 aluminium matting. Flying from the FOB enabled KC-130 crews supporting operations in Iraq to have shorter transit times and faster turnarounds when making multiple trips into Iraq, while allowing aircraft to return to Sheikh Isa for maintenance and crew replacement when needed.

Left: In addition to aerial refuelling, Marine 'Herks' can provide aviation-delivered ground refuelling, or ADGR. During ADGR operations, the crewmasters man the fuel hoses, with one pilot outside the aircraft serving as ADGR safety supervisor and the other on the flight deck monitoring fuel transfer and other systems.

Right: Though automation and digital avionics have simplified many of the tasks performed by enlisted aircrew on the KC-130J, 'Battleherk' crewmasters perform a multitude of duties, both inside and out of the aircraft. Here, crewmaster SSgt David Law from VMGR-152 connects hose fittings while establishing an ADGR site at Twentynine Palms.
(**Both:** Joe Copalman)

The last of the Marine Corps' 'legacy' model C-130s, the KC-130T remains in service with VMGR-452 based in Newburgh, New York. As of this writing, the 'Yankees' of VMGR-452 are currently undergoing transition to the KC-130J. (Joe Copalman)

When Operation Iraqi Freedom started on the night of 20/21 March 2003, the KC-130s of the HAG flew round-the-clock aerial refuelling missions, helping Marine F/A-18s and AV-8Bs extend mission times over the various interdiction 'kill boxes' in eastern Iraq. Marine 'Herks' continued to provide aerial refuelling throughout the initial phase of combat operations, a service that became more critical as ground forces advanced closer to Baghdad. The distances between central Iraq and Kuwait and the carriers in the Northern Arabian Gulf, and the need for extended time on station – especially for F/A-18Ds flying strike coordination and reconnaissance and forward air controller (airborne) missions – demanded abundant tanker support.

Marine KC-130s also provided a crucial logistics capability for the Regimental Combat Teams (RCTs) advancing on Baghdad. Though capable of carrying far more cargo farther and more quickly than the Corps' CH-53E Super Stallions, Marine 'Herks' required much longer landing zones, and it was not until the Marines began seizing Iraqi airfields that KC-130s started landing inside Iraq to offload cargo. Utilising captured airfields, the pilots and aircrews of the HAG delivered much-needed ammunition, food, fuel, supplies, personnel, and even mail to Marines in the field, while also ferrying casualties back to Kuwait for treatment. Marine KC-130s even operated from

an Iraqi highway as ground forces closed in on Baghdad. Known as the QualCom FARP (forward arming and refuelling point – all FARPs in Iraq were named after American Major League Baseball stadiums), the site comprised a long stretch of Iraq's Shaykh Hantush highway 100 miles (160km) south of Baghdad, with the first KC-130 landing there on 31 March 2003. QualCom proved critical for the final push on Baghdad as the HAG delivered vital supplies to Marines preparing to enter the capital. The site also served as a transload point for casualties, which would arrive at QualCom via helicopter to be transferred to waiting KC-130s, which would rush them to Kuwait.

In addition to the standard KC-130 missions of moving troops and materiel and providing fuel for Marine aircraft, the HAG operated three KC-130s as airborne direct air support centres (DASCs). Though the Marines maintained two DASCs in Kuwait to synch up aircraft with the needs of ground forces in Iraq, the DASCs relied on electronic line of sight to maintain communications with aircraft operating deep within Iraq. With most fixed-wing aircraft flying at 10,000ft (3,048m) or higher, communications were generally not an issue. But for helicopters operating at 100ft (30m) above the ground hundreds of miles away, distance and terrain degraded or blocked line-of-sight between Marine rotorcraft and the DASCs in Kuwait. Anticipating these communications issues, 3rd MAW leadership directed the HAG to provide three KC-130s for dedicated use as DASC-A aircraft. For this mission, the Herks each carried an AN/UYQ-3A communications van with the radio suite needed for DASC-A operations. In combat, the DASC-A concept proved critical to success on the ground, as AH-1W Cobras flew missions in excess of 16 hours in the opening days of the war, and were able to maintain contact with the DASC-As for updated mission taskings and directions to the nearest FARPs for the fuel and weapons to continue the mission. The HAG maintained one KC-130 DASC-A overhead around the clock from 21 March through the fall of Baghdad on 12 April.

From legacy 'Herks' to the KC-130J – heavier, faster and further

At the turn of the century, most KC-130s in Marine service were of a vintage that included not only Desert Storm service, but in some cases, pre-dated the Vietnam War. While the three active-duty squadrons flew the 1960s-era KC-130F and 1970s-era KC-130R, the two reserve VMGRs flew the 1980s-era KC-130T, which was derivative of the Air Force's C-130H, outfitted with Alison T56-A-16 turboprop engines and four-bladed metal propellers. Still in service with reserve squadron VMGR-452 'Yankees' based at Stewart Air National Guard Base in Newburgh, New York, the KC-130T functions with a crew of six. In addition to the pilot and co-pilot, the flight deck accommodates a flight engineer and a Tactical Systems Operator (TSO, formerly known as a navigator), while the rear cargo compartment has historically been manned by a flight mechanic and a loadmaster. In addition to 24 KC-130Ts, the Marines operated a pair of KC-130T-30 stretched-fuselage aircraft with a 15-foot (4.57m) longer cargo hold than the standard T. This stretched configuration gave the -30 the ability to carry 128 combat-loaded troops versus 92 in the KC-130T, 97 casualty litters versus 76, and five additional pallets of cargo. With one each initially going to the two reserve VMGRs, the

Marine KC-130J crews are as comfortable operating at night as they during the day. The KC-130J was designed with night-vision-goggle-compatible cockpits from the beginning, whereas those of 'legacy' USMC 'Herks' had to be modified for night operations.
(Joe Copalman)

pair ended up together at VMGR-452 before being de-configured as tankers and transferred to the Navy reserve in the early 2010s. All F and R-model KC-130s have been retired and replaced by the KC-130J as of 2007.

With the first example being delivered to the Marine Corps on 7 September 2001, the KC-130J is approaching its 20th year in USMC – and the Marines are still accepting new ones. Based on the Air Force's C-130J 'Super Hercules', which first flew in April 1996, the KC-130J offers significantly expanded capabilities over the legacy models it replaced. Externally, the one major observable difference between the J and the T is the newer model's six-bladed composite propeller with 'scimitar'-style blades. The engines turning those new propellers are Rolls-Royce AE 2100 D3 turboprops offering 4,637shp of power, an upgrade over the Allison T56's 4,590shp for the KC-130T that yields a top speed for the J in excess of 40mph (64km/h) over the legacy types it replaced.

The KC-130J can pass fuel to receiving aircraft almost twice as quickly as the KC-130T due to being outfitted with Flight Refuelling Ltd's Mk 32B-901E refuelling pods equipped with ram-air boost pumps. Faster refuelling means tactical aircraft spend less time 'on the hose' and more time above the Marines who need their assistance.

KC-130J crews

With a 'glass' cockpit outfitted with modern avionics, many of the tasks performed by navigators, flight engineers and flight mechanics have been automated by software in the KC-130J. This automation resulted in a different crew model, with the elimination of the TSO/navigator, engineer and flight mech positions, with navigation and systems monitoring being split between the pilots and a crew chief manning an augmented crew station on the flight deck. Two enlisted loadmasters manned the cargo compartment during early KC-130J operations, responsible for loading and offloading cargo and passengers, dispensing flares during battlefield illumination missions, managing airdrop operations, setting up ADGR sites, observing aerial refuelling operations, and serving as safety lookouts through the rear troop door windows. Beginning in 2011, the USMC consolidated the crew chief and loadmaster jobs into a single position called a 'crewmaster', resulting in a standard KC-130J crew now consisting of two pilots and a senior crewmaster on the flight deck, and two junior crewmasters in the back, an arrangement that persists to this day.

Describing the role of the crewmaster at the augmented crew station up front, KC-130J crewmaster Sergeant Jonathan Ruiz said, '*The role up front is to help out the pilots. When they start getting task saturated, we're able to monitor systems while the pilots are aviating and communicating. It definitely helps having that extra crewmember up there to take some of the workload off. Everybody has their piece of the puzzle to bring it all together.*' Though the pilots are capable of extending and retracting the refuelling hoses and monitoring fuel transfer, this is typically done by the crewmaster up front. In back, the two crewmasters function much like loadmasters under the previous crew construct, but the goal for all crewmasters is the ability to man any aircrew position in the aircraft. Though the training progression to get from the back to the front is not on a firmly established schedule, most crewmasters are

The KC-130J is a low-density, high-demand asset, with even the two reserve squadrons routinely providing support for USMC air and ground units worldwide.
(Joe Copalman)

ready to begin training on the augmented crew station position within 18 to 24 months of arriving at their squadron, with the deciding factors being proficiency and motivation.

The first KC-130J combat deployment came in February 2005, when six Battleherks from VMGR-252 deployed to Al Asad, Iraq as part of an ongoing rotation shared among all VMGR squadrons. The KC-130Js performed the same missions in Iraq as the old legacy-model Herks – general transport, aerial refuelling and battlefield illumination (BI). The latter mission dates back to the Vietnam War for Marine Herks. Then, as in Iraq, BI was largely a means of denying the enemy the cover of darkness, especially when it came to IED emplacement. During BI operations, crewmasters place a LAU-74 flare chute assembly in a gap between a partially lowered rear ramp and upwards-opening door, then set timers on the flare to determine the altitude they open at. The two flares used most often are the LUU-2 illumination flare that burns at 1.8 million candlepower for four-to-five minutes and the LUU-19 'covert' illumination flare that burns primarily in the infrared spectrum and provides significant illumination for anyone wearing night vision devices.

In September 2006, responsibility for training KC-130 pilots and aircrew transitioned from VMGRT-253 'Titans' – long the Corps' Hercules fleet replacement squadron – to VMGR-252 'Otis' at MCAS Cherry Point. While primarily a deployable, active-duty VMGR-252 retains a training detachment in-house for pilot and aircrew production for the fleet, as well as an abbreviated syllabus for pilots coming back to the 'Herk' after a non-flying tour.

Battleherk goes kinetic – Harvest HAWK

In October 2010, the Marine KC-130 fleet gained multi-sensor imagery reconnaissance (MIR) and Close Air Support (CAS) capabilities in the form of the Harvest HAWK sensor and weapons kit. This upgrade remains limited in capacity, with only 10 modified airframes in two US-based squadrons – VMGR-252 on the east coast and VMGR-352 on the west coast. The Harvest HAWK kit consists of a fire control console in the cargo hold, a Target Sight Sensor (TSS) under the aft portion of the port underwing fuel tank, a hardpoint for an M299 quad-rail launcher for AGM-114 Hellfire missiles in place of the portside aerial refuelling pod and a 'derringer' door with two launch tubes for AGM-176 Griffin missiles. To accommodate the kit, Harvest HAWK-equipped KC-130Js lost some capacity and capability. Internally, the palletised fire control officer (FCO) workstation reduces the space available for cargo or troops, and the 'derringer' door with the vertical launch tubes for the Griffin missiles at the rear of the left side of the aircraft limits the egress option for parachute insertions to the right side. Externally, the fuel tank under the left wing loses some capacity due to the TSS at the rear of the tank, and the left aerial refuelling pod is traded for the Hellfire rails. This limits the Harvest HAWK KC-130Js to refuelling only from the right wing, though passing fuel to other aircraft limits the Harvest HAWK's time on station.

Of all the capabilities Harvest HAWK brings to the fight, its endurance has proven to be the most critical in both the MIR and CAS roles. Major Tyler Burnham, a Harvest HAWK instructor, said that missions in Afghanistan could exceed 11 hours in duration. Praising this endurance, Burnham stated, '*If you think of continuity, most CAS assets*

Left: Since October 2010, the two CONUS-based active-duty VMGR squadrons (-252 at Cherry Point and -352 at Miramar) have operated a handful of KC-130Js equipped as Harvest HAWK. Visible in the background is the 'Derringer' door with two launch tubes for Griffin air-to-surface missiles. (Joe Copalman)

Right: The Harvest HAWK aircraft employ two primary precision-guided weapons systems – the AGM-176 Griffin and AGM-114 Hellfire (pictured here). (USMC/Cpl Samantha Arrington)

have to conduct, depending on the mission duration, multiple battlefield handovers between assets that are coming in. The beauty of Harvest HAWK is that we can facilitate both the infil and the exfil (of ground forces) and provide additional capabilities while we're on station. So really, we were the continuity for a lot of those missions. Once new players checked in, we gave them a situation update if the FAC or the JTAC was unable to contact them. A lot of the time, they'd push it to us because we had really good situational awareness of what was going on in that area of operations.' Major Andrew Myers, KC-130 Division head at Marine Aviation Weapons and Tactics Squadron One (MAWTS-1), worked with Harvest HAWK KC-130Js from the ground as a forward air controller (FAC) on a combat tour in Afghanistan. While he never had the opportunity to control fires from a Harvest HAWK, he frequently relied on the overwatch the type provided, using video from its sensors to maintain visual contact on validated targets to direct fires from other assets like Harriers and AH-1 Cobras.

Harvest HAWK Plus – expanding capability, restoring capacity

For as effective as the Harvest HAWK KC-130Js were, several issues limited the cargo and refuelling utility of aircraft configured with the kit and prevented the full potential of the system from being realised. Some of these issues – such as the need for a palletised Fire Control Console and the loss of the port-side troop door lookout window to the derringer-style reloadable tube launchers for the Griffin missiles – are difficult to remedy. Others, like the loss of overall fuel capacity due to the placement of the Target Sight System in the rear of the port-side external tank, and the sensor masking issues that often result from the TSS being placed there, are relatively easy to fix. The Harvest HAWK Plus (HH+) is the second-generation of the Harvest HAWK system, intended to – in the words of a KC-130J crewmaster – 'give us more of our airplane' back.

By relocating the sensor turret underneath the nose of the KC-130J, the HH+ modification solves the problems of fuel capacity and sensor masking. Additionally, the Marines upgraded the turret from the Lockheed Martin AN/AAQ-30 Target Sight System with the L3 Wescam MX-20. For as much use as Harvest HAWK crews got out of the TSS, it is a system designed for a use on a low-flying attack helicopter bolted

The Harvest HAWK Plus (HH+) upgrade improved on the original Harvest HAWK concept by upgrading the sensor to an MX-20 and relocating it to the 'chin' of the aircraft. In addition to resolving some sensor masking issues, this restored the port-side external fuel tank to full capacity. (USMC/Cpl Paige Stade)

on to a much higher-flying aircraft. The MX-20 brings far better image resolution and longer-ranged targeting capabilities. Additional engineering and testing has cleared the Harvest HAWK KC-130Js for additional hardpoints outboard of the refuelling pods at a location known as outer wing station 430. Current plans call for the movement of the M299 quad-rail Hellfire launchers to station 430, not only allowing for the left-hand refuelling pod to be re-mounted, but also the carriage of eight total AGM-114s with launch rails under both wings. Moving the sensor from the left underwing fuel tank to the nose and reinstalling the port-wing refuelling pod restores the aircraft's 58,500lb (26,535kg) fuel capacity and ability to refuel two aircraft simultaneously. When the Harvest HAWK was first announced in 2009, the initial concept included a door-mounted, sideways-firing 30mm cannon, but accuracy issues kept the gun from the final fit. The Navy's 2020 budget includes USD6 million for two Mk 44 Bushmaster 30mm cannons for integration into the HH+ weapons kit beginning in 2023. With the potential for deeper magazines and a high rate of fire, the Bushmaster would give Harvest HAWK crews kinetic flexibility and persistence, as well as a low-collateral damage option where even the smaller high-explosive warheads of the Griffin and Viper Strike are perhaps too much. The Harvest HAWK fleet is also scheduled to being using the Lockheed Martin AGM-179 Joint Air-To-Ground Missile (JAGM) once it becomes available as a Hellfire replacement.

While the Marines intend to keep the kinetic capabilities of the Harvest HAWK restricted to VMGR-252 and VMGR-352 (each with five aircraft modified for the kit and three kits total), several of the HH+ upgrades are intended for the entirety of the Corps' KC-130J community. In alignment with the 'every platform a sensor, shooter and node' mandate, all Marine Herks are getting the chin-mounted MX-20 modification and the

Given the vast distances involved in supporting Special Purpose MAGTF – Crisis Response – Africa, KC-130Js are a critical component of USMC operations in Africa. Here a 'Battleherk' assigned to SPMAGTF-CR-AF supports and embassy-reinforcement exercise in Bamako, Mali in August 2019. (USMC/Capt Clay Groover)

capability to carry and employ the Intrepid Tiger II EW pods. On top of that, all Marine KC-130Js are also receiving the Department of the Navy Large Aircraft InfraRed CounterMeasure (DoNLAIRCM) defensive system to replace the BAE AN/ALQ-157 infrared countermeasures system.

'Battleherks' over Africa

After the 11 September 2012 terror attacks on a diplomatic facility and a CIA annex in Benghazi, Libya claimed the lives of four Americans, including US Ambassador to Libya, Chris Stevens, the Marine Corps established Special Purpose Marine Air-Ground Task Force – Crisis Response – AFRICOM (SPMAGTF-CR-AF). The primary role of SPMAGTF-CR-AF is to prevent future Benghazi-like attacks by providing a battalion-sized force of Marines to respond to potentially deadly situations and an aviation combat element (ACE) to rapidly move them wherever they are needed. The SPMAGTF's ACE consists of six MV-22 Ospreys and two KC-130Js, both detachments being on six-month rotations.

The complementary capabilities of the SPMAGTF's Herks and Ospreys were first put to the test in early 2014, when sectarian violence threatened the US embassy in the South Sudanese capital of Juba. Anticipating a possible need for evacuation, the SPMAGTF's leadership sent the Ospreys and 'Battleherks' from Morón, Spain to east Africa, with the Ospreys flying to Camp Lemonnier in Djibouti, while the KC-130Js flew to Entebbe, Uganda. On 3 January 2014, the order to evacuate the embassy came, with the Ospreys lifting embassy personnel and transporting them to the waiting KC-130s in Uganda for transport out of the region.

Staying connected

While the introduction of the Osprey has helped the Marines overcome the 'tyranny of distance' characterising operations in Africa (as well as in the Pacific), the considerable distances the MV-22B can travel – especially when aerial refuelled by KC-130Js – introduced another problem: staying connected to headquarters, fielded units and other aircraft.

One of the top priorities for Marine aviation in recent years has been the integration of digital interoperability (DI) technology. With the different digital 'languages' native to the various aircraft in the Marine Corps, one of the service's DI goals was to create a common infrastructure where all users in a network utilise the same digital language, as well as a common means of accessing it. For the KC-130 community, DI currently takes a few forms, most centred around ruggedised Android-based tablets called Marine Air-Ground Tablets, or MAGTabs. One of the most widely used MAGTab apps, KILSWITCH (Kinetic Integration Lightweight Software Individual Tactical Combat Handheld), was initially developed for aviation fires management but has been adapted for non-kinetic applications that are useful for Battleherk crews. Major Burnham explained, '*We use KILSWITCH, especially for the Harvest HAWK, but also for the normal KC-130 fleet. We'll use that for things like air delivery, for imagery, run-in, threat plotting, and then battlefield illumination for drift.*' The USMC is also using tablets for networked situational awareness. Using other apps like Tactical Chat, Marines are able to update other units in the network on a mission's progress, unexpected threats, or changes in the situation using pre-determined brevity codes. For example, if a raid force is inserted on an objective via MV-22s, the MV-22 flight lead can hold down the line item for 'raid force inserted' on a MAGTab, and anyone else in that network monitoring mission progress on a MAGTab will know that the insertion was successful.

Though digital interoperability systems have been used in the active VMGR fleet, DI is still a developing capability. One current limitation is proximity. As MAWTS-1 KC-130 instructor pilot Captain James O'Hara explained, '*It's a line-of-sight thing, you've got to be close to all the players to make it work. But when you're on the objective, it frees up communications. There's a lot to be done with it yet, there's a lot they need to improve, but for the most part, being able to take someone's routing and put it on KILSWITCH, have it automatically upgrade, do X check items so you can see progression through the objective area, and do all that without radio communications – it is a benefit. It is an absolute benefit.*'

One means of overcoming the proximity limitations of DI is satellite communications. Major Burnam, who helped evaluate SatCom systems for the Marine Corps explained, '*Some of the networking we've been exploring and even using forward-deployed are things like ViaSat, which is a company that has an over-the-horizon SatCom capability for data, voice, video, you name it.*' When used, ViaSat's antenna is mounted in the hatch above the KC-130J's flight deck and has been used operationally by Marine Herks assigned to support SPMAGTF-CR-AF, where the distances involved necessitate reliable over-the-horizon communications. Burnham continued, '*I did the demo of that years ago on Harvest HAWK. We had one installed, I was on a little headset talking on Skype to the east coast, they had video of our feed, and I had T-Chat up and I was providing them with information on what we were doing that way too, so talking all at once. It was beautiful.*'

Making it RAIN

Harvest HAWK is not the only kinetic weapons systems Marine KC-130Js bring to the fight. Beginning in 2014, the VMGR community added the M142 HIMARS (High-Mobility Artillery Rocket System) long-range rocket artillery system to its arsenal. HIMARS is a smaller, more mobile launch platform for the same munitions fired by the M270 Multiple Launch Rocket System (MLRS), a heavy tracked vehicle that carries two six-shot launchers. By contrast, the M142 is based on the US Army's M1140 Family of Medium Tactical Vehicles truck chassis, which carries a single six-shot MLRS launcher and is small enough for a single launcher to be carried aboard a C-130. While the HIMARS can fire most rocket/warhead combinations in the MLRS family of munitions, the weapon currently employed by Marine HIMARS batteries is the M31A1 Guided MLRS (GMLRS, pronounced 'Gimmlers') rocket. The M31A1 relies on GPS guidance to accurately service targets with its 200lb (90kg) blast-fragmentation warhead at ranges of up to 43 miles (70km).

Employing a tactic known as HI-RAIN – short for HIMARS Rapid Insertion – Marine KC-130J crews will embark an M142 launcher aboard a 'Herk' and plug it into the aircraft's GPS navigation system. This ensures that no matter where the aircraft lands, the launcher 'knows' precisely where it is in the world, meaning that the launch crew can simply roll the M142 out of the back of a 'Herk' at an austere landing site, drive the launcher to a minimum safe distance from the aircraft, launch however many rockets are needed to adequately service a target, and then drive back to the waiting aircraft for departure. As the US military emerges from 15 years of low-intensity conflict and counterinsurgency in benign threat environments and is once again focusing heavily on fighting and winning in high-end conflicts with near-peer competitors, anti-access/area denial is a legitimate real-world challenge, and one the HI-RAIN tactic is intended to overcome.

While this tactic is effective against targets with known locations, Marine HIMARS battalions are leveraging another aviation asset in the process of finding, fixing and finishing enemy targets of opportunity. With the stealth capabilities of the Lockheed Martin F-35B Lightning II allowing it to operate undetected by radar, the Marines are counting on the type to penetrate deep into enemy airspace to locate targets and relay the coordinates to HIMARS batteries for them to engage.

An extended-range variant of the M31 rocket, known as GMLRS-ER, is currently under development and should be entering service in the early 2020s. GMLRS-ER is expected to have a maximum range of 93 miles (150km), giving Marines the ability to shape conditions in the battlespace from much further over the horizon.

JPADS – revolutionising aerial delivery

Though not a direct modification to the KC-130J per se, the Joint Precision Airdrop System (JPADS) brings significantly expanded capabilities to the Battleherk when performing the air delivery (AD) mission. Conceived of as one solution to the multifaceted problem of anti-access/area denial operations, JPADS relies on a GPS guidance package called a Modular Autonomous Guidance Unit (MAGU) and a steerable parachute to 'fly' an air-dropped load to land very close to, if not directly on top of, the intended drop coordinates. The system allows cargo aircraft to drop loads from outside the engagement range of short and medium-ranged weapons, and also to drop multiple loads intended for different landing zones in a single pass, further minimising aircraft exposure to enemy threats.

From a ground perspective, JPADS collapses the traditionally long and wide drop zones into far more manageable (and defencible) areas, limiting the amount of time Marines on the ground spend retrieving air-delivered cargo and significantly reducing their exposure if enemy fire is a threat. JPADS also increases the number of possible drop zones, as the smaller patches of ground needed for successful precision airdrops are more plentiful than the kinds of zones demanded by traditional air delivery systems.

The Marines have used JPADS since 2008, upgrading to an improved guidance system in 2013 that increased the accuracy of drops to within 450ft (150m) of the designated point of impact from a release point up to 15.5mi (25km) away. Until recently, the maximum weight of JPADS loads topped out at 2,200lb (998kg), requiring more pallets to be dropped on a single pass in cases where a single load lacked the capacity for all necessary supplies for the Marines or joint/coalition force troops on the

Modern Marine KC-130J crews rely on the Joint Precision Air Delivery System, which utilizes GPS guidance and steerable parachutes that can deliver loads near their intended impact points from up to 15.5mi (25km) away.
(USMC/Cpl Carlos Jimenez)

ground. The new JPADS 10k system allows for loads as heavy as 10,000lb (4,536kg) to be dropped and is just now being fielded.

The Marines of VMGR-252 'Otis' conducted the first live JPADS 10k drop outside of testing on 7 November 2019 during MAGTF Warfighter Exercise 1-20 at Marine Corps Air-Ground Combat Center Twentynine Palms. Captain Robert Vachon, a logistics officer with the 2nd Marine Logistics Group who witnessed the 7 November drop, conveyed the logistics community's excitement for JPADS 10k, telling the author, '*When it starts being utilised, it's going to be a big shift in how we look at the logistical question and how we utilise that air integration.*'

YANKY72 – tragedy over Mississippi

On 10 July 2017, a KC-130T from VMGR-452 'Yankees', operating under the callsign YANKY72, departed MCAS Cherry Point on a flight transporting a team of seven special operators from the 2nd Raider Battalion to Naval Air Facility El Centro in southern California. While cruising at 20,000ft (6,096m) over Mississippi, the aircraft broke apart, caught fire and plummeted to the farmland below, killing all seven Raiders as well as the two pilots and seven enlisted aircrew aboard. The crash resulted in the grounding of all Navy and Marine KC-130Ts pending the results of an investigation. The investigation concluded that faulty maintenance at a US Air Force C-130 depot facility resulted in corrosion on a propeller blade being painted over, rather than treated, in 2011. Untreated, the corrosion in this blade continued to spread, ultimately resulting in the failure of the blade, which separated from the spinner, passed through the left side of YANKY 72's fuselage, and embedded itself on the interior of the right side of the fuselage. The shock of the blade impacting the right side of the fuselage was strong enough to dislodge the right inboard propeller assembly, completely separating it from its mount and causing it to impact the right side of the fuselage before streaking along the length of the aircraft and impacting the right horizontal stabiliser, shearing most of it off. Weakened by propeller impacts on both sides, the fuselage quickly failed, with the forward cabin separating forward of the wing.

Prior to this mishap, the VMGR squadrons already comprised the most overworked community within USMC aviation. Five squadrons fulfilled constant demand for KC-130s to support ongoing contingency operations, 'tethered' support for seaborne MEUs, detachments in support of Special Purpose MAGTFs and Marine Rotational Forces worldwide, and multiple Integrated Training Exercise and Weapons and Tactics Instructor course iterations throughout the year – on top of the day-to-day demands for aerial refuelling from the fixed-wing, tiltrotor and CH-53E communities, and a Marine Corps in constant need of airlift to move people and gear from one place to another. Losing a complete squadron to the KC-130T grounding while still attempting to meet demands that did not diminish in the wake of the crash placed a heavier burden on the rest of the VMGR community, with all squadrons doing what they could to increase their own operational tempos to meet the needs of the fleet. With the source of the mishap identified and inspections and repairs complete to prevent a similar one from occurring, the KC-130Ts are back in the air, with VMGR-452 preparing to transition to the KC-130J beginning in FY2020.

Continued combat

The KC-130J's ability to operate from short, unimproved surfaces continues to make it a valuable asset in the continuing war against Islamist terrorists. With VMGRs constantly providing 'Herk' detachments to SPMAGTF-CR-Central Command in the Middle East, Marine KC-130Js support Operation Inherent Resolve (OIR), the fight against the so-called Islamic State in Iraq and Syria (ISIS) by transporting personnel and equipment into and out of austere sites in Syria, with at least two such sites in northern Syria being utilised between 2017 and 2019. Marine 'Herk' support helped sustain operations like the liberation of Raqqa in summer and autumn 2017, where a Marine artillery battalion expended 35,000 rounds of 155mm (6.1in) ammunition against ISIS terrorists while supporting Syrian Democratic Forces troops over a five-month period. Additionally, KC-130Js assigned to SPMAGTF-CR-CC provide aerial refuelling for Harriers, Hornets and Ospreys flying OIR missions, as well as aerial logistics support for continuing operations in Afghanistan under Operation Freedom's Sentinel.

A 'glass' cockpit with digital display screens and heads-up displays set the cockpit of the KC-130J apart from the 'legacy' models it replaced.
(Joe Copalman)

Initiatives and moving forward

While all three active-component VMGRs have received their full primary mission aircraft inventory (PMAI) of 15 aircraft each, the KC-130J transition continues for the two reserve VMGRs. As of 2019, VMGR-234 had received seven of a planned 12 KC-130Js, while VMGR-452 still operates the KC-130T, with transition planned to begin in FY2020. Once the active and reserve PMAIs are reached, the Marines will continue accepting another ten KC-130Js, with two going to each of the five VMGRs as backup aircraft. Additionally, the 2019 Aviation Plan includes an initiative to expand the reserve PMAI to 15 aircraft each, bringing the reserve squadrons in 100 per cent alignment with the active-component VMGRs. The biggest challenge for the Marine 'Battleherk' community remains manpower, as the constant demand for KC-130 support consistently gives the VMGR squadrons the shortest dwell times between deployments in Marine aviation.

VMR AND H&HS | MARINE OPERATIONAL SUPPORT AIRLIFT

The Marine Corps operates a small fleet of commercial-derivative jet and turboprop light transport aircraft in the Operational Support Airlift (OSA) role, which mostly involves transporting senior leadership. Marine OSA capability is spread among two types of squadrons – Headquarters and Headquarters Squadrons (H&HS), which are assigned to various Marine Corps Installations Commands and operate the base flight detachments for most Marine Corps Air Stations, and Marine Transport Squadrons (VMRs), which are assigned to Marine Air Wings and have traditionally served higher headquarters units.

Four primary types comprise the Marine OSA fleet – the Beech UC-12 Huron, Gulfstream C-20, Cessna UC-35 Citation and Boeing C-40 Clipper. At 14 and 12 examples of each, respectively, the UC-12 and UC-35 are the most numerous OSA types in the Marines Corps, with the C-20 and C-40 limited two examples each (the C-40s pending delivery). The UC-12 fleet has been undergoing an upgrade from the legacy UC-12F and UC-12M models to the new UC-12Ws, which offer expanded capacity, higher speed and extended range. The C-40s – intended exclusively for VMR-1 'Roadrunners' at NAS JRB Fort Worth – are being acquired to replace a long-serving pair of C-9B Skytrain IIs the service retired in April 2017 at Andrews Air Force Base in Washington, DC. The move of VMR-1 to Fort Worth accompanied a consolidation of VMR squadrons to the

The Marine Corps operates a pair of Gulfstream C-20Gs, which provide transportation for leadership from Marine Corps Base Hawaii at Kaneohe Bay throughout the Pacific. (USMC/LCpl Matthew Bragg)

4th Marine Air Wing, the aviation element of Marine Forces Reserve. The H&HS unit at Marine Corps Base Hawaii at Kaneohe Bay operates the Corps' two C-20Gs, which offer longer range and a roomier cabin than the UC-35. The Marine Corps is currently seeking a common aircraft to replace its C-20Gs, UC-35Cs and UC-35Ds, though no specific type has been identified yet.

The OSA community serves a vital purpose during both home-station and deployed operations. In the Continental United States (CONUS), Marine OSA units provide cost-effective and time-critical movement of leadership personnel from one base to another without having to rely on rigid commercial flight schedules or imposing on the already over-tasked KC-130 community. Marine OSA aircraft also transport maintainers and smaller spare parts to airfields throughout the United States to repair aircraft that have broken down and need to be repaired in place. In addition to supporting USMC leadership movements, Marine OSA units also support the Joint Operational Support Airlift Command by taking joint force taskings throughout the United States.

The H&HS and VMR units routinely deploy detachments overseas to support intra-theatre airlift, especially for the Special Purpose Marine Air-Ground Task Forces (SPMAGTFs) assigned to Africa and to Central Command in the Middle East. Support for SPMAGTFs differs from domestic 'people and parts' runs in that the missions can be slightly more consequential. Recounting VMR taskings in support of SPMAGTF-CR-Africom, Major Miguel Peña, a UC-12W and UC-35C pilot with VMR Belle Chasse said, '*The Special Purpose MAGTF commanding officer views his center of gravity as his ability to be mobile and agile, to go around the rim of the Mediterranean and provide support for our embassies to relocate personnel – including forced relocation if needed to protect them. He uses us as a tertiary means to ensure that those aviation assets are always ready.*' While on an AFRICOM deployment, Peña flew considerable distances in support of both security cooperation missions and the Centers for Disease Control during the Ebola Crisis of 2014-16. Peña recalls, '*The Special Purpose MAGTF CO was tasked with the humanitarian aid there and coordinating with the CDC. We moved him from Djibouti to Entebbe, Uganda. He did his business (with the CDC) there, and then for security cooperation, we moved him to Burundi. I think at the time the area was going through some civil strife. That's what we do.*'

Workhorses of the Marine OSA fleet are the Beech C-12 Huron and Cessna UC-35 Citation. The UC-12W is the most recent and most capable C-12 variant currently employed by the US military. The UC-35 fleet is due for replacement by a yet-to-be-determined business jet that will also replace the Corps' two Gulfstream C-20s. These aircraft are from VMR Belle Chasse at Joint Reserve Base Naval Air Station New Orleans. (Joe Copalman)

Chapter 13

VMU | MARINE UNMANNED AERIAL VEHICLE

The Marine Corps' experience with unmanned aerial vehicles dates to June 1984, when Detachment T, Target Acquisition Battery, 10th Marine Regiment was established at Camp Lejuene. Though lacking any aircraft at the time, Detachment T's mission was to employ unmanned aerial vehicles (UAVs) – at the time called remotely piloted vehicles (RPVs) – as spotters for the 10th Marines' artillery batteries. Before the unit had taken delivery of its first aircraft – Israeli-built Mastiff RPVs – it was re-designated as the 1st RPV Platoon and reassigned from the artillery-focused 10th Marines directly to the 2nd Marine Division. By the end of 1984, the Platoon had two Mastiffs operated and maintained by crews that had been trained in Israel. In October 1986, the unit had grown enough to be re-designated the 1st RPV Company.

RQ-2 Pioneer

By July 1987, the Marines had replaced the aging Mastiffs with the RQ-2 Pioneer, a joint endeavour designed by Israeli Aircraft Industries and AAI. The Pioneer offered increased endurance and higher-fidelity sensors than the Mastiff, employing the Wescam DS-12 Electro-Optical/Infrared sensor, which could provide near-real time

The USMC was an early adopter with unmanned aerial systems, acquiring IAI Mastiff UAVs from Israel in 1984. By 1987, the Marines replaced the Mastiff with the RQ-2 Pioneer, pictured here, a type the Corps operated for over 20 years, finally retiring the type in 2008. (USMC)

analogue video by day and either white-hot or black-hot IR footage at night. With a 26-horsepower Fitchel & Sachs SF2-350 two-cylinder two-stroke engine and 12 gallons (47 litres) of fuel, the RQ-2 provided 5.5 hours of flight time, giving ground commanders a degree of persistence that fixed and rotor-winged aircraft at the time could not provide.

The Pioneer was an ideal platform for the Marines in its time, largely due to its ability to operate from both land and sea. For launch, Pioneer relied on either a truck-mounted, pneumatic rail-type catapult, or on JATO (jet-assisted take-off) rocket motors to propel it to launch speeds from a ship's deck or a short runway. Pioneer offered flexibility on recovery as well, as it carried a small arrester cable to snag the arresting wire of a purpose-built system for conventional runways, or could simply be flown into a recovery net on land or aboard ship. This flexibility gave the Marines a single-type programme of record that could provide reconnaissance, surveillance and target acquisition (RSTA) services for any Marine Air-Ground Task Force (MAGTF), regardless of whether it was land-based or aboard amphibious shipping as a Marine Expeditionary Unit (MEU).

Renaming, realignment and expansion

Two additional RPV companies stood up in 1987 at Marine Corps Air Ground Combat Center Twentynine Palms to provide west coast units with UAS coverage. The 1st RPV Co at Camp Lejeune was re-designated the 2nd RPV Co, while the two new units established at Twentynine Palms were the 1st and 3rd RPV Cos, which subsequently merged into a single unit, the 1st RPV company.

Aligning with the emerging nomenclature for remotely piloted vehicles in the early 1990s, the Corps' two RPV companies re-designated as UAV companies in January 1993. Three years later, the units re-designated as Marine Unmanned Aerial Vehicle Squadrons (VMUs) and were realigned under Marine Aircraft Groups. This move saw VMU-2 relocate from Camp Lejeune to MCAS Cherry Point and from Marine Air Control Group 28 to Marine Aircraft Group 14. In 2000, the Marine Corps shifted the VMUs back to the MACGs, a decision that remained unpopular within the community for over a decade.

From 2004 onward, VMU-1 'Watchdogs' and VMU-2 'Night Owls' deployed almost constantly, at times supporting concurrent detachments in Afghanistan and Iraq while also supporting contractor-operated UAVs aboard amphibious shipping attached to MEUs. The Marines helped ease this operational pressure by standing up a third unmanned squadron, VMU-3 'Phantoms' at 29 Palms on 12 September 2008. The three active-duty VMUs were augmented by a reserve squadron – VMU-4 'Evil Eyes' – which stood up at MCAS Yuma on 1 July 2010.

Pioneers over Iraq

The Pioneer began contributing to Operation Iraqi Freedom in March 2003 before the invasion even started. The 'Watchdogs' of VMU-1 detected the Rumaylah oil fields burning several days prior to the planned start of the ground offensive, the result of Saddam Hussein trying to create an environmental catastrophe as he did in 1991. This resulted in the invasion starting two days earlier than planned. Given the speed of the ground forces' advance through southern Iraq, VMU-1 and VMU-2 had to revise their tactics to be able to set up and break down operations quickly to keep pace with the

Regimental Combat Teams (RCTs) making their way towards Baghdad. To maximise mobility, both squadrons reduced the amount of equipment they took with them. The two units conducted day and night RSTA, route reconnaissance and battle damage assessment (BDA) along the Marines' route of advance, employing hunter-killer tactics to locate targets and coordinate artillery strikes on them. Multiple Iraqi artillery batteries – by far the most potent threat facing ground forces – were destroyed using this tactic. Ground commanders were so impressed with the RQ-2 that VMUs received priority for artillery missions. Even with this priority, and the use of RQ-2s to locate targets for aerial attack – too often the Pioneers located valid targets but could not get artillery or air attacks on them quickly enough, driving home the need an armed UAV.

Redeploying to Iraq beginning in 2004 to assist in the fight against insurgents, the VMU squadrons employed the RQ-2 for persistent surveillance during the battles of Fallujah and Ramadi. Given the concerns over civilian casualties, Pioneer operators became adept at performing pattern-of-life surveillance, observing routines that enabled intelligence analysts to determine the best times to conduct raids against insurgents in various communities. The RQ-2 continued to serve in Afghanistan and Iraq through 2008, amassing a 22-year record of Marine Corps service.

RQ-7 Shadow

The Corps' long relationship with the RQ-2 came to an end in January 2008 when it was replaced by the AAI RQ-7B Shadow. At the core of the RQ-7B's RSTA capabilities was the Israel Aerospace Industries POP-300D Electro-Optical/Infrared (EO/IR) sensor turret with a laser designator. The POP-300D enabled RQ-7 to provide near-real time colour video by day and either white-hot or black-hot IR footage at night, with image quality comparable to that provided by the US Air Force's MQ-1 Predator. Equipped with a laser designator, the POP-300 could also designate targets for laser-guided munitions. Unmanned aerial systems (UAS – the term for UAVs plus all necessary support equipment) are classified into five 'groups' organised by size and weight, with Group

Introduced in 2008, the AAI RQ-7B Shadow replaced the RQ-2 as the Marine Corps' UAV programme of record. (Joe Copalman)

1 referring to small, hand-launched drones and Group 5 being large systems like the General Atomics MQ-9 Reaper. The Shadow, being a Group 3 UAV, falls in the middle.

The Marines fielded three variants of the basic RQ-7B – the short-wing, the long-wing and the v2. There was little difference between the long-wing and short-wing variants aside from wingspan. The short-wing Shadow had a wingspan of 14ft (4.2m), allowing it to carry 11.6 US gal (44 lit) of fuel for a total endurance of six hours. The long-wing variant had a 20ft (6.1m) wingspan, giving it a fuel capacity of 15.3 US gal (58 lit) for endurance up to nine hours.

The third variant – the RQ-7Bv2 (version 2) – was an upgrade of the long-wing Shadow in response to numerous deficiencies with the basic RQ-7B. Unlike larger UAVs operated by the Air Force like the MQ-1 Predator and MQ-9 Reaper, which were controlled via satellite uplinks with remote ground control stations sometimes half-way around the world, the RQ-7B relied on electronic line-of-site with the Ground Control Station. At maximum range (about 55 miles/89km), turning at certain angles could obscure the Shadow's datalink, resulting in a disruption of the command signal. To remedy this, Marine RQ-7Bs received a new datalink called the Tactical Common Datalink (TCDL) that included a mast atop the fuselage for the antenna, greatly reducing the likelihood of loss-of-signal due to wing obscuration. Along with increased signal reliability, the TCDL brought greater data security to the Shadow. Additional features of the v2 included an upgraded engine with electronic fuel injection for increased reliability and hardpoints under the wings for external stores should any have been approved, though none were.

In addition to providing RSTA services, the RQ-7B carried a communications system enabling Marines in the field to maintain contact with headquarters over long distances or while operating in mountains or valleys where terrain features obscure electronic line of sight. Known as the Communications Relay Package (CRP), the system consisted of a pair of AN/PRC-125 tactical multiband radios in the wingtips, a wiring harness and a relay that enables to radios to 'talk' to the RQ-7's main computer. Shadows performed both the RSTA and communications relay missions simultaneously.

The IAI POP-300D sensor of the RQ-7B brought an increase in sensor fidelity over the RQ-2, as well as a laser designator. (Joe Copalman)

The RQ-7B saw extensive use in Afghanistan during Operation Enduring Freedom, providing RSTA service for the Marine and UK forces operating in Helmand Province. Staff Sergeant Christopher Herr deployed to Afghanistan in 2009 with VMU-3 'Phantoms' as an RQ-7B operator. On the opening night of Operation Moshtarak – the 15,000-troop multinational effort to wrest the town of Marjah from Taliban control – Herr served as the night shift non-commissioned officer in charge. Recalling the squadron's contribution to Moshtarak, Herr said, '*We conducted aerial reconnaissance in support of the ground units that were assaulting the city. We were covering the entry points into the city, providing general overwatch. It was a different mentality during that operation, because each battalion had their own sector of the city, and at any given time, the Shadow would be in support of one of those sectors. The AirO (air officer – senior aviation advisor to a battalion or regimental commander) or JTAC for those battalions would be controlling us for that sector. It was definitely a very, very busy time.*'

One of those AirOs on the ground in Marjah was Major Alex Ramthun, a Harrier pilot on an AirO tour with 1st Battalion, 6th Marine Regiment. Explaining how he and the other battalions employed the RQ-7s during Moshtarak, Ramthun said, '*A lot of the time we'd do hunter-killer teams where we would use the Shadow to locate targets. It*

flies a little lower, and even though it makes a little bit of noise, the Taliban would kind of ignore it, so we could get it into spots where other aircraft couldn't. We would have the Harriers waiting out of jet noise area, and the Shadow would find targets and either pass the coordinates through me to the aircraft or it would use its own IR marker to illuminate a target for a Harrier to strike. Both of those were very effective.'

After a 2009 Afghan deployment during which commanders repeatedly observed hostile acts such as IED emplacement through RQ-7 video feeds, but could not stop these acts or immediately respond to them with kinetic force, the Marines began exploring the possibility of arming RQ-7s with small munitions to be able to enable engagement of time-sensitive targets when other kinetic assets were not available. Picking up on a stagnating Army initiative to arm that service's RQ-7Bs, the USMC announced in 2011 that it would be arming its Shadows, receiving clearance that August to begin initial experimental work to evaluate the feasibility of several different munitions. This evaluation was largely conducted at the contractor level, with AAI working with different companies on fitting and firing their own proposed weapons from an AAI Shadow. Among the munitions tested between 2012 and 2014 were the General Dynamics 10lb (4.5kg) 81mm (3.2in) Air-Dropped Mortar, Lockheed Martin's 11lb (5kg) Shadow Hawk laser-guided glide bomb and Textron's 12.7lb (5.75kg) Fury precision-guided munition. While all munitions tested for the RQ-7 were successful, the Marines ran out of funding for arming the Shadow in May of 2015, with no further test or development work on the concept occurring.

Like most aircraft at the end of their service lives in USMC service, the RQ-7B remained relevant until the end. On the type's final combat deployment in 2017, VMU-3 supported a joint US/Philippines task force combating Islamic State militants in the Philippines. During this deployment, VMU-3 used RQ-7Bv2 aircraft to locate and track high-value targets for allied (presumably Philippines Air Force) aircraft to attack. The

An RQ-7B catches an arresting wire at an expeditionary airfield. While the RQ-7B brought enhanced capabilities over the RQ-2, it lacked the ability to be recovered aboard amphibious ships, restricting it to land-based operations. (Joe Copalman)

'Phantoms' operated on a 'spoke' system, in which small launch, recovery and control teams were positioned in remote locations closer to operating areas to extend the squadron's reach by over a hundred miles. Two RQ-7B operators from VMU-3 were awarded the Navy and Marine Corps Achievement Medal with Remote Impact Device for their actions during the Philippines deployment. This award is for sailors and Marines not physically present during a battle, but who played a significant role in its outcome. The Marines, Sgt Joseph Latsch and Sgt Ethan Mintus, were the first to receive awards with the 'R' device.

The final flight of any RQ-7B in Marine Corps service occurred during the culminating event of the Rim of the Pacific (RIMPAC) exercise in July 2018. Over 11 years of service, the Corps' four VMU squadrons deployed with the RQ-7B a combined total of 11 times, with the Shadow fleet accumulating more than 39,000 flight hours before retirement.

To cover a need for UAVs that exceeded the capacity of USMC RQ-7B Shadows in service at the time, and to maintain an amphibious UAV capability, the Marine Corps operated ScanEagle UAVs on a contractor-owned, contractor-operated basis. (USMC/GySgt Shannon Arledge)

Scan Eagle and Aerosonde

To augment the RQ-2 fleets of the VMUs deployed to Iraq and Afghanistan, the Marines turned to contractor-owned/contractor-operated (COCO) solutions. The first 'COCO' UAV employed by the Marines was the Insitu Scan Eagle. At the time of its introduction into combat in Iraq in 2005, the Scan Eagle boasted the longest endurance of any Marine UAV – 20 hours. Sensor-wise, Scan Eagle was initially daylight-only, lacking an IR sensor until the introduction of the 'NightEagle' in 2009. Even then, Scan Eagle was an either/or asset, as only the EO or IR sensor could be fitted at once, and it lacked a laser designator, limiting its utility for fires coordination. The AAI Aerosonde-G UAV replaced Scan Eagle in June 2012 as the Marine Corps' 'COCO' UAV to augment the Shadow, making its combat debut on 2 December 2012, completing a 10-hour ISR flight with VMU-3. The Aerosonde-G offered shorter endurance than the Scan Eagle – around ten hours – but brought EO and IR sensors in one package, as well as a laser pointer. While incapable of designating targets for laser-guided weapons like the Shadow, laser pointers can highlight areas of interest for ground troops or other aircraft to get their targeting pods onto for surveillance or target designation. While both Scan Eagle and Aerosonde filled the amphibious deployment gap to provide MEUs with organic UAV capabilities, both systems routinely augmented VMU squadrons flying the RQ-7B in Iraq and Afghanistan. With the reintroduction of an organic amphibious UAV capability in the Boeing-Insitu RQ-21A Blackjack, Marine reliance on 'COCO' unmanned solutions tapered off until the introduction of the MQ-9 Reaper into VMU-1 on a 'COCO' contract for operations in Afghanistan.

Unmanned cargo

One of the more innovative unmanned aerial systems employed by the USMC is the Lockheed Martin CQ-24A K-Max. Also known as the Cargo Resupply Unmanned Aircraft System (CRUAS), the CQ-24 is an optionally manned rotorcraft based on the proven Kaman Aerospace K1200 K-Max helicopter. The CQ-24A resulted from a 2007 partnership between Kaman and Lockheed Martin to market an optionally manned air-

craft to the DOD as a means of transporting supplies to remote outposts while bypassing overland routes vulnerable to insurgent ambushes and improved explosive devices.

CRUAS became a Marine Corps programme in response to a 2009 urgent operational needs statement. The two CQ-24s deployed to Afghanistan in November 2011, flying the first unmanned cargo resupply mission the following month. The CRUAS was so effective that what was initially only supposed to be a seven-month deployment continued for almost three years, coming to an end in 2014 when a drawdown of Marine forces in Afghanistan reduced the need for the system. During the Afghan deployment, the two CQ-24s moved 4.5 million pounds (2,041,166kg) of cargo over the course of over 2,000 sorties. Per a Kaman press release, this amounted to the work of 900 convoys and 46,000 hours of exposure to possible IEDs and other common threats to ground convoys.

The two CQ-24As – BuNos 169221 and 169222 – had been at MCAS Yuma with VMX-1 since 7 May 2016, with the intent the pair would be used to inform the development of future unmanned cargo systems and establish tactics, techniques and procedures for the employment of those systems and others. This included plans to fit the aircraft with EO/IR sensors, external fuel tanks and a satellite communications system for further trials flights to expand the envelope of Marine unmanned rotorcraft operations through 2028. Having sat dormant at Yuma since arriving, the CQ-24s recently received a second lease on life. On 1 May 2019, Kaman announced the award of a Marine contract to reactivate the two CQ-24s to flight readiness for additional test work. With some of the systems aboard the CQ-24s nearly ten years out of date, Kaman is swapping out old technology for new components, including a new autonomous flight system. As of this writing, it is unclear when this work will be complete and what base or unit the aircraft will go to, though returning to Yuma and VMX-1 makes sense.

The CQ-24A is not the only unmanned rotor-winged logistics platform the Marines have evaluated. The Aurora Flight Sciences Autonomous Aerial Cargo/Utility System (AACUS) is an optionally manned Bell UH-1H helicopter equipped with LiDAR (Light Detection and Ranging) sensors and cameras for terrain and obstacle avoidance, enabling precision operations, even in urban environments. While the UH-1H was used for demonstration flights in late 2017, the system is designed to give any helicopter autonomous flight capability. Rotorcraft equipped with the AACUS system are controlled by

Left: Between 2011 and 2014, the Marines operated a pair of Lockheed Martin CQ-24A optionally-manned cargo helicopters in Afghanistan. A development of the Kaman K-Max, the CQ-24A allowed the marines to resupply remote outposts in Helmand province without exposing them to potential ambushes and roadside bombs. (USMC/Cpl Justin Boling)

Right: In 2017, the Marine Corps tested another unmanned cargo system developed by Aurora Flight Sciences and the Office of Naval Research. Known as the Autonomous Aerial Cargo/Utility System (AACUS), the system is a set of platform-agnostic autonomous flight controls that were mated to a UH-1H 'Huey' for these tests. During testing, the system was 'flown' by enlisted infantry Marines to prove ease of operation. (USMC)

a tablet computer, with control and flight programming being simple enough for infantrymen with no flying experience to competently operate the system with only a few hours of training. The Marines are also considering AACUS for casualty evacuation.

For all the capabilities that systems like CRUAS and AACUS bring in terms of resupply, the Marines see smaller, even cheaper systems as the way forward. While heavy equipment requires a dedicated heavy-lift asset like the CH-53 to move, loads in the range between 500 and 1,000lb (227 and 454kg) suffice for bringing the food, water, ammunition and other necessities to keep Marines in the field combat-effective. Some Marines in the UAS community see something like a larger quadcopter-based system as the way forward for unmanned resupply, with podded cargo containers reducing drag and allowing higher speeds for faster delivery and eliminating the need for complex sling load operations.

RQ-21A Blackjack

The RQ-21 is a development of Boeing-Insitu's 'Integrator' UAV, chosen to replace the RQ-7B through a 2010 contract. Known as the Blackjack, the RQ-21 holds numerous advantages over the RQ-7, including twelve-hour endurance versus the Shadow's nine, and a smaller logistics, maintenance and ground control footprint, enabling greater mobility. Foremost among the Blackjack's advantages is its ability to operate from amphibious shipping using the same pneumatic catapult launch and 'Skyhook' recovery systems as the Scan Eagle. Additionally, the Blackjack's communications relay sys-

The Blackjack brings most of the capabilities of the RQ-7B to the VMU squadrons (albeit with the absence of a laser designator), with the addition of a payload bay for sensors, jammers, or other useful systems as well as the ability to be recovered at sea via the same 'Skyhook' system employed by the ScanEagle (seen in the background). (Joe Copalman)

tem facilitates both UHF and VHF waveforms, whereas the Shadow only supported VHF communications.

The RQ-21 is comparable in many aspects to the RQ-7. Both types rely on electronic line-of-sight for control signals, limiting their range to around 55 miles (89km). Like the Shadow, this can be extended for the Blackjack through hub-and-spoke operation. While sensor options remained similar, including electro-optical sensors for daylight full-motion colour video and infrared sensors for night, a laser rangefinder and an IR pointer, the Blackjack's sensor currently lacks a laser designator. While Blackjack operators still use the sensors to develop targeting information for artillery and air-strikes, the RQ-21 currently cannot host laser-guided weaponry. Unlike the Shadow, the Blackjack has a payload bay allowing for integration of sensors, jammers and other systems weighing up to 39lb (18kg). Current payloads approved for the RQ-21 include the AN/PDY-2 'Split Aces' synthetic aperture radar and ground moving target indicator and the AN/DSY-4 'Spectral Bat' signals intelligence (SIGINT) system, capable of signal detection and geo-location. Another sensor, Logos Technologies' 'Redkite' wide-area motion imagery sensor, completed successful integration flights aboard an RQ-21 in February 2017.

Marine Corps leadership has long expressed optimism about using UAVs for electronic warfare (EW), and the type's payload bay was a major selling point for the RQ-21, as the USMC planned on retiring its fleet of EA-6B Prowler EW aircraft and shifting much of the service's EW burden to unmanned systems. The primary EW system employed by Marine aircraft is the Intrepid Tiger II (IT-II) communications EW pod, which had been programmed for integration into the RQ-21 from before its acquisition through 2019, when it no longer appeared as a future upgrade initiative for the

The RQ-21 is operated by a crew of two – an Air Vehicle Operator, typically an enlisted Marine, and an Unmanned Aircraft Commander, typically a commissioned officer seated side-by-side in a truck-transportable ground control station. Though capable of missions as long as 12 or more hours, most RQ-21 missions are shorter than that. (Joe Copalman)

Since entering service in 2014, the Marine RQ-21 fleet has undergone a sensor upgrade, from the EO/IR2 payload to the EO/IR4, which offers a smoother transition between the pictures generated by the electro-optical and infrared sensors. The USMC Blackjack fleet is due for a further sensor upgrade that will incorporate a laser designator – a capability lost in the transition from the RQ-7B. (Joe Copalman)

Blackjack in the 2019 Marine Aviation Plan. Given the size and weight of the IT-II pod, many in the VMU community expressed scepticism about the possibility of integrating the system into the Blackjack, with one operator saying, '*They'd have to make the RQ-21 a lot bigger to slap one of those on it.*'

Entering USMC service in 2014, the RQ-21 made its combat debut in Afghanistan that April on deployment with VMU-2. Marine Blackjacks provided aerial reconnaissance for Marine, British and Afghan forces operating in Helmand Province before the drawdown of US forces brought VMU-2 back to Cherry Point in September 2014. Data from this deployment informed the refinement of RQ-21 TTPs and identified required software tweaks and hardware changes, leading to declaration of initial operational capability in January 2016. By that summer, the Blackjack had deployed again, this time to Iraq in support of Marine Raiders fighting against Islamic State in Iraq and Syria (ISIS) insurgents in Operation Inherent Resolve (OIR).

The Marines have employed the RQ-21 extensively in Iraq and Syria during OIR, supporting special operations forces as well as the anti-ISIS Syrian Defence Forces. The VMUs flew the Blackjack so much in 2017 and 2018 that units involved exceeded their budgeted flight hours by more than 300 per cent, requiring the navy to request the reallocation of funds to cover the increased operational tempo.

In addition to development work on new radar and SIGINT payloads, Marine RQ-21s received a sensor upgrade. As Gunnery Sergeant Jonathan Salasibarra, an RQ-21 instructor pilot at Marine Aviation Weapons and Tactics Squadron One (MAWTS-1) explained, '*We went from the EO/IR2 to the EO/IR4. It was a huge shift in the camera. When I go from EO to IR, it used to be where I'm not looking at the same thing anymore when I do the shift. But with them redesigning the turret, it gives more ease in transitioning.*' Marine RQ-21s are set to receive another sensor turret upgrade, with EO/IR5 including a laser designator, restoring a capability VMU lost in the transition from the Shadow.

MUX

Until its cancellation in March 2020 as a costly, overly-ambitious do-it-all system, the MAGTF UAS Expeditionary, or MUX, had been one of the highest-priority Marine Corps development programmes. Several designs were proposed prior to cancellation, including Bell's V-247, illustrated. (Bell)

Aware that Group 3 systems were not ideal for the long-time priorities of armed UAVs and shifting its EW burden to unmanned systems, the Marine Corps developed a concept in 2016 known as Marine Air-Ground Task Force Unmanned Expeditionary Capability, or MUX. MUX was to be a Group 5 system in the same class as the Air Force's MQ-9 Reaper, though runway-independent and capable of shipboard operation, with a focus on fighting peer-level threats in addition to the insurgents and pirates the VMUs faced off against since 2001. As described in the 2019 Marine Aviation Plan, '*MUX will be multi-sensor and will provide early warning, electronic warfare, a C4 bridge, ISR, strike capability, and logistics at ranges complementary to those of MV-22 and F-35, giving MAGTF commanders flexible, persistent, and lethal reach.*'

Proposed MUX designs included Bell's V-247 tiltrotor UAV and Northrop-Grumman's TERN, a tail-sitter capable of vertical take-off and landing. Though a high priority project for successive deputy commandants for aviation since 2016, MUX drew criticism for both its complexity and the space the system would take up aboard amphibious shipping. In the end, the airborne early warning (AEW) requirement proved to be the programme's Achilles heel, as the weight of systems needed for that mission would

have strained the type's vertical take-off capability. Marine leadership cancelled the MUX programme in March 2020, announcing in its place a two-tiered approach utilising land-based Group 5 systems and smaller (Group 3 or 4) ship-based systems. Further, Commandant David Berger seeks systems capable of interchangeable payloads, 24-hour endurance and interoperability with multiple ships for distributed maritime operations. Berger has also expressed interest in an unmanned aerial refuelling system similar to the navy's RQ-25 Stingray.

Scout UAS and 'Quads for Squads'

In addition to the group 3 UAS flown by the VMUs, the Marines employ multiple Group 1 unmanned systems operated by infantry units. Known as Small Unit Remote Scouting System (SURSS) Family of Small Unmanned Aircraft Systems (FoSUAS), these systems give small unit leaders an organic means of enhancing their situational awareness in near-real time. Until recently, the Marines utilised three small hand-launched fixed-wing systems – the RQ-11B Raven, RQ-12A Wasp and RQ-20A Puma, with only the Raven and Puma still in use.

Additionally, small quad-rotor drones have been used at the squad level under a programme called 'Quads for Squads'. In early 2018, Marine rifle squads began training with small 'Instant Eye' quadcopters under the Quads for Squads initiative championed by then-Commandant General Robert Neller. Concerns over cybersecurity grounded the programme later that year, but as this grounding was aimed primarily at commercial-off-the-shelf drones manufactured in China, the Marines secured an exemption to continue utilising the US-built Instant Eye. Inclusion of SURSS has led to the establishment of a designated UAS operator position in every rifle squad. Moving forward, Marine SURSS acquisition will be based on a capabilities model, with nano, micro and

Reconnaissance Marines with the 26th MEU's Maritime Raid Force launch an RQ-20 Puma from a combat rubber raiding craft in the Arabian Gulf. As the largest SUAS under the Small Unit Remote Scouting System, the RQ-20 has a range of ten miles (16km) and can remain airborne for up to 90 minutes. (USMC/Cpl Gary Jayne III)

short range/short endurance quadrotor UAVs, tethered systems and three fixed-wing capability sets – short, medium and long range/endurance hand-launched UAVs.

Administrative changes

Until 2012, most commissioned officers serving in VMU squadrons did so in a temporary capacity. These officers came from outside the UAV community and were mostly command and control officers or aviators from fixed or rotor-wing communities serving temporarily with a VMU unit much in the same way an aviator would serve with a ground unit on a forward air controller tour. The creation of an official military occupational specialty (MOS) – 7315 – for UAS officers established a career path for commissioned officers to serve their entire careers in VMU squadrons. This enhanced the professionalism of the VMU community and provided it with advocates who understand the capabilities that unmanned systems provide to the MAGTF and the long-term needs of the VMUs to ensure maximum combat effectiveness.

Though undeniably flying units meeting all the demands and facing the same challenges as any other flying community in the Marines Corps, the VMU squadrons fell under the control of Marine Air Control Groups, rather than MAGs like their brethren in manned aircraft communities. Looking back on the challenges of reporting to an MACG, Gunnery Sergeant Salasibarra – who has been a UAV operator since 2004 recalled, '*Prior to our transition to the MAG, maintenance was – I wouldn't say bottom of the barrel, but we were scraping for parts. We were scraping for assistance from an MACG who has really got nothing to do with aviation and trying to get our maintenance up to a point where we can go out and support and actually train the way we need to.*' In addition to maintenance, the VMUs struggled with crew training under the MACGs. As then-Staff Sergeant Christopher Herr recalled when interviewed

Marine ground units employ a number of Small Unmanned Aircraft Systems (SUAS) under the umbrella of the Small Unit Remote Scouting System, which are short-range, man-portable UAVs for 'over the hill' intelligence, surveillance and reconnaissance. This is the hand-launched RQ-11B Raven. (USMC/Sgt Andy Martinez)

in 2016, '*The aircrew still had to keep up with all the aviation requirements, whether that was NATOPS checks or currency and proficiency. It was just a completely different training and readiness mindset.*'

On 13 May 2013, VMU-2 'Night Owls' became the first unmanned squadron to transition from a control group back to an aircraft group, moving from MACG-28 to MAG-14. As part of this transition, those VMUs not already assigned to a Marine Corps Air Station (MCAS) relocated, with VMU-1 moving from Twentynine Palms to Yuma and VMU-3 relocating from Twentynine Palms to Kaneohe Bay, Hawaii. Praising this transition, Salasibarra said, '*Getting underneath a MAG, there's an aviation mindset. We definitely have that support that we needed.*'

The transition from MACG to MAG control was preceded by a similar change within MAWTS-1. In 2012, the UAS division transferred from MAWTS-1's command, control and communications (C3) department to its TACAIR department. Explaining the significance of this, Staff Sergeant Herr said, '*When the UAS division changed from C3 to TACAIR, that required a drastic revision of a lot of our curriculum because it was a paradigm shift in every sense of the phrase. It was no longer quite as Marine Air Command and Control Section-centric. Now there's a much greater depth of focus on things like weaponry, integration with aviation assets, TTPs for those assets. That was a big shift.*'

Unmanned systems have proven so effective that the Marine Corps recently reorganized its rifle squads to include a position for a UAS operator to employ a small quadcopter-type drone under a program known as 'Quads for Squads.' (USMC/PFC Rhita Daniel)

Marine Reapers

With the most ambitious MUX timetable envisaging an early operational capability in 2026, and with the RQ-21's limited operational radius, line-of-sight dependence and lack of armament, the Marine Corps issued an urgent needs request in 2018 for a Group 5 UAS such as the MQ-9 Reaper. In addition to providing much greater range, longer endurance and the capability to employ precision-guided munitions, the Reaper would give the VMU community experience operating a Group 5 UAS, informing the development of the MUX.

The first – and currently the only – Marine unit operating the Reaper is VMU-1 'Watchdogs' based at MCAS Yuma. Since September 2018, VMU-1 has partnered with General Atomics Aeronautical Systems, Inc (GA-ASI) to operate MQ-9As in Afghanistan as a 'COCO' asset. Over the first year of this contract, VMU-1 Reapers provided over 4,800 hours of ISR support in Afghanistan. As with the US Air Force Reapers, Marine MQ-9s are launched and recovered by personnel in-theatre but are flown by aircrews in the continental United States.

Whereas the RQ-21 is too small to carry robust EW systems like the Intrepid Tiger II pod, the Group 5 MQ-9 could easily carry the pod (if the USMC chose to so equip it), giving the Marines a platform that can provide credible, persistent EW coverage in alignment with the Corps' new MAGTF-EW construct, which places a heavy emphasis on unmanned systems for EW.

In 2020, the Marine Corps' MQ-9 contract will transition from contractor-owned/contractor-operated to government-owned/government-operated. Under this 'GOGO' arrangement, the Marine Corps plans on reaching IOC with the MQ-9 in late 2020. The navy intends to purchase three more MQ-9s for the USMC in its 2021 budget. With cancellation of the MUX, the Marines may very well invest even more heavily in the Reaper moving forward.

Initially contracting two General Atomics MQ-9 Reapers on a contractor-owned, contractor-operated arrangement to gain experience operating Group 5 unmanned aircraft systems to inform the service's MUX acquisition priorities, the Marine Corps has decided to transition to a government-owned, government operated construct to cover the UAS gaps left by the cancellation of the MUX. (USAF/SrA Haley Stevenss)

HMX AND VMX | MARINE HELICOPTER AND MARINE OPERATIONAL TEST AND EVALUATION

Since 1957, the 'Nighthawks' of Marine Helicopter Squadron One (HMX-1) have been responsible for short-haul air transportation of the President of the United States (POTUS). While the Marine Corps initially shared this responsibility with the US Army, HMX-1 became the sole unit tasked with the Presidential helicopter mission in 1976.

Established on 1 December 1947 as the Marines Corps' first helicopter squadron, HMX-1 was tasked with assessing the utility of helicopters to move Marines ashore for amphibious assaults, to test and evaluate Marine rotorcraft and to develop the Corps' tactics, techniques and procedures for an operational concept the Marines dubbed 'vertical envelopment'. Though initially established as a test and evaluation unit, other units assumed responsibility for these tasks, leaving HMX-1 to focus almost solely on executive transport.

Whiteside – the Executive Flight Detachment

HMX-1 is divided into two branches – the Executive Flight Detachment (EFD), also known as the 'whiteside' due to the white-painted upper fuselages of the detachment's aircraft, and the 'greenside', which provides support for Presidential movements. The primary mission of the 'whiteside' is transporting the President (who may be accompanied by family, staff, high-ranking government officials, or foreign dignitaries) in and around the Washington, DC area, most frequently between the White House and

Despite the type's age and the increasing difficulty in supporting it, the iconic VH-3Ds operated by HMX-1 as Presidential transports continue to perform the job admirably. (USMC/Sgt Michael Cifuentes)

Andrews Air Force Base or the Presidential retreat at Camp David, Maryland. Currently, the EFD operates two types of Presidential transport helicopters – the Sikorsky VH-3D Sea King and VH-60N 'White Hawk'. Most VH-3s and VH-60s wear a metallic green paint scheme with gloss white upper fuselages, a pair of white cheatlines running the length of the fuselage, an American flag graphic on each engine nacelle, and 'United States of America' stencilled on the tail boom.

In addition to supporting Presidential movement in the Washington, DC area, the EFD supports local movements for Presidential visits, both within the United States and overseas, as both the VH-3D and VH-60N are air-transportable via Lockheed C-5 Galaxy or Boeing C-17 Globemaster III transports. The VH-3D typically requires 12 to 16 hours to prepare for air transport, and to unload and prepare for flight.

By contrast, the VH-60N can be prepared for air transport in less than two hours, making it ideal for short-notice trips. Though based in Quantico, the EFD maintains a presence at Naval Support Facility Anacostia, 3 miles (4.8km) from the White House. Just as the President's Boeing VC-25A flies with the callsign 'Air Force One' when the President is aboard, 'whiteside' aircraft fly as 'Marine One' while carrying the President.

Presidential Sea Kings

Since 1962, the VH-3 has been the primary helicopter used for Presidential transport, beginning with the VH-3A and transitioning to the VH-3D in 1976. HMX-1 operates 11 VH-3Ds, along with a single UH-3D used for training. Of note, the navy continues to operate a single VH-3A assigned to HX-21 at NAS Patuxent River for test work in support of HMX-1. With a scheduled sunset of spring 2023, HMX-1's VH-3 are undergoing a service life extension programme (SLEP) to keep the type mission-capable through the last few years of its service life. A recent cockpit upgrade included a satellite weather feed, GPS moving maps and night-vision compatible cockpit displays.

VH-60N

Complementing the VH-3D is another Sikorsky 'white top' – the VH-60N, which arrived at HMX-1 in November 1988. Numbering eight aircraft (plus a single UH-60N for crew training), the EFD's VH-60Ns provide the same service as the VH-3D. Whereas the VH-3D flies with a crew of three, the VH-60N operates with a crew of four – pilot, co-pilot, crew chief and a communications systems operator. The VH-60 can seat up to ten passengers.

Though a minor detail in operational military use, the lower-slung ceiling of the VH-60N cabin requires passengers to 'hunch' when entering and exiting the aircraft. With its ample headroom and correspondingly taller main cabin door, the VH-3D facilitates a more dignified movement into and out of the aircraft, making it preferable for executive transport, especially if foreign dignitaries are aboard. According to former HMX-1 commanding officer (2004-2006) Major General Andrew O'Donnell (USMC, Ret), *'If you're doing something like the G8 and you're in London, they liked the H-3 because it's more 'Presidential'. You lower the steps and they walk out. Whereas the -60, pilot-wise, it was more manoeuvrable, has more power, and is faster.'*

Additionally, the VH-60 was typically chosen over the VH-3 for flights in hot, high and heavy environments. During his command tour with HMX-1, O'Donnell deployed to Pakistan and Afghanistan in support of a March 2006 trip by President George W. Bush to meet with Afghan President Hamid Karzai and visit US troops. Recalling this

particular trip, O'Donnell said, '*I flew President Bush, he was on a classified trip into Pakistan and Afghanistan, and he took a -60. We had three 60s, and nobody knew we were going. We covered up the white paint and the American flag with a kind of wash-off green paint. From a distance it looked like another Army Black Hawk. Of course, we had all the equipment and all the instrumentation that would keep us out of harm's way from all the hand-held (SAMs) and whatever else they might have had. It worked out good.*'

Given HMX-1's mission and the frequency with which the aircraft operate overseas, the VH-60N is equipped with extensive aircrew survival equipment. The current fit includes the AN/APR-39 radar warning receiver and missile plume detection system, the AN/AAR-47 missile warning system, the AN/AVR-2 laser detector, the AN/AAQ-24(V)25 Large Aircraft Infrared Countermeasures system and AN/ALE-47 chaff and flare dispensers .

Under a mid-life upgrade completed in 2002, the HMX-1 VH-60N fleet received a communications system upgrade, enabling secure communications between VH-60Ns, VH-3Ds, VC-25 'Air Force One' aircraft, E-4B National Emergency Airborne Command Post aircraft and the White House Communications Agency. A 2015 SLEP also upgraded the type's engines to the General Electric T700-GE-401C, offering better performance at high altitudes and reinforced the airframe to allow an additional 4,000 hours of flight time to sustain the fleet through its final phase-out in FY 2023.

While the VH-3D remains the preferred 'Marine One' platform due to its tall cabin and doors allowing 'dignified' boarding and egress, the VH-60 is easier to transport aboard US Air Force cargo aircraft, making it an ideal choice for overseas visits and short-notice domestic movements. (Joe Copalman)

The greenside – presidential support

The 'greenside', which historically flew several different aircraft, currently operates a single type, the Bell-Boeing MV-22B Osprey. In the Presidential support role, HMX-1 'greenside' aircraft transported Presidential staffers, Secret Service protective details, media and essential equipment needed to support Presidential visits, a mission the squadron's Ospreys continue to be used for today.

Along with supporting Presidential movements, 'greenside' HMX-1 remained committed to providing OT&E for the Corps' assault support helicopters, maintaining a small fleet that mirrored those of the medium (HMM) and heavy (HMH) helicopter squadrons throughout Marine aviation. The types of OT&E support HMX-1 provided included the development of TTPs for the UH-34, CH-46 and CH-53 communities, the integration of new avionics or defensive systems and aviation support for ground units aboard Quantico.

When not directly supporting Presidential movements, HMX-1 'greenside' supports various USMC units in the Washington, DC area. The Nighthawks have a longstanding relationship with the Marine Corps Combat Development Center (MCCDC), also based at Quantico, helping the infantry develop and revise the TTPs used for working with helicopters and tiltrotor aircraft. Utilising the various ranges at Quantico, including an urban 'combat town' facility, HMX-1 provides aircraft and aircrews to assist with tactical skills like egressing aircraft, securing landing zones, fast-roping, tactical recovery of aircraft and personnel (TRAP), and other essential tasks and missions in which the ground and aviation components work together.

The Secret Service also utilises the 'greenside' aircraft for tactical training, ensuring their protective and counter-assault teams are prepared for any contingency. 'Greenside' aircraft also support the Officer Candidate School (OCS) at Quantico, providing both aircraft demonstrations for candidates considering careers in aviation, and facilitating the movement of candidates during tactical phases of the course.

Left: The CH-46F was a longtime mainstay of the HMX-1 'greenside' Presidential support fleet. Though painted in a VIP scheme, the HMX-1 'Phrogs' retained the spartan interior of fleet CH-46s and were largely used for transporting Secret Service agents, Presidential staffers, and members of the media.
(Joe Copalman)

Right: With the CH-46 on its way out of service, HMX-1 began replacing the 'Phrog' with the MV-22 Osprey in May 2013 to continue the Presidential support mission.
(Marcus Jellyman)

'Greenside' changes

Though often referred to as VH-46 and VH-53 aircraft, respectively, HMX-1's Sea Knights and Super Stallions were effectively standard production models with little modification. This enabled HMX-1 to support MCCDC and OCS seamlessly, as if they were receiving support from fleet HMM and HMH squadrons. Further, it allowed the Nighthawks to test new avionics or other systems aboard H-46s and H-53s as part of its OT&E mission. The squadron's transition away from OT&E began in 2009, when Marine Operational Test and Evaluation Squadron 22 (VMX-22) at MCAS New River assumed the CH-53E OT&E mission. The squadron continued to operate 'greenside' CH-53Es through April 2011, after which the Super Stallion pilots re-trained on the CH-46E, flying the Sea Knight until it was replaced by the Osprey.

VMX-22 'Nighthawks'
Aug 2003 – May 2016

On 4 May 2013, the squadron held an induction ceremony for six Ospreys at Quantico, the first of 12 intended to replace both the CH-46E and CH-53E. Upon induction, HMX-1 immediately put its Ospreys to work fulling 'greenside' requests, supporting an OCS class. By early 2014, the Nighthawks fully integrated the Osprey into their Presidential support operations, enabling HMX-1 to retire its CH-46s.

Prior to the introduction of the Osprey, the 'greenside' had been a proving ground for prospective 'whiteside' pilots. Recalling the typical career progression at HMX-1 prior to the V-22, Major General O'Donnell said, '*Everybody started off on the greenside, flying -46s and -53s. While you're flying the support aircraft, you're going through the ground school and the syllabuses and the simulators and then you start flying the white tops, both the H-3 and the -60. That's a four-year tour. And after you've been there for about a year, you start flying as a White House co-pilot, then you do that for about a year. And then you become a White House HAC, helicopter aircraft commander, and that allows you to fly everybody but the President. You could fly co-pilot with POTUS, but you could fly everybody but POTUS – visiting heads of state, the Vice President, etc. And then if you get selected to be a Marine One pilot, the CO picks four or five guys that he decides are going to fly the President, and that's usually the last year you're there.*' This progression ceased with the introduction of the Osprey. As O'Donnell explained, '*It used to be you started off as a -46 or -53 pilot, then you'd transition into the VH-3 and the VH-60, but now the V-22 guys, they don't do any of that stuff. They just fly the V-22 the whole time they're there. It put a real burden on the pure helicopter guys that are flying the white tops.*' With no rotor-wing aircraft organic to 'greenside' HMX-1 feeding prospective pilots into the 'whiteside' roster, new helicopter pilots coming to the squadron immediately start out in the VH-3 and VH-60.

AgustaWestland VH-71 Kestrel – first attempt at a new New Marine One

By the early 2000s, the VH-3D had been in service and out of production for nearly 25 years. With any out-of-production aircraft, spare part stocks deplete and supportability becomes more challenging, the VH-3D being as susceptible to this as any aircraft. The Marines initiated the search for a helicopter to replace the VH-3D in February 2002 with a study of viable alternatives in production or development. The US Department

The first attempt to replace the VH-3D and VH-60N with a single type came in January 2005, with Agusta-Westland, in partnership with Lockheed Martin and Bell Helicopter, selected to produce the next 'Marine One' platform based on the AW101 Merlin. Designated as the VH-71 Kestrel, the program ran into development delays and cost overruns that resulted in the project being terminated in April 2009. (Lockheed Martin)

of Defense made the search for a 'Marine One' replacement official, issuing a request for proposal (RFP) for 23 aircraft to replace the VH-3D and VH-60N fleets in what became known as the Presidential Helicopter Replacement Program, or VXX. The VXX RFP yielded two proposals – the Sikorsky S-92 and the AgustaWestland AW101, rebranded as the US101 as the result of a partnership between Lockheed Martin, AgustaWestland and Bell Helicopter. Though AgustaWestland (now Leonardo) was a European company, the partnership with Lockheed Martin and Bell resulted in an aircraft that was 64 per cent American-made.

Despite criticism from Sikorsky and others that the US101 was a 'foreign' helicopter built by a 'socialist' company – and the optics of an American President flying on a 'European' helicopter – the Lockheed-Martin/AgustaWestland/Bell partnership won out, with the DOD announcing on 28 January 2005 that the US101 would be the new Presidential helicopter. While the US101 – redesignated as the VH-71 Kestrel – offered speed and range advantages over the VH-3 and VH-60, engineering issues encountered during modification of the aircraft resulted in delays and cost overruns. The programme continued to miss key development benchmarks and projected costs skyrocketed.

With US President Barack Obama attempting to cut government spending, the VH-71 programme stood in stark contrast with his efforts. On 23 February 2009, during a Fiscal Responsibility Summit in Washington, DC, President Obama remarked '*The helicopter I have now seems perfectly adequate to me.*' Secretary of Defense Robert Gates recommended termination of the VH-71 programme on 6 April 2009, citing out of control costs and concerns that the aircraft might not perform as needed. Included in Obama's FY2010 budget proposal, however, was a proposal for a new VXX programme to replace the Presidential fleet. When the final FY 2010 House and Senate Defense Appropriations Bill reached President Obama's desk for signature, it included USD130 million in funding for the renewed Marine One replacement programme.

VH-92 – 21st-century 'Marine One'

Having watched the VH-71 programme from the sidelines, Sikorsky believed it had a winning aircraft with the S-92 and teamed up with its prior VXX rival – Lockheed Martin – on a revised S-92A 'Superhawk' proposal. On 7 May 2014 Sikorsky accepted the contract to produce the next Presidential Transport Helicopter, which would be known as the VH-92A. In addition to the 21 VH-92As being acquired for 'White Top' Presidential transport, the contract includes two non-VIP CH-92As for pilot training.

Following the type's first flight on 28 July 2017, a pair of engineering development models began a planned 12-month, 250-hour flight test programme. Additionally, Lockheed Martin/Sikorsky manufactured four system demonstration test article (SDTA) aircraft, which are production-representative VH-92As currently being used for fit and integration tests of the avionics, communications gear, environmental control systems and defensive systems to ensure compatibility and determine a standardised configuration prior to low-rate initial production. To avoid possible test or delivery delays as a result of new systems not keeping pace with aircraft development, Lockheed Martin/Sikorsky is utilising mature, proven avionics and components as much as possible to deliver an aircraft that is mission-ready on day one. Once testing is complete, the SDTA aircraft will become part of HMX-1's fleet of 21 'white top' VH-92As.

The S-92 series feature a rotor ice protection system, anti-ice windshields and a heated cockpit and cabin for cold-weather flying. It is also equipped with enhanced

The cancellation of the VH-71 left HMX-1 without a replacement for its aging 'Marine One' fleet. After another competition pitting an AW101 derivative against Sikorsky's S-92, the DOD chose Sikorsky's offering, designated as the VH-92. Pictured here, HMX-1 crews conduct landings on the south lawn of the White House in September 2018 during testing. (USMC/Sgt Hunter Helis)

active vibration control for smoother flying and a rear ramp alternative for entering and exiting the aircraft. A pair of General Electric CT7-8A6 turboshaft engines connected to a 4,170shp main gearbox enables improved 'hot and high' performance. Features specific to the VH-92 include a mission communications system designed by Naval Air Systems Command, avionics and electronics 'hardened' against the effects of electromagnetic pulse and electromagnetic interference and an improved environmental control system. Importantly for a VIP helicopter, the height of the main cabin door is 6ft (2m), permitting 'dignified' movement on and off the aircraft. For air transportability, the VH-92 can fit inside a C-17 without having to fold the tail pylon and a main rotor head featuring manual blade fold capability.

Testing benchmarks

With integrated developmental and operational flight testing commencing at NAS Patuxent River in August 2018, the program has remained on track, hitting critical benchmarks to the expected performance standards with only slight delays that – so far – have fallen within the allowable tolerances. Additionally, projected overall costs have declined, dropping from USD5.18 billion to USD4.95 billion between April 2014 and May 2018. One of the more notable test events happened on 22 September 2018, when a crew from HMX-1s operational test team landed one of the SDTA VH-92s on the south lawn of the White House for the first time, conducting a total of 14 landings and take-offs.

As tiltrotor technology continues to mature, and with the introduction of compound rotorcraft like the Sikorsky/Boeing SB-1 Defiant, the VH-92A may be the last conventional helicopter acquired for Presidential transport. Having said that, HMX-1 managed to keep the VH-3D fleet operational, relevant and effective over what will be 47 years by the time it finally bows out, so we may be seeing American Presidents waving to television cameras as they board a waiting VH-92 for decades to come.

VMX-1 – Consolidating Marine Aviation Operational Test

Given the close relationship between US Navy and Marine Corps aviation, testing of Marine aircraft has historically fallen under the umbrella of the navy's test and evaluation community. The community serves two primary functions – developmental test and evaluation (DT&E) and OT&E. Squadrons tasked with DT&E work closely with manufacturers and focus primarily on engineering and whether new aircraft can meet the expected performance metrics. Units that perform OT&E evaluate the systems and armaments that make an aircraft a weapons system and develop the TTPs needed to effectively employ those aircraft.

Having moved away from most aspects of test work, HMX-1 has passed the Marine OT&E torch to the 'Argonauts' of Marine Operational Test and Evaluation Squadron One (VMX-1). The Argonauts' story dates to April 2000, when an MV-22B belonging to the Marine Corps' V-22 fleet replacement squadron, Marine Medium Tiltrotor Squadron 204 (VMMT-204) crashed at a small airport in Marana, Arizona. While on approach for a night landing, the aircraft entered a vortex ring state, a condition in which a helicopter settles into its own highly-turbulent recirculated rotor wash and loses considerable lift, causing it to roll quickly and descend nose first into the ground, killing all

19 Marines aboard. This mishap occurred amidst a test programme that was behind schedule and over budget, having barely survived multiple cancellation threats. Adding insult to injury, the commanding officer of VMMT-204, Lieutenant Colonel Odin Leberman, was relieved of command on 18 January 2001 after revelations he had ordered his maintainers to falsify reports to make it appear as if the squadron's aircraft were in better shape than they were. Though investigators found no connection between the falsified maintenance records and the fatal crash at Marana, the very public nature of both incidents led many to conclude that Marine leadership wanted the Osprey so bad, they were willing to cut corners to get it.

On 28 August 2003, the Marines established Marine Operational Test and Evaluation Squadron 22 (VMX-22) at MCAS New River, the squadron's mission being getting the V-22 programme back on track. VMX-22 reported directly to the US Navy Operational Test and Evaluation Force and accepted Air Force and Navy pilots as well as Marines. The justification for the joint force pilots and direct reporting to the navy was to restore credibility to the MV-22 test programme in the wake of the crashes and groundings and falsified maintenance records.

Initially designated VMX-22 and established to reign in the floundering MV-22 Osprey development program in 2003, the charter of the 'Argonauts' has expanded to include operational test and evaluation for all tilt-rotor and rotor-winged aircraft in Marine service, as well as the F-35B under a new designation, VMX-1. (Joe Copalman)

With Osprey OT&E squarely on their shoulders, the Marines of VMX-22 quickly got to work doing their part trying to get the program back on track. By October 2006, the squadron was ready to put the Osprey to the test as an assault support aircraft in simulated combat conditions at MCAS Yuma. VMX-22 brought a pair of MV-22s to participate in long-range raid and casualty evacuation (CASEVAC) events designed to test the Osprey's capabilities. During this detachment, the two crews flew infantrymen from Yuma to several landings zone aboard the expansive ranges of the Marine Corps Air Ground Combat Center at Twentynine Palms, inserting and extracting them, and performing simulated CASEVAC. Success in these events validated systems and TTPs VMX-22 developed and generated data for further testing and revisions.

For the next six years, the MV-22 remained the sole focus of VMX-22 test and evaluation efforts, developing the initial TTPs for the Osprey community and validating the efficacy of various avionics, defensive system, weapons and tactics, helping prepare the type for entrance into the fleet and into the deployment rotation cycle. Though the squadron has expanded its focus over recent years, the 'Argonauts' have remained committed to supporting the Osprey community. In April 2015, the squadron sent a detachment to New Mexico to test upgraded software in a reduced-visibility landing environment. Crews on this detachment also test-fired the Defensive Weapons System, a belly-mounted 7.62mm (0.3in) Gatling-type gun that has proven problematic over the course of multiple attempts to provide additional firepower to the Osprey.

A CH-53E Super Stallion operated by VMX-1 at low altitude over the Colorado River north of MCAS Yuma. The 'Argonauts' relocated from MCAS New River to Yuma in July 2015 to be closer to the vast range complexes in the area and to work more closely with Marine Aviation Weapons and Tactics Squadron One at Yuma. (Kevin Whitehead)

Super Stallion OT&E

As the Osprey community made several successful operational deployments on land and at sea, validating much of the test and evaluation work VMX-22 had done on the MV-22, the Marines expanded the squadron's portfolio to include the CH-53E in 2009. Since the addition of the CH-53A Sea Stallion to its 'greenside' fleet in 1967, HMX-1 managed the OT&E needs of the CH-53 community. The passing of this torch to VMX-22 at New River represented the first major step towards consolidating Marine aviation OT&E under a single squadron. In August 2014, the 'Argonauts' sent a CH-53E detachment to test the Joint Precision Airdrop System (JPADS) over the US Army's Yuma Proving Ground. The JPADS system combines a GPS guidance system with a steerable parachute system to drastically increase the accuracy of air-delivered supplies and equipment. While at Yuma, VMX-22's Super Stallion crews worked closely with Marines from the 1st Marine Logistics Group, who assisted in rigging the JPADS system to palletised loads for the drop tests.

Now permanently based at Yuma under the redesignated VMX-1, the Marines' CH-53E OT&E fleet continues to provide valuable test and evaluation service to ensure the Super Stallion remains tactically relevant through the end of the type's service. Once CH-53K initial operational testing is completed at MCAS New River, two CH-53Ks will join VMX-1's fleet. The 'Argonauts' have been assisting with the CH-53K programme, supporting testing of the number two engine backflow duct installation and instrumentation at both New River and Patuxent River in FY2018, as well as other 'King Stallion' test initiatives.

C3 and UAVs

Further expansion of VMX-22 occurred in 2013, when the squadron established a Command, Control and Communications (C3) department and an unmanned aerial systems (UAS) division. Since its establishment, the C3 department – under the re-designated VMX-1 – has assisted in the test and evaluation of aviation-related command and control systems in support of Marine Corps Operational Test and Evaluation Activity (MCOTEA) objectives. With air defence being a major focus of USMC C3, the VMX-1 C3 department supports several projects aimed at protecting the total force from aerial threat.

One ground-based air defence system recently tested by VMX-1 is the Compact Laser Weapons System (CLaWS), a low-power, medium-range energy weapon designed to neutralise hostile unmanned aerial vehicles. Another recent focus of C3 efforts is testing of the AN/TPS-80 Ground/Air Task Oriented Radar (G/ATOR) on behalf of MCOTEA, and helping assist in the development and evaluation of the Light Marine Air Defense Integrated System (L-MADIS). Moving forward, the C3 department will assist in operational testing of MAGTF digital interoperability systems, refining the Tactical Air Control Element concept and providing command and control subject matter expertise to the testing of different types of aircraft.

Relocation and redesignation

On 16 July 2015, VMX-22 relocated from New River to Yuma. Planning for the move began in April 2014, resulting in construction of a new, modern hangar at Yuma to support not just the squadron's Ospreys, but multiple examples of almost every deployable aircraft in the USMC inventory. With responsibility for MV-22, F-35B, CH-53E, C3

Operating its own fleet of almost every type of aircraft in Marine Corps service, VMX-1 can test interoperability of most Marine aircraft with the F-35, all in-house. (Joe Copalman)

and UAS operational test & evaluation, the move came amid a continuing expansion of the VMX-22 charter to include even more aircraft.

The move to Arizona yielded immediate benefits. Foremost among these is Yuma being the home to Marine Aviation Weapons and Tactics Squadron One (MAWTS-1), the Marine aviation centre of excellence. Established in 1978 to train Marine Weapons and Tactics Instructors to standardise tactical aviation training programmes, MAWTS-1 writes and revises the training and readiness syllabi for all deployable aircraft in the Marine Corps. One of VMX's primary jobs is developing initial TTPs for new aircraft entering the active fleet, effectively producing the rough draft of the T&R syllabus for these aircraft. Being co-located at Yuma enables closer integration between MAWTS and VMX. Other advantages include year-round permissive flying weather and easy access to the Barry M. Goldwater Range, the Yuma Proving Ground and the Chocolate Mountain live-fire ranges. As an acknowledgment of the squadron's growth beyond supporting only the MV-22, the 'Argonauts' formally redesignated as VMX-1 on 13 May 2016.

Skid test

With the squadron firmly in place at Yuma by the end of July 2015, the 'Argonauts' made another move to consolidate Marine OT&E at a single location. Testing for the USMC 'skid' community – the AH-1W SuperCobra, AH-1Z Viper and the UH-1Y Venom – had long been conducted by VX-9 'The Vampires', a navy OT&E squadron based at Naval Air Weapons Station China Lake. In August 2015, responsibility for 'skid' OT&E transferred from VX-9 to VMX at Yuma. Recent test projects the H-1 division has participated in include firing the Advanced Precision Kill Weapons System with the M282 Penetrator Warhead, evaluating the Digital Interoperability – Full Motion Video (DI-FMV) system and testing of the Joint Air-to-Ground Missile (JAGM). The 'Argonauts' also helped verify deficiencies in a new Joint Service Aircrew Mask designed for operating in chemical, biological, radiological and nuclear environments. Looking ahead, the VMX-1 'skids' will stay busy participating in further testing of the DI-FMV system, assessment of the Distributed Aperture Infrared Countermeasure system, software upgrades for JAGM compatibility and evaluation of the APR-39D(v)2 Radar Signals Detecting Set.

F-35 testing – VMX-1 Det Edwards

With OT&E for the Lockheed-Martin F-35 Lightning II being a major focus for VMX-1, the squadron maintains a detachment of six F-35Bs at Edwards Air Force Base in California as the Marine Corps' contribution to the Joint Operational Test Team (JOTT). As the F-35 is a joint programme, the TTPs for all three F-35 variants among all operators are standardised to a degree rarely seen before, if ever. The JOTT is comprised of US Air Force, US Navy and Marine Corps personnel and F-35s, as well as aircraft, pilots and maintainers from the British Royal Air Force and Royal Navy and the Royal Netherlands Air Force. Most tactics being developed by the JOTT will be employed by all F-35 users, regardless of the air arm or variant.

Despite this unprecedented level of jointness, VMX-1 Det Edwards still participates in multiple Marine-specific OT&E events and has even supported some F-35B developmental test in what is known at 'DT assist'. Among these USMC-centric events are at-sea periods for intensive shipboard flight, maintenance and weapons testing, as well as other projects like integrated fire control and expeditionary operations like Agile Lightning. During this, in February 2017, crews and aircraft from VMX-1 and VMFA-211 conducted expeditionary operations at austere landing sites and received aviation-delivered ground refuelling from MV-22s, validating several expeditionary operations TTPs.

With the concurrent nature of F-35 development and fielding, VMX-1 Det Edwards is closely linked to the Corps' operational F-35 squadrons. If a specific system or function is proving problematic, the fleet squadrons can reach out to VMX-1 to notify them of the issue and – hopefully – get a solution.

The final hurdle for the JOTT to clear for the F-35 to enter full-scale production is completion of initial operational test and evaluation (IOT&E), which began in December 2018. Though initially expected to conclude in late 2019, numerous testing delays, specifically with the Joint Testing Environment, have pushed that back, possibly as far out as early 2021. Once IOT&E concludes, the Edwards det will relocate to Yuma, further consolidating OT&E under one roof – minus a few exceptions.

Harriers, Hornets and Herks

While the test force being consolidated at Yuma represents every aircraft that will eventually grace the flight decks of amphibious assault ships in support of Marine Expeditionary Units (MEU) once all the transitions currently underway are complete, a few Marine tactical aircraft have not, and likely will not come under the VMX-1 umbrella. Responsibility for OT&E for the AV-8B Harrier and F/A-18A-D Hornet – still the Corps' two most numerous tactical jets – rests with VX-31 'The Dust Devils' at China Lake.

Over the past two decades, VX-31 managed some of the most critical upgrades and systems to be integrated into the Harrier and Hornet fleets, like the LITENING targeting pod, the GBU-54 Laser JDAM and the Intrepid Tiger II electronic warfare pod. For the Marine KC-130 Hercules community, OT&E is conducted by VX-20 at Patuxent River. While VX-20 had a KC-130J (BuNo 166743) assigned to the squadron for the better part of the first decade of the 21st Century, that aircraft has been reassigned to VMGR-234 'Ranger', one of two Marine Forces Reserve KC-130J squadrons. Despite not having any 'Herks' currently assigned, VX-20 retains the OT&E mission for Marine C-130s, most recently completing testing of the Harvest HAWK Plus upgrade for the Corps' small fleet of armed KC-130Js.

'Mihi Cura Futuri'

The end state of operational test consolidation under VMX-1 at Yuma will be an OT&E force that flies the same mix of aircraft assigned to MEU Aviation Combat Elements – F-35B, AH-1Z, UH-1Y, CH-53E/K, RQ-21 and MV-22. Just as an ACE working up to deploy trains as it fights, VMX-1 will be able to test as the ACE fights, able to not just work out platform-specific testing of systems and tactics, but also the interoperability of those systems and tactics with other aircraft in the ACE. Such test work is increasingly crucial with digital interoperability becoming a core capability within Marine aviation. Having most of the Marine OT&E force located at a single base, flying out of a single hangar and sharing the same ready room, less than a block away from MAWTS-1 will only serve to benefit the operational squadrons at the tip of the spear in the decades to come.

A 'Dust Devils' Harrier during testing of the centreline-mounted LITENING targeting pod and wearing the remnants of an experimental paint scheme. (Joe Copalman)

THE FUTURE

The majority of this book was written between summer 2019 and summer 2020. In that short span of time, it sometimes seemed as if the Marine Corps published new policies or acquisition priorities every week. The appointment of General David Berger as the 38th Commandant of the Marine Corps (CMC) in July 2019 brought about considerable changes in the Marines Corps' roadmap for how it will organise, equip, train and fight over the coming decades. General Berger aims to align the size, shape and orientation of the Marine Corps with the United States' 2018 National Defense Strategy, which shifts the Department of Defense's main priority from combatting terrorism and insurgencies in the Middle East and South Asia to the 'Great Power Competition' with peer threats like China and Russia. In his 2019 Commandant's Planning Guidance, Berger broadcast that no concept, formation, organisation, or weapons system is immune to change or cancellation, with the litmus test for everything the Marine Corps owns or does being its utility in fighting peer-level competitors states from within their own weapons engagement zones.

In November 2019, the Second Marine Expeditionary Force (II MEF) participated in the Marine Air-Ground Task Force Warfighter Exercise (MWX) at Marine Corps Air-Ground Training Center Twentynine Palms in the desert east of Los Angeles, California. During the exercise, II MEF's command, ground, logistics and aviation elements faced off against the 7th Marine Regiment, augmented by 40 Commando, UK Royal Marines as the opposition force utilising a free-play, attrition-based model in which forces 'killed' in simulated combat do not regenerate. The purpose was to stress-test the MAGTF concept itself against a peer-level threat in accordance with Berger's assertion that '*the MAGTF cannot be our only solution for all crisis.*' Results from this and a second MWX held in spring 2020 are being used to help refine the ways in which the Marine Corps – including its aviation units – organise for combat against peer competitors like China and Russia.

In just the few weeks prior to submitting this manuscript for review, Commandant Berger released numerous changes to align the Marine Corps with his planning guidance – which in turn is aligned with the 2018 National Defense Strategy orienting the entirety of the US military for success in peer-state conflict. In early March 2020, the MAGTF Unmanned Expeditionary concept – a do-everything short take-off vertical landing unmanned aerial vehicle Marine Corps leadership had hoped would fill critical gaps in persistent surveillance, attached tiltrotor escort and electronic warfare – was cancelled in favour of acquiring more MQ-9 Reaper land-based UAVs.

On 23 March 2020, the Marine Corps published a new force design initiative that, among other things, cuts one light attack helicopter squadron, one medium tiltrotor

With its ability to operate within an adversary's weapons engagement zone and share data with other aircraft and ships via multiple datalinks, the F-35 will play a central role in the future of Marine Corps aviation. (Jamie Hunter/Aviacom)

Use this QR code to access a photo gallery with more pictures by Joe Copalman.

squadron and one heavy helicopter squadron over the next decade. Additionally, this initiative reduces the primary aircraft authorised number for F-35 squadrons from 16 aircraft per squadron to ten aircraft per squadron, a decision made based on the current pilot shortage and the high cost of acquiring and operating the F-35. Though no corresponding announcement in the total number of F-35s being acquired from the USMC has been announced, the likelihood of such an announcement before publication of this book is highly likely.

The dynamism that has so far characterised Berger's tenure as Commandant will likely produce further, possibly more drastic changes to how the Marines operate and interoperate with other armed services. The omission of any such changes in the preceding pages is not deliberate, but simply a result of publishing lead times.

Regardless of what path Berger and his successors chart for the Marine Corps of the future, it is obvious Marine aviation will continue to evolve in capability and continue play a critical role in the defence of the United States and its allies for decades to come.

APPENDIX I: USMC AIR UNITS

Headquarters USMC (HQ USMC)

HMX-1
'The Nighthawks'
MV-22B, VH-3D, VH-60N, VH-92

MAWTS-1
'none'

VMX-1
'Argonauts'
AH-1Z, CH-53E/K, CQ-24A, F-35B, MV-22B, RQ-21A, UH-1Y

1st Marine Air Wing (1st MAW)

MWHS-1
'America's Finest'

MAG-12

MALS-12
'Marauders'

MWSS-171
'The Sentinels'

VMFA-121
'Green Knights'
F-35B

VMFA-242
'Bats'
F/A-18D, F-35B

VMGR-152
'Sumos'
KC-130J

MAG-24

HMH-463
'Pegasus'
CH-53E

HMLA-367
'Scarface'
AH-1Z, UH-1Y

MALS-24
'Warriors'

MWSD-24
'Gryphons'

VMM-268
'Red Dragons'
MV-22B

VMM-363
'Lucky Red Lions'
MV-22B

VMU-3
'Phantoms'
RQ-21A

MAG-36

MALS-36
'Bladerunner'

MWSS-172
'Firebirds'

VMM-262
'Flying Tigers'
MV-22B

VMM-265
'Dragons'
MV-22B

MACG-18

MACS-4
'Vice Squad'

MASS-2
'Pacific Vagabonds'

MTACS-18
'Keep Charging'

MWCS-18
'Warriors From The Ground Up'

2nd Marine Air Wing (2nd MAW)

MWHS-2
'Snake Eyes'

MAG-14

MALS-14
'Dragons'

MWSS-271
'Workhorse'

VMA-223
'Bulldogs'
AV-8B

VMA-231
'Ace of Spades'
AV-8B

VMA-542
'Tigers'
AV-8B

VMAT-203
'Hawks'
AV-8B, TAV-8B

VMGR-252
'Otis'
KC-130J

VMU-2
'Night Owls'
RQ-21A

MAG-26

MALS-26
'Patriots'

MWSS-272
'Untouchables'

VMM-162
'Golden Eagles'
MV-22B

VMM-261
'Raging Bulls'
MV-22B

VMM-263
'Thunder Chickens'
MV-22B

VMM-264
'Black Nights'
MV-22B

VMM-266
'Fighting Griffons'
MV-22B

VMM-365
'Blue Knights'
MV-22B

VMMT-204
'Raptors'
MV-22B

MAG-29

HMH-366 'Hammerheads' CH-53E	HMH-461 'Ironhorse' CH-53E	HMH-464 'Condors' CH-53E	HMHT-302 'Phoenix' CH-53E
HMLA-167 'Warriors' AH-1Z, UH-1Y	HMLA-269 'The Gunrunners' AH-1Z, UH-1Y	MALS-29 'Wolverines'	MWSS-274 'Ironmen'

MAG-31

MALS-31 'Stingers'	MWSS-273 'Sweat Hogs'	VMFA-115 'Silver Eagles' F/A-18C	VMFA-251 'Thunderbolts' F/A-18C (F-35C)	
VMFA-312 'Checkerboards' F/A-18C	VMFA(AW)-224 'Bengals' F/A-18D	VMFA(AW)-533 'Hawks' F/A-18D	VMFAT-501 'Warlords' F-35B	VMFAT-502 'Nightmares' F-35B

MACG-28

MACS-2 'Eyes of the MAGTF'	MASS-1 'Chieftain'	MTACS-28 'Olympians'	MWCS-28 'Spartans'	2nd LAAD Bn 'Death From Below'

3rd Marine Air Wing (3rd MAW)

MWHS-3
'Eagles'

MAG-11

MALS-11
'Devilfish'

MWSS-273
'Ace Support'

VMFA-225
'Vikings'
F-35B

VMFA-232
'Red Devils'
F/-18C

VMFA-314
'Black Nights'
F-35C

VMFA-323
'Death Rattlers'
F/A-18C

VMFAT-101
'Sharpshooters'
F/A-18C&D

VMGR-352
'Raiders'
KC-130J

MAG-13

MALS-13
'Black Widows'

MWSS-371
'Sand Sharks'

VMA-214
'Black Sheep'
AV-8B

VMA-311
'Tomcats'
AV-8B

VMFA-122
'Flying Leathernecks'
F-35B

VMFA-211
'Wake Island Avaengers'
F-35B

VMU-1
'Watchdogs'
MQ-9A, RQ-21A

MAG-16

HMH-361
'Flying Tigers'
CH-53E

HMH-462
'Heavy Haulers'
CH-53E

HMH-465
'Warhorse'
CH-53E

HMH-466
'Wolfpack'
CH-53E

MALS-16
'Forerunners'

MWSS-374
'Rhinos'

VMM-161
'Greyhawks'
MV-22B

VMM-163
'Ridge Runners'
MV-22B

VMM-165
'White Knights'
MV-22B

VMM-166
'Sea Elk'
MV-22B

VMM-362
'Ugly Angels'
MV-22B

MAG-39

HMLA-169
'Vipers'
AH-1Z, UH-1Y

HMLA-267
'Stingers'
AH-1Z, UH-1Y

HMLA-369
'Gunfighters'
AH-1Z, UH-1Y

HMLA-469
'Vengeance'
AH-1Z, UH-1Y

HMLAT-303
'Atlas'
AH-1Z, UH-1Y

MALS-39
'Hellhounds'

MWSS-372
'Diamondbacks'

VMM-164
'Nightriders'
MV-22B

VMM-364
'Purple Foxes'
MV-22B

MACG-38

MACS-1
'Falconers'

MASS-3
'Blacklist'

MTACS-38
'Phoenix'

MWCS-38
'Red Lightning'

3rd LAAD Bn
'Feel The Sting'

4th Marine Air Wing (4th MAW)

VMR Belle Chasse
'Easy'
UC-12W, UC-35C

MAG-41

HMLA-775
'Coyotes'
AH-1Z, UH-1Y

MALS-41
'Desperados'

MWSS-471
'Red Wolf'

MWSS-473
'The Gargoyles'

VMFA-112
'Cowboys'
F/A-18A++/C+

VMFT-401
'Snipers'
F-5F, F-5N

VMGR-234
'Rangers'
KC-130J

VMM-764
'Moonlight'
MV-22B

VMR-1
'Roadrunners'
C-40A

VMU-4
'Evil Eyes'
RQ-21A

MAG-49

HMH-772(-)
'The Hustlers'
CH-53E

HMLA-773
'Red Dogs'
AH-1W/Z, UH-1Y

MALS-49
'Magicians'

MWSS-472
'Dragons'

VMGR-452
'Yankees'
KC-130T, KC-130J

VMM-774
'Wild Goose'
MV-22B

MACG-48

MACS-24
'Earthquake'

MASS-6
'Lighthouse'

MTACS-48
'none'

MWCS-48
'Roar of the Corps'

Marine Corps Installations Command (MCI)

MCIEAST

H&HS Beaufort
'Swamp Foxes'
UC-12M

H&HS Cherry Point
'Rams'
UC-35D

H&HS New River
'Ka-Bar'
UC-12F/W

MCIWEST

H&HS Miramar
'Grizzlies'
UC-12W, UC-35D

H&HS Camp Pendeleton
'Stampede'
UC-12W

H&HS Yuma
'Guardians'
UC-12F

MCIPAC

H&HS Futenma
'Magic'
UC-12W

H&HS Iwakuni
'Torii'
UC-12W

H&HS Kaneohe Bay
'Ghost'
C-20G

BIBLIOGRAPHY

COPALMAN, J., '21st Century 'Battleherk', *AirForces Monthly*, Issue 366, September 2018: 46–52

COPALMAN, J., 'Arizona Snipers', *Combat Aircraft*, Volume 20, No. 11 (November 2019): 74–83

COPALMAN, J., 'Avengers Arise', *AirForces Monthly*, Issue 342 (September 2016): 64–65

COPALMAN, J.,'Fusing Fighters for the Future', *AirForces Monthly*, Issue 338 (May 2016): 48–53

COPALMAN, J., 'Heavy Metal', *US Navy and Marine Corps Airpower Yearbook 2018*: 28–35

COPALMAN, J., 'Texas Cowboys', *Combat Aircraft*, Volume 20, No. 3 (March 2019): 44–51

COPALMAN, J., 'The Prowler and Beyond', *AirForces Monthly*, Issue 360 (March 2018): 74–79

COPALMAN, J., 'Unsung Hero', *AirForces Monthly*, Issue 342 (September 2016): 56–60

COPALMAN, J., 'Waging Peace', *AirForces Monthly*, Issue 340 (July 2016): 48–53

CUTLER, T. J., *The U.S. Naval Institute on Marine Corps Aviation* (Annapolis: Naval Institute Press, 2016) ISBN 978-1-6824-7040-4

DAVIS, LtGen J., Marine Aviation Plan 2015 (October 2014) (https://www.aviation.marines.mil/Portals/11/2015%20Marine%20Aviation%20Plan%20Final_%2010%20Oct%202014_1110%20EDT.pdf)

ELWARD, B., *Legacy Hornets: Boeing's F/A-18A-D Hornets of the USN and USMC* (Anglen, PA: Schiffer, 2017) ISBN 978-0-7643-5434-2

GLOVER, D., 'Twice the Sting', *AirForces Monthly*, Issue 345 (December 2016): 38–42

Holmes, T., *US Marine Corps and RAAF Hornet Units of Operation Iraqi Freedom* (Oxford: Osprey Publishing, 2006) ISBN 978-1-8417-6847-2

Hunter, J., 'The Big Test', *Combat Aircraft*, Volume 20, No. 2 (February 2019): 80–87

Lake, J., 'Keeping the Legacy Alive', *AirForces Monthly*, Issue 373, April 2019: 50–55

Lowery, Col N. S., *U.S. Marines in Afghanistan, 2001-2002: From the Sea* (Quantico: History Division, United States Marine Corps, 2011) ISBN 978-1-4700-9555-0

Mersky, P. B., *U.S. Marine Corps Aviation Since 1912: 4th Edition* (Annapolis: Naval Institute Press, 2009) ISBN 978-1-5911-4516-5

Nordeen, L., *AV-8B Harrier II Units of Operation Iraqi Freedom I-VI* (Oxford: Osprey Publishing, 2013) ISBN 978-1-7809-6310-5

Nordeen, L., *AV-8B Harrier II Units of Operation Enduring Freedom* (Oxford: Osprey Publishing, 2014) ISBN 978-1-7820-0344-1

Rudder, LtGen St., 2018 Marine Aviation Plan (December 2017) (https://www.aviation.marines.mil/Portals/11/2018%20AvPlan%20FINAL.pdf)

Rudder, LtGen St., 2019 Marine Corps Aviation Plan (April 2019) (https://www.aviation.marines.mil/portals/11/2019%20avplan.pdf)

Saint, Col P. D., *23 Days to Baghdad: U.S. Marine Aviation Combat Element in Iraq, 2003* (Quantico: History Division, United States Marine Corps, 2017) ISBN 978-1-9449-6121-3

Sherrod, R., *History of Marine Corps Aviation in World War II* (Washington: Combat Forces Press, 1952) 978-1-1178-7805-8

Stout, J. A., *Hammer From Above: Marine Air Combat Over Iraq* (Presidio Press, 2005) ISBN 978-0-8914-1865-8

West, B., *No True Glory: A Frontline Account of the Battle for Fallujah* (New York City: Bantam, 2005) ISBN 978-0-5533-8319-5

Whitten, H. W., *Silent Heroes: U.S. Marines and Airborne Electronic Warfare, 1950-2012: 5th Edition* (Colonel H. Wayne Whitten & Associates, 2013) ISBN 978-0-8712-1025-8

Whittle, R., *The Dream Machine: The Untold History of the Notorious V-22 Osprey* (New York: Simon & Schuster, 2010) ISBN 978-1-4165-6296-2

Download this bibliography plus further selected reading from the author via this QR code.

INDEX

ACCURATE TECHNICAL DRAWINGS
AVIATIONGRAPHIC.COM
Phone: +39.338.487.3171
Email: info@aviationgraphic.com
Address: Via Enrico Lai 35, 09128
Cagliari - ITALY
The Italian Excellence
AVIATIONGRAPHIC.COM SINCE 2003
ROYAL AIR FORCE
VMFA-251
765
166765
MARI